THE HANDBOOK OF
JAPANESE
ADJECTIVES
AND
ADVERBS

THE HANDBOOK OF
JAPANESE
ADJECTIVES
AND
ADVERBS

Taeko Kamiya

KODANSHA USA

Published by Kodansha USA, Inc.
451 Park Avenue South
New York, NY 10016

Distributed in the United Kingdom and continental Europe
by Kodansha Europe Ltd.

ISBN 978-1-56836-416-2

First published in Japan in 2002 by Kodansha International
First US edition 2012 published by Kodansha USA

22 21 20 19 18   7 6 5 4

www.kodanshausa.com

CONTENTS

APPENDIXES   289

P R E F A C E

The Japanese language is said to be rich in modifiers—adjectives and adverbs. If you pick up a book or magazine and read a page or two, you will see how adjectives go with nouns, and adverbs with verbs, to convey accurate, vivid descriptions. In fact, these modifiers add indispensable nuance and flavor to the language.

The purpose of this book is to help students obtain a basic knowledge of Japanese adjectives and adverbs so that they may use them effectively in sentences.

Adjectives are presented in two parts. Part I deals with the conjugations of the two types of adjectives—*i*-adjectives and *na*-adjectives—and of some of the basic auxiliary adjectives. A conjugation practice follows the description of each adjective or group of adjectives. Part II deals with the usage of various adjectival forms. Each usage is illustrated with example sentences, and practices are provided every few lessons to allow you to test your understanding. Adverbs are presented by grouping them according to what they express—time, quantity, degree, circumstance and so forth. Each adverb is illustrated with examples sentences, and practices are provided every few lessons.

It is my wish that this book will prove useful, that you will come to better understand the meanings of Japanese adjectives and adverbs and be able to express yourself in "true Japanese."

I thank my editors, Shigeyoshi Suzuki and Michael Staley at Kodansha International, for making the publication of this book possible.

ADJECTIVES

INTRODUCTION

This section deals with some of the main features of Japanese adjectives as well as their similarities to and differences from English adjectives. You are advised to read it carefully before moving on to the main text.

TYPES OF ADJECTIVES

Japanese adjectives may be divided into two types: (a) *i*-adjectives, which end with *i*, and (b) *na*-adjectives, which end with *na*. *I*-adjectives are Japanese in origin while *na*-adjectives are mostly Chinese-origin words.

atarashii	新しい	new	shizukana	静かな	quiet
isogashii	忙しい	busy	sukina	好きな	favorite
omoshiroi	面白い	interesting	benrina	便利な	convenient

NOUN MODIFIERS

When used as noun modifiers, Japanese adjectives, like their English counterparts, precede the nouns they modify. Foreign words used as adjectives in Japanese become *na*-adjectives.

(a) **ōkii** ie   **kuroi** kuruma
大きい家   黒い車
a big house   a black car

(b) **kireina** hana
きれいな花
a pretty flower

modanna biru
モダンなビル
a modern building

genkina hito
元気な人
a healthy person

yunīkuna aidia
ユニークなアイディア
a unique idea

ADJECTIVAL PREDICATES

I-adjectives, when used as predicates, behave like verbs. For example, when *ōkii* 大きい (big) or *kuroi* 黒い (black) is used as a predicate, it means "is big" or "is black," not just "big" or "black."

Tanaka-san no ie wa **ōkii**.
田中さんの家は**大きい**。
Mr. Tanaka's house is big.

Watashi no kuruma wa **kuroi**.
私の車は**黒い**。
My car is black.

Na-adjectives, when used as predicates, behave like nouns. That is, the stem form (the form without *na*) must be followed by the copula (be-verb) *da*, as must an ordinary noun. For this reason, *na*-adjectives are sometimes called "nominal (nounlike) adjectives" or "adjectival nouns."

Kono hana wa **kirei da**.
この花は**きれいだ**。
This flower is pretty.

Yamada-san wa **genki da**.
山田さんは**元気だ**。
Miss Yamada is healthy.

Some *na*-adjectives can be used as nouns when functioning as the subject or object of a sentence.

anzenna asobiba → Kodomo ni totte **anzen** ga taisetsu da.
安全な遊び場　　　子供にとって**安全**が大切だ。
a safe playground　　　Safety is important for children.

zeitakuna kurashi → Sonna **zeitaku** wa dekinai.
ぜいたくな暮らし　　そんな**ぜいたく**は出来ない。
luxurious living　　　I can't afford such a luxury.

EXCEPTIONS: The *i*-adjectives *ōkii* 大きい (big), *chiisai* 小さい (small) and *okashii* おかしい (funny) may be used as *na*-adjectives when modifying certain nouns such as those given in the examples below.

ōkina kōen　　　　**大きな公園**　　a big park
chiisana ike　　　　**小さな池**　　　a small pond
okashina hanashi　　**おかしな話**　　a funny story

AUXILIARY ADJECTIVES

Auxiliary adjectives are adjectives that are attached to other adjectives or verbs. Some are *i*-adjectives (Examples 1, 2, 3, 4), while others are *na*-adjectives (Examples 5, 6).

1. Ano resutoran wa takai **rashii**.
    あのレストランは高い**らしい**。
    That restaurant seems to be expensive.

2. Kono mondai wa jūdai **kamoshirenai**.
    この問題は重大**かもしれない**。
    This problem might be serious.

3. Fuji-san ni nobori**tai**.
    富士山に登り**たい**。
    I want to climb Mt. Fuji.

4. Kono kigu wa tsukai**yasui**.
    この器具は使い**やすい**。
    This utensil is easy to use.

5. Kono pai wa oishi**sō da**.
    このパイはおいし**そうだ**。
    This pie looks delicious.

6. Sumisu-san wa sumō ga sukina **yō da**.
    スミスさんはすもうが好きな**ようだ**。
    Mr. Smith appears to like sumo.

In addition to auxiliary adjectives, there are also auxiliary verbs. These, too, can attach to adjectives.

(a) Kono heya wa sema**sugiru**.
    この部屋は狭**すぎる**。
    This room is too small.

(b) Kare wa majime **sugiru**.
    彼はまじめ**すぎる**。
    He is too serious.

TENSES OF ADJECTIVES

Japanese adjectives conjugate and have two tenses: present and past. The same adjectival form is used to express both present and future tenses.

(a) Shiken wa **yasashii**.
    試験は**易しい**。
    The exam is/will be easy.

    Shiken wa **yasashikatta**.
    試験は**易しかった**。
    The exam was easy.

(b) Tetsuzuki wa **kantan da**.
    手続きは**簡単だ**。
    The procedure is/will be simple.

    Tetsuzuki wa **kantan datta**.
    手続きは**簡単だった**。
    The procedure was simple.

LEVELS OF SPEECH

Japanese adjectives have plain, polite and superpolite forms or levels of speech. The plain form is used among family and friends, as well as in publications. The polite form is used among adults who are not close friends. The super-polite form is seldom used by younger speakers except in such greetings as *o-hayō gozaimasu* おはようございます (Good morning) or *o-medetō gozaimasu* おめでとうございます (Congratulations).

	(a) "It is interesting."	(b) "It is simple."
PLAIN	Omoshiroi. 面白い。	Kantan da. 簡単だ。
POLITE	Omoshiroi **desu**. 面白いです。	Kantan **desu**. 簡単です。
SUPERPOLITE	Omoshirō **gozaimasu**. 面白うございます。	Kantan **de gozaimasu**. 簡単でございます。

MORE MODIFIERS

Japanese has various other kinds of modifiers besides the *i-* and *na-* adjectives explained above.

1. Demonstratives

There are two sets of demonstratives ("this," "that," etc.) that are used like adjectives before nouns.

kono この this ~	sono その that ~	ano あの that ~ over there	dono どの which ~ ?
konna こんな this kind of ~	sonna そんな that kind of ~	anna あんな that kind of ~	donna どんな what kind of ~ ?

When items are in sight, **kono** and *konna* indicate items near the speaker, e.g., **kono** *zasshi* この雑誌 (this magazine); *sono* and *sonna* indicate items near the listener, e.g., **sonna** *tokei* そんな時計 (that kind of watch); *ano* and *anna* indicate items away from but seen by both, e.g., **ano** *tatemono* あの建物 (that building over there). *Dono* and *donna* are used in interrogative sentences, e.g., *Sore wa **donna** tokoro desuka* それは**どんな**所ですか？(What kind of place is it?). When items are not in sight, *sono* and *sonna* refer to items known by the speaker or previously referred to in the course of conversation, e.g., **sono** *hito* その人 (that person (I met/just mentioned)). *Ano* and *anna* refer to items known by both the speaker and the listener, e.g., **anna** *kuruma* あんな車 (that kind of car (we saw)).

2. Special Adjectives

Some adjectives do not conjugate and are only used as noun modifiers.

aru hi	ある日	a certain day
tonda sainan	とんだ災難	a terrible misfortune
taishita gakusha	大した学者	a great scholar
sugureta hon	すぐれた本	an excellent book
arayuru shudan	あらゆる手段	every possible means
naki chichi	亡き父	my late father

3. Noun + *no* + Noun

A noun followed by the particle *no* forms a phrase that modifies the noun that follows it. The use of *no* also applies to pronouns: *Watashi no* 私の (my), *anata no* あなたの (your), *kare no* 彼の (his), *kanojo no* 彼女の (her), *karera no* 彼らの (their). However, pronoun forms are often avoided in Japanese unless there is a special need for them.

Nihongo no hon	日本語の本	a book on/in Japanese
gakkō no sensei	学校の先生	a school teacher
watashi no namae	私の名前	my name

This *no* can also be added to a noun phrase that already has a particle attached.

tomodachi kara no tegami
友達からの手紙
a letter from my friend

Shikago de no shigoto
シカゴでの仕事
a job in Chicago

4. Relative Clauses

Relative clauses (noun-modifying clauses) precede the nouns they modify. In Japanese, there are no relative pronouns equivalent to the English words "which," "that" or "who." Japanese adjectives may appear in any tense in the predicate of a relative clause, as may Japanese verbs.

Samukunai hi wa niwa de hatarakimasu.
寒くない日は庭で働きます。
On the days that are not cold, I work in the yard.

Tanoshikatta natsuyasumi ga owatta.

楽しかった夏休みが終わった。

The summer vacation that was enjoyable ended.

Genki datta koinu ga kyū ni shinda.

元気だった子犬が急に死んだ。

The puppy that had been healthy died suddenly.

PART I

CONJUGATION

As we have seen earlier, there are two types of Japanese adjectives—*i*-adjectives and *na*-adjectives—as well as a variety of auxiliary adjectives. They all conjugate. The following charts show how.

 1 *I*-adjectives

I-adjectives are similar to verbs and conjugate like verbs.

samui 寒い "cold"

FORMS	CONJUGATION	
Stem	samu- 寒-	
Prenominal	samui 寒い	cold ∼
Present	samui 寒い	is cold
Negative	samu**kunai** 寒くない	is not cold
Past	samu**katta** 寒かった	was cold
Negative Past	samu**kunakatta** 寒くなかった	was not cold
Conjunctive/*Te*	samu**ku**/samu**kute** 寒く/寒くて	cold and ∼
Adverbial	samu**ku** 寒く	(become) cold
Conditional	samu**kereba** 寒ければ	if … is cold
Tara (Conditional)	samu**kattara** 寒かったら	if … is cold

Tari	samu**kattari** 寒かったり	sometimes … is cold and sometimes ～
Noun	samu**sa** 寒さ	coldness

EXAMPLES OF EACH FORM:

Prenominal form

samui fuyu
寒い冬
a cold winter

Present form

Shikago no fuyu wa **samui**
シカゴの冬は**寒い**。
Chicago winters are cold.

Negative form

Kyō wa **samukunai**.
今日は**寒くない**。
Today is not cold.

Past form

Kinō wa **samukatta**.
昨日は**寒かった**。
Yesterday was cold.

Negative Past form

Kyonen no fuyu wa **samukunakatta**.
去年の冬は**寒くなかった**。
Winter last year was not cold.

Conjunctive/*Te* form

Soto wa **samuku** uchi wa atatakai.
外は**寒く**、内は暖かい。
It's cold outside and warm inside.

Heya ga **samukute** benkyō dekinai.
部屋が**寒くて**勉強出来ない。
The room is cold and I can't study.

Adverbial form	Kinō kara kyū ni **samuku** natta. 昨日から急に**寒く**なった。 It suddenly became cold as of yesterday.
Conditional form	**Samukereba** hītā o tsukete kudasai. **寒ければ**ヒーターをつけてください。 If it's cold, please turn on the heater.
Tara form	**Samukattara** dekakemasen. **寒かったら**出かけません。 If it's cold, I won't go out.
Tari form	Saikin, **samukattari atsukattari** suru. 最近、**寒かったり暑かったり**する。 These days, it's sometimes cold and sometimes hot.
Noun form	Hidoi **samusa** o kanjiru. ひどい**寒さ**を感じる。 I feel a bitter cold.

The adjective *ii* is an irregular one. It is usually only used in the prenominal and present forms. In all other conjugation forms, *yoi* is used.

ii/yoi いい/よい "good"

FORMS	CONJUGATION	
Stem	i-/yo- い-/よ-	
Prenominal	ii/yoi いい/よい	good ~
Present	ii/yoi いい/よい	is good
Negative	yokunai よくない	is not good
Past	yokatta よかった	was good
Negative Past	yokunakatta よくなかった	was not good
Conjunctive/*Te*	yoku/yokute よく/よくて	good and ~
Adverbial	yoku よく	well
Conditional	yokereba よければ	if ... is good
Tara (Conditional)	yokattara よかったら	if ... is good
Tari	yokattari よかったり	sometimes ... is good and sometimes ~
Noun	yosa よさ	goodness

EXAMPLES OF EACH FORM:

Prenominal form **ii/yoi** tenki
いい/よい 天気
good weather

Present form Koko wa itsumo tenki ga **ii/yoi**.
ここはいつも天気が**いい/よい**。
The weather here is always good.

Negative form	**Kyō wa tenki ga yokunai.** 今日は天気がよくない。 The weather is not good today.
Past form	**Kinō wa tenki ga yokatta.** 昨日は天気がよかった。 The weather was good yesterday.
Negative Past form	**Bosuton no tenki wa yokunakatta.** ボストンの天気はよくなかった。 The weather in Boston was not good.
Conjunctive/*Te* form	**Tenki ga yoku pikunikku wa tanoshikatta.** 天気がよくピクニックは楽しかった。 The weather was good and the picnic was enjoyable.
	Keshiki ga yokute takusan shashin o totta. 景色がよくてたくさん写真をとった。 The scenery was good and I took a lot of pictures.
Adverbial form	**Gogo wa tenki ga yoku natta.** 午後は天気がよくなった。 The weather became better in the afternoon.
Conditional form	**Tenki ga yokereba gorufu o shimasu.** 天気がよければゴルフをします。 If the weather is good, I will play golf.

Tara form	Ashita kibun ga **yokattara** shigoto ni iki-masu.
	明日気分が**よかったら**仕事に行きます。
	If I feel better tomorrow, I'll go to work.

Tari form	Ano resutoran no sābisu wa **yokattari warukattari** suru.
	あのレストランのサービスは**よかったり悪かったり**する。
	The service at that restaurant is sometimes good and sometimes bad.

Noun form	Watashi wa kono e no **yosa** ga wakaranai.
	私はこの絵の**よさ**が分からない。
	I cannot appreciate what is good about this picture.

PRACTICE 1

A. Give the negative form of the following words.

1. atsui 暑い hot   2. mushiatsui 蒸し暑い humid
3. atatakai 暖かい warm   4. suzushii 涼しい cool

B. Give the past and negative past forms of the following words.

1. nagai 長い long   2. mijikai 短い short
3. ōi 多い many/much   4. sukunai 少ない few/little

C. Give the *te* form of the following words.

1. hayai 早い early   2. hayai 速い speedy   3. osoi 遅い late/slow
4. takai 高い high/expensive   5. yasui 安い inexpensive
6. hikui 低い low

D. Give the adverbial form of the following words.

1. yoi よい good   2. warui 悪い bad   3. isogashii 忙しい busy
4. yakamashii やかましい noisy

E. Give the conditional forms (*ba/tara*) of the following words.

1. muzukashii 難しい difficult   2. yasashii 易しい easy
3. omoshiroi 面白い interesting   4. tsumaranai つまらない boring

F. Give the *tari* form of the following words.

1. atarashii 新しい new/fresh   2. furui 古い old
3. omoi 重い heavy   4. karui 軽い light

G. Give the noun form of the following words.

1. tōi 遠い far   2. chikai 近い near
3. wakai 若い young   4. tanoshii 楽しい enjoyable

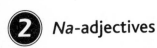 ## *Na*-adjectives

Na-adjectives are similar to nouns in that they conjugate with the copula *da*.

shizukana 静かな "quiet"

FORMS	CONJUGATION	
Stem	shizuka 静か	
Prenominal	shizuka**na** 静かな	quiet ~
Present	shizuka**da** 静かだ	is quiet
Negative	shizuka**de (wa) nai** 静かで(は)ない	is not quiet
Past	shizuka**datta** 静かだった	was quiet
Negative Past	shizuka**de (wa) nakatta** 静かで(は)なかった	was not quiet
Te	shizuka**de** 静かで	quiet and ~
Adverbial	shizuka**ni** 静かに	(become) quiet
Conditional	shizuka**nara (ba)** 静かなら(ば)	if … is quiet
Tara (Conditional)	shizuka**dattara** 静かだったら	if … is quiet
Tari	shizuka**dattari** 静かだったり	sometimes … is quiet and sometimes ~
Noun	shizuka**sa** 静かさ	quietness

EXAMPLES OF EACH FORM:

Prenominal form 　　　**shizukana** hoteru

　　　　　　　　　　静かなホテル

　　　　　　　　　　a quiet hotel

Present form	**Kono hoteru wa shizuka da.** このホテルは**静かだ**。 This hotel is quiet.
Negative form	**Ano resutoran wa shizuka dewa nai.** あのレストランは**静かではない**。 That restaurant is not quiet.
Past form	**Toshokan wa shizuka datta.** 図書館は**静かだった**。 The library was quiet.
Negative Past form	**Hito ga ōzei ite, kōen wa shizuka dewa na-katta.** 人が大勢いて、公園は**静かではなかった**。 There were many people, so the park wasn't quiet.
Te form	**Koko wa shizuka de yoku benkyō dekiru.** ここは**静かで**よく勉強出来る。 This place is quiet and I can study well here.
Adverbial form	**Nikai no heya ga shizuka ni natta.** 二階の部屋が**静かに**なった。 The room upstairs became quiet.
Conditional form	**Nami ga shizuka nara oyogimasu.** 波が**静かなら**泳ぎます。 If the waves are quiet, I'll swim.

Tara form	**Shizuka dattara** yoku nemurareru.
	静かだったらよく眠られる。
	If it's quiet, I can sleep well.
Tari form	Kono resutoran wa **shizuka dattari nigi-yaka dattari** suru.
	このレストランは静かだったりにぎやかだったりする。
	This restaurant is sometimes quiet and sometimes lively.
Noun form	Tori no nakigoe ga mori no **shizukasa** o yabutta.
	鳥の鳴き声が森の静かさを破った。
	The bird's cry broke the calm of the wood.

PRACTICE 2

A. Give the negative form of the following words.

1. kantanna 簡単な simple   2. fukuzatsuna 複雑な complicated

B. Give the past and negative past forms of the following words.

1. jōzuna 上手な skillful   2. hetana 下手な unskillful
3. benrina 便利な convenient   4. fubenna 不便な inconvenient

C. Give the *te* form of the following words.

1. anzenna 安全な safe   2. kikenna 危険な dangerous
3. hitsuyōna 必要な necessary

D. Give the adverbial form of the following words.

1. himana ひまな free (not busy)   2. taihenna 大変な difficult
3. mendōna 面倒な troublesome

E. Give the conditional forms (*nara(ba)*/*tara*) of the following words.

1. sukina 好きな favorite   2. kiraina 嫌いな hateful
3. jūdaina 重大な important

F. Give the *tari* form of the following words.

1. shiawasena 幸せな happy   2. fukōna 不幸な unhappy
3. kenkōna 健康な healthy

G. Give the noun form of the following words.

1. rippana 立派な excellent   2. seikakuna 正確な accurate

 3 Auxiliary Adjectives

Auxiliary adjectives attach to other adjectives or verbs. Some are *i*-adjectives, e.g., *tai* たい (want to), *rashii* らしい (seem), *yasui* やすい (easy to), while others are *na*-adjectives, e.g., *yō da* ようだ (seem) and *sō da* そうだ (look, appear to). They conjugate in the same way as other *i*- or *na*-adjectives. The following charts show the conjugations of *tai* and *sō da* as examples of each category.

Tai たい

Tai is attached to the stem of the *masu* form of a verb to express a first-person (I, we) desire to do something.

iku 行く go

FORMS	CONJUGATION	
Present	(iki)tai （行き）たい	want to (go)
Negative	(iki)takunai （行き）たくない	do not want to (go)
Past	(iki)takatta （行き）たかった	wanted to (go)
Negative Past	(iki)takunakatta （行き）たくなかった	did not want to (go)
Conjunctive/*Te*	(iki)taku/(iki)takute （行き）たく/（行き）たくて	want to (go) and ~
Adverbial	(iki)taku （行き）たく	(become) eager to (go)
Conditional	(iki)takereba （行き）たければ	if … want to (go)
Tara (Conditional)	(iki)takattara （行き）たかったら	if … want to (go)
Tari	(iki)takattari （行き）たかったり	sometimes … want to (go) and sometimes ~
Noun	(iki)tasa （行き）たさ	desire to (go)

PRACTICE 3

A. Attach the present form of *tai* to the following words.

1. kaimasu 買います buy   2. urimasu 売ります sell
3. mimasu 見ます see

B. Attach the negative form of *tai* to the following words.

1. yamemasu 辞めます quit   2. okurimasu 送ります send
3. arukimasu 歩きます walk

C. Attach the past and negative past forms of *tai* to the following words.

1. naraimasu 習います learn
2. benkyō shimasu 勉強します study

D. Attach the *te* form of *tai* to the following words.

1. kakimasu 書きます write   2. yomimasu 読みます read

E. Attach the conditional forms (*ba/tara*) of *tai* to the following words.

1. tabemasu 食べます eat   2. nomimasu 飲みます drink
3. kimasu 来ます come

F. Attach the noun form of *tai* to the following words.

1. asobimasu 遊びます play   2. aimasu 会います meet

Sō da そうだ

Sō da is attached to the stem of an *i*- or a *na*-adjective to express conjecture based on what the speaker sees or feels. There is no noun form.

ureshii 嬉しい glad

FORMS	CONJUGATION	
Present	(ureshi) **sōda** （嬉し）そうだ	look(s) (glad)
Negative	(ureshi) **sōde (wa) nai** （嬉し）そうで**(は)ない**	do(es) not look (glad)
Past	(ureshi) **sōdatta** （嬉し）そう**だった**	looked (glad)
Negative Past	(ureshi) **sōde (wa) nakatta** （嬉し）そうで**(は)なかった**	did not look (glad)
Conjunctive/*Te*	(ureshi) **sōde** （嬉し）そう**で**	look(s) (glad) and ~

Adverbial	(ureshi) sōni (嬉し)そうに	(glad)ly
Conditional	(ureshi) sōnara(ba) (嬉し)そうなら(ば)	if ... look(s) (glad)
Tara (Conditional)	(ureshi) sōdattara (嬉し)そうだったら	if ... look(s) (glad)
Tari	(ureshi) sōdattari (嬉し)そうだったり	sometimes ... look(s) (glad) and sometimes ~

genkina 元気な healthy

FORMS	CONJUGATION	
Present	(genki) sōda (元気)そうだ	look(s) (healthy)
Negative	(genki) sōde (wa) nai (元気)そうで(は)ない	do(es) not look (healthy)
Past	(genki) sōdatta (元気)そうだった	looked (healthy)
Negative Past	(genki) sōde (wa) nakatta (元気)そうで(は)なかった	did not look (healthy)
Te	(genki) sōde (元気)そうで	look(s) (healthy) and ~
Adverbial	(genki) sōni (元気)そうに	(vigorous)ly
Conditional	(genki) sōnara(ba) (元気)そうなら(ば)	if ... look(s) (healthy)
Tara (Conditional)	(genki) sōdattara (元気)そうだったら	if ... look(s) (healthy)
Tari	(genki) sōdattari (元気)そうだったり	sometimes ... look(s) (healthy) and sometimes ~

PRACTICE 4

A. Attach the present form of *sō da* to the following words.

1. oishii おいしい delicious   2. mazui まずい unsavory
3. daijina 大事な important

B. Attach the negative form of *sō da* to the following words.

1. amai 甘い sweet   2. karai 辛い salty/hot
3. kikenna 危険な dangerous

C. Attach the past and negative past forms of *sō da* to the following words.

1. tsuyoi 強い strong   2. benrina 便利な convenient
3. hitsuyōna 必要な necessary

D. Attach the *te* form of *sō da* to the following words.

1. yawarakai 柔かい soft   2. mezurashii 珍しい rare
3. kōkana 高価な expensive

E. Attach the adverbial form of *sō da* to the following words.

1. kanashii 悲しい sad   2. omoshiroi 面白い interesting
3. meiwakuna 迷惑な annoying

F. Attach the conditional forms (*nara/tara*) of *sō da* to the following words.

1. yowai 弱い weak   2. hiroi 広い spacious
3. fukuzatsuna 複雑な complicated

USAGE OF ADJECTIVES

In Part I we saw how Japanese adjectives conjugate and make numerous forms. Part II deals with how each of these forms is used in connection with sentence structures. Let us begin with the simplest case —adjectives used to modify nouns—and then move on to adjectival predicates, expressions following adjectival predicates, auxiliary adjectives and so forth on to more complex forms. The boxed sentence patterns listed under each form are numbered and arranged from easiest to most difficult. Non-conjugating adjectives are not covered here.

 Noun Modifiers

1.1 | **Adj + N** |

(a) akai hana   (red flower)
     赤い 花

(b) nigiyakana machi   (bustling city)
     にぎやかな 町

An *i-* or a *na*-adjective modifies the noun that follows it. Note that two or more adjectives may be used to modify a single noun (Example 3), just as in English.

EXAMPLES:

1. **aoi** sora 青い空 (blue sky), **shiroi** kumo 白い雲 (white cloud), **kiiroi** ribon 黄色いリボン (yellow ribbon)

2. **kireina** e きれいな絵 (pretty picture), **azayakana** iro 鮮やかな色 (bright color), **daijina** koto 大事なこと (important matter)

3. **ōkii shiroi** ie 大きい、白い家 (big, white house), **kireina**, **akai** kutsu きれいな、赤いくつ (pretty, red shoes), **sunaona**, **kashikoi** kodomo 素直な、かしこい子供 (obedient, smart child)

1.2 ┌─────────────┐
    │ Adj + **no** の │   "one"
    └─────────────┘

(a) chiisai no   (small one)
    小さい の

(b) jōbuna no   (durable one)
    丈夫な の

The particle *no* attached to an *i-* or a *na*-adjective functions as a pronoun: it replaces a noun when the noun is understood from context.

EXAMPLES:

1. Ano **chiisai** no o misete kudasai.
   あの小さいのを見せてください。
   Please show me that small one over there.

2. **Jōbuna** no o erabimashita.
   丈夫なのを選びました。
   I chose a/the durable one.

36

1.3 | **motto** もっと + Adj | "-er," "more"

(a) motto tsuyoi   (stronger)
    もっと 強い

(b) motto fukuzatsuna   (more complicated)
    もっと 複雑な

The word *motto* placed before an *i-* or a *na*-adjective creates the comparative form of that adjective.

EXAMPLES:

1. **Motto tsuyoi** himo o kudasai.
   もっと強いひもをください。
   Give me a stronger cord, please.

2. Kore wa (sore yori) **motto fukuzatsuna** mondai desu.
   これは（それより）**もっと複雑な**問題です。
   This is a more complicated problem (than that).

1.4 | **ichiban** 一番 + Adj | "-est," "most"

(a) ichiban wakai   (youngest)
    一番 若い

(b) ichiban taisetsuna   (most important)
    一番 大切な

The word *ichiban* placed before an *i-* or a *na-*adjective creates the superlative form of that adjective.

EXAMPLES:

1. Kaisha de **ichiban wakai** hito wa Minami-san desu.
   会社で**一番若い**人は南さんです。

   The youngest person in the company is Mr. Minami.

2. Kono naka de kore ga **ichiban taisetsuna** jisho desu.
   この中でこれが**一番大切な**辞書です。

   Among these, this is the most important dictionary.

 Adjectival Predicates

When used as predicates, Japanese adjectives have two tenses: present and past. The following charts show these tenses and their negative forms in both the plain and polite styles of speech.

takai 高い expensive

	AFFIRMATIVE (AFF)	NEGATIVE (NEG)
Present	takai 高い takai desu* 高いです is expensive	takakunai 高くない takakunai desu/takaku arimasen* 高くないです/高くありません is not expensive
Past	takakatta 高かった takakatta desu* 高かったです was expensive	takakunakatta 高くなかった takakunakatta desu/takaku arimasen deshita* 高くなかったです/高くありませんでした was not expensive

*Polite style of speech

kireina きれいな pretty

	AFFIRMATIVE (AFF)	NEGATIVE (NEG)
Present	kirei da きれいだ kirei desu* きれいです is pretty	kirei de wa/ja** nai きれい では/じゃ ない kirei de wa/ja** arimasen* きれい では/じゃ ありません is not pretty
Past	kirei datta きれいだった kirei deshita* きれいでした was pretty	kirei de wa/ja** nakatta きれい では/じゃ なかった kirei de wa/ja** arimasen deshita* きれい では/じゃ ありませんでした was not pretty

*Polite style of speech   **Ja is more colloquial than *de wa*.

The following boxed entries (2.1–2.3) represent the three basic constructions in which adjectival predicates are used in the present, past and negative forms.

2.1 | **N wa/ga は/が + Adj aff** | "NOUN is ADJECTIVE"

(a) takai/takakatta   (is/was expensive)
　　高い/高かった

(b) kirei da/kirei datta   (is/was pretty)
　　きれいだ/きれいだった

The affirmative adjective used as a predicate provides information about a noun, which may be either the topic or the subject of the sentence. When the noun is the topic, it is marked by the particle *wa*, and when it is the subject, it is marked by *ga*. The topic is often the same as the subject.

1. Hoteru no resutoran wa **takai/takai desu**.
   ホテルのレストランは**高い/高いです**。
   The restaurants in hotels are expensive.

2. Umi no iro ga **kirei datta/kirei deshita**.
   海の色が**きれいだった/きれいでした**。
   The color of the ocean was pretty.

2.2 | **N wa/ga は/が + Adj neg** | "NOUN is not ADJECTIVE"

(a) takakunai/takakunakatta   (is/was not expensive)
    高くない/高くなかった

(b) kirei de wa nai/kirei de wa nakatta   (is/was not pretty)
    きれいではない/きれいではなかった

The negative form of an *i*- or a *na*-adjective used as a predicate provides information about a noun, which may be either the topic or the subject of the sentence.

EXAMPLES:

1. Konsāto no kippu wa **takakunakatta/takaku arimasen deshita**.
   コンサートの切符は**高くなかった/高くありませんでした**。
   The concert ticket was not expensive.

2. Mada kōen no sakura no hana wa **kirei de wa nai/kirei de wa arimasen**.

まだ公園の桜の花は**きれいではない/きれいではありません**。

The cherry blossoms in the park are not pretty yet.

2.3 | N1 wa は N2 ga が + Adj |

"As for NOUN 1, NOUN 2 is ADJECTIVE"

(a) nagai/nagakatta   (is/was long)
長い/長かった

(b) jōzu da/jōzu datta   (is/was skillful)
上手だ/上手だった

In the *wa ... ga* construction, the topic marked by *wa* and the subject marked by *ga* appear in one sentence.

EXAMPLES:

1. Watashi no inu wa mimi ga **nagai/nagai desu**.
   私の犬は耳が**長い/長いです**。
   My dog has long ears. (lit. As for my dog, his ears are long.)

2. Haruko-san wa piano ga **jōzu datta/jōzu deshita**.
   春子さんはピアノが**上手だった/上手でした**。
   Haruko was good at piano. (lit. As for Haruko, piano was her forte.)

3. Tomu wa sakana ga **suki de wa nai/suki de wa arimasen**.
   トムは魚が**好きではない/好きではありません**。
   Tom does not like fish. (lit. As for Tom, fish is not his favorite.)

4. Watashi wa atarashii kuruma ga **hoshii/hoshii desu**.

私は新しい車が**欲しい/欲しいです**。

I want a new car. (lit. As for me, a new car is desirable.)

5. Watashi wa kare no shinsetsu ga **ureshikatta/ureshikatta desu**.

私は彼の親切が**嬉しかった/嬉しかったです**。

I was pleased by his kindness. (lit. As for me, his kindness was pleasing.)

PRACTICE 1 (2.2–2.3)

A. Change the following sentences into the negative form.

1. **Kōen no ike wa fukai.**

公園の池は深い。

The pond in the park is deep.

2. **Kono kaban wa benri desu.**

このかばんは便利です。

This bag is convenient.

3. **Watashi-tachi no kyōshitsu wa akarui desu.**

私達の教室は明るいです。

Our classroom is bright.

4. **Kono heya wa tenjō ga takai.**

この部屋は天井が高い。

This room has a high ceiling.

B. Change the following sentences into the past form.

1. Ano resutoran wa yūmei da.
   あのレストランは有名だ。
   That restaurant is famous.

2. Kare no heya wa semai desu.
   彼の部屋は狭いです。
   His room is small.

3. Depāto no ten'in wa shinsetsu desu.
   デパートの店員は親切です。
   The salespeople at the department store are kind.

4. Jimu wa tenisu ga heta da.
   ジムはテニスが下手だ。
   Jim is poor at tennis.

C. Change the following sentences into the negative past form.

1. Watashi no kaisha wa eki kara tōkatta.
   私の会社は駅から遠かった。
   My company was far from the train station.

2. Kinō no shiken wa muzukashikatta desu.
   昨日の試験は難しかったです。
   Yesterday's exam was difficult.

3. Sono machi no chikatesu wa kirei datta.
   その町の地下鉄はきれいだった。
   That city's subway was clean.

4. Buraun-san wa sashimi ga kirai deshita.
   ブラウンさんはさしみが嫌いでした。
   Mr. Brown disliked sashimi.

D. Fill in the blanks with the appropriate forms of the adjectives given in parentheses.

1. Kanji no kuizu wa _____ ta. (yasashii)
   漢字のクイズは _____ た。（易しい）
   The kanji quiz was easy.

2. Koko no kikō wa _____ desu. (ondanna)
   ここの気候は _____ です。（温暖な）
   The climate here is mild.

3. Kono sūji wa _____ desu ka. (tashikana)
   この数字は _____ ですか。（確かな）
   Is this number accurate?

4. Ano mise no kēki wa _____ arimasen. (oishii)
   あの店のケーキは _____ ありません。（おいしい）
   The cakes at that store are not good.

5. Kono shiroi kōto wa _____ ta. (yasui)
   この白いコートは _____ た。（安い）
   This white coat was not cheap.

6. Gakusei wa ii kyōkasho ga _____ da. (hitsuyōna)
   学生はいい教科書が _____ だ。（必要な）
   Students needed good textbooks.

7. Watashi wa haha no shi ga _____ ta desu. (kanashii)
   私は母の死が _____ たです。（悲しい）

   I was saddened by my mother's death.

③ Expressions Following Adjectival Predicates (Adj pred)

Adjectival predicates in the present, past or negative forms are combined with other elements such as auxiliaries, particles or phrases to create various expressions.

3.1 | Adj pred + **darō** だろう | "probably"

(a) tsumetai/tsumetakatta darō   (is/was probably cold)
   冷たい/冷たかった だろう

(b) tekisetsu*/tekisetsu datta darō   (is/was probably appropriate)
   適切*/適切だった だろう   *Da だ drops.

Darō, the presumptive form of the copula (be-verb) *da*, is used as an auxiliary to indicate the speaker's conjecture. *Deshō* is the polite form of *darō*.

EXAMPLES:

1. Umi no mizu wa **tsumetai** darō.
   海の水は**冷たい**だろう。

   The ocean water is probably cold.

2. Shiga Kōgen wa **suzushikatta** deshō.
志賀高原は**涼しかった**でしょう。

The Shiga Highlands were probably cool.

3. Isha no shochi wa **tekisetsu datta** deshō.
医者の処置は**適切だった**でしょう。

The doctor's treatment was probably appropriate.

3.2 | **Adj pred + ka か** | "…?"

(a) oishii/oishikatta ka   (is/was … delicious?)
おいしい/おいしかった か

(b) genkaku*/genkaku datta ka   (is/was … strict?)
厳格*/厳格だった か   *Da だ drops.

The particle *ka* at the end of a sentence turns the sentence into a question.

EXAMPLES:

1. Furansu ryōri wa **oishikatta** desu ka?
フランス料理は**おいしかった**ですか。

Was the French meal delicious?

2. Kono kawa wa **fukakunai** desu ka.
この川は**深くない**ですか。

Isn't this river deep?

3. Anata no gakkō no kisoku wa **genkaku** desu ka.
あなたの学校の規則は**厳格**ですか。

Are the regulations of your school strict?

3.3 | **Adj pred + ne ね** | "…, isn't it/he?" "…, is it/he?"

(a) amai/amakatta ne
甘い/甘かった ね
(is/was sweet, isn't/wasn't it?)

(b) genki da/genki datta ne
元気だ/元気だった ね
(is/was healthy, isn't/wasn't he?)

The particle *ne* at the end of a sentence indicates the speaker's request for confirmation.

EXAMPLES:

1. Kono orenji wa **amai** ne.
このオレンジは**甘い**ね。

These oranges are sweet, aren't they?

2. Ano resutoran no hanbāgā wa **oishikunakatta** desu ne.
あのレストランのハンバーガーは**おいしくなかった**ですね。

The hamburger at that restaurant wasn't good, was it?

3. Akira wa itsumo **genki da** ne.
明はいつも**元気だ**ね。

Akira is always in good spirits, isn't he?

3.4 | Adj pred + **yo** よ | "I tell you"

(a) omoshiroi/omoshirokatta yo   (is/was interesting, I tell you)
面白い/面白かった よ

(b) benri da/benri datta yo   (is/was convenient, I tell you)
便利だ/便利だった よ

The particle *yo* at the end of a sentence indicates strong conviction on the part of the speaker.

EXAMPLES:

1. Yūbe no eiga wa **omoshirokatta** yo.
ゆうべの映画は**面白かった**よ。
Last night's movie was interesting, I tell you.

2. Kono dōgu wa totemo **benri** desu yo.
この道具はとても**便利**ですよ。
This tool is very convenient, I tell you.

3. Ano gaka wa **yūmei ja nakatta** desu yo.
あの画家は**有名じゃなかった**ですよ。
That painter wasn't famous, I tell you.

3.5 | Adj pred + **ga** が | "but"

(a) yasui/yasukatta ga   (is/was inexpensive, but …)
安い/安かった が

(b) jōzu da/jōzu datta ga   (is/was good at (something), but …)
　　上手だ/上手だった が

The particle *ga* is used as a conjunction to combine two sentences that express contrastive ideas.

EXAMPLES:

1. Kono kōto wa **yasui** ga shitsu ga **warui**.
　このコートは**安い**が質が**悪い**。
　This coat is inexpensive, but its quality is bad.

2. Watashi no apāto wa **hirokunakatta** ga **kaiteki** deshita.
　私のアパートは**広くなかった**が**快適**でした。
　My apartment wasn't spacious, but it was comfortable.

3. Ane wa ryōri ga **jōzu** desu ga watashi wa **heta** desu.
　姉は料理が**上手**ですが私は**下手**です。
　My older sister is good at cooking, whereas I am poor at it.

3.6 | Adj pred + **keredomo けれども** | "although"

(a) muzukashii/muzukashikatta keredomo
　　難しい/難しかった けれども   (although … is/was difficult)

(b) hitsuyō da/hitsuyō datta keredomo
　　必要だ/必要だった けれども   (although … is/was necessary)

The particle *keredomo* is, like *ga,* used as a conjunction to combine two sentences that express contrastive ideas.

EXAMPLES:

1. Kono shigoto wa **muzukashii** keredomo omoshiroi desu.
   この仕事は**難しい**けれども面白いです。

   Although this work is difficult, it is interesting.

2. Atarashii konpyūtā ga **hitsuyō da** keredomo ima wa kaenai.
   新しいコンピューターが**必要だ**けれども今は買えない。

   Although I need a new computer, I can't buy one now.

3. Kare wa gorufu ga **jōzu ja nakatta** keredomo suki deshita.
   彼はゴルフが**上手じゃなかった**けれども好きでした。

   Although he wasn't good at golf, he liked it.

PRACTICE 2 (3.1–3.6)

Fill in the blanks with the appropriate forms of the adjectives given in parentheses.

1. Raishū no shiken wa _____ darō. (kantanna)
   来週の試験は _____ だろう。(簡単な)

   Next week's exam will probably be simple.

2. Yūbe no opera wa _____ desu ne. (subarashii)
   ゆうべのオペラは _____ ですね。(すばらしい)

   Last night's opera was splendid, wasn't it?

3. Ano mise no sakana wa itsumo _____ desu ka. (shinsenna)
   あの店の魚はいつも _____ ですか。(新鮮な)

   Are the fish at that store always fresh?

4. Toshokan wa chikatesu no eki kara _____ nai desu yo. (tōi)
図書館は地下鉄の駅から _____ ないですよ。(遠い)
The library is not far from the subway station, I tell you.

5. Koko wa _____ da ga kaimono ni _____ da. (shizukana)
(fubenna)
ここは _____ だが買い物に _____ だ。(静か)(不便な)
This place is quiet, but inconvenient for shopping.

6. Ano resutoran wa _____ keredomo ryōri wa _____ nai.
(yūmeina) (oishii)
あのレストランは _____ けれども料理は _____ ない。
(有名な)(おいしい)
Although that restaurant is famous, the food isn't good.

7. Kono kutsu wa _____ keredomo _____ ja nai deshō.
(kireina) (jōbuna)
このくつは _____ けれども _____ じゃないでしょう。
(きれいな)(丈夫な)
Although these shoes are pretty, they are probably not durable.

3.7 | Adj pred + **dake da** だけだ | "only," "just," "that's all"

(a) ōkii/ōkikatta dake da   (is/was only big)
    大きい/大きかった だけだ

(b) majimena*/majimedatta dake da   (is/was only serious)
    まじめな*/まじめだった だけだ   *Da だ changes to na な.

51

Used after an adjective, the particle *dake* limits someone or something to the state expressed by that adjective. The particle *bakari* may be used in place of *dake* (Example 2).

EXAMPLES:

1. Ano sutēki wa **ōkikatta** dake da.
   あのステーキは**大きかった**だけだ。
   The steak was big, that's all.

2. Kare wa **majimena** bakari de, shigoto wa dekinai.
   彼は**まじめな**ばかりで、仕事は出来ない。
   He is too conscientious and cannot do (good) work.

3. Honda-san wa gorufu ga **sukina** dake da. Jōzu ja nai.
   本田さんはゴルフが**好きな**だけだ。上手じゃない。
   Mr. Honda just loves golf. It's not that he's good at it.

3.8 | **Adj pred + hazu da はずだ** | "I expect that 〜"

(a) mijikai/mijikakatta hazu da
    短い/短かった はずだ
    (I expect that ... is/was/will be short)

(b) seiketsuna*/seiketsu datta hazu da
    清潔な*/清潔だった はずだ
    (I expect that ... is/was/will be clean)
    *Da だ changes to *na* な.

Used after an adjective, *hazu* expresses the speaker's expectation or belief that someone or something is, was or will be in some state. *Hazu* is a pseudonoun—a noun never used independently.

EXAMPLES:

1. Kyō no kaigi wa **mijikai** hazu da.
   今日の会議は**短い**はずだ。
   I expect that today's meeting will be short.

2. Byōin wa mina **seiketsuna** hazu desu.
   病院はみな**清潔な**はずです。
   The hospitals are most certainly clean.

3. Tetsuzuki wa **kantan datta** hazu da.
   手続きは**簡単だった**はずだ。
   The procedure was no doubt simple.

3.9 Adj pred + **koto ga aru** ことがある

"There are/were times when ～"

(a) furui/furukatta koto ga aru
    古い/古かった ことがある
    (There are/were times when ... is/was old)

(b) kikenna*/kiken datta koto ga aru
    危険な*/危険だった ことがある
    (There are/were times when ... is/was dangerous)
    *Da だ changes to *na* な.

Used after an adjective, the phrase *koto ga aru* indicates that a state exists or has existed from time to time.

EXAMPLES:

1. Ano mise no pan wa **furui** koto ga aru.
   あの店のパンは**古い**ことがある。

   There are times when the bread at that store is old.

2. Wāpuro ga totemo **takakatta** koto ga arimasu.
   ワープロがとても**高かった**ことがあります。

   There was a time when word processors were very expensive.

3. Tozan wa **kikenna** koto ga arimasu.
   登山は**危険な**ことがあります。

   Mountain climbing can be dangerous at times.

3.10 | **Adj pred + no/koto の/こと** |　　"that ～"

(a) ii/yokatta no/koto　　　　　　　　　(that ... is/was good)
    いい/よかった の/こと

(b) shōjikina*/shōjiki datta no/koto　　　(that ... is/was honest)
    正直な*/正直だった の/こと　　　　　*Da だ changes to na な.

Both *no* and *koto* are nominalizers that turn adjectival clauses into noun phrases. They are used interchangeably.

EXAMPLES:

1. Kudamono ga karada ni **ii** no wa dare demo shitte imasu.
   果物が体に**いい**のはだれでも知っています。
   Everybody knows that fruits are good for the body.

2. Kinō no shiai ga **yokatta** koto o kikimashita ka.
   昨日の試合が**よかった**ことを聞きましたか。
   Did you hear that yesterday's game was good?

3. Ano hito ga **shōjiki datta** koto wa tashika desu.
   あの人が**正直だった**ことは確かです。
   It is certain that he was honest.

3.11 | Adj pred + **kashira/kana かしら/かな** | "I wonder"

(a) shitashii/shitashikatta kashira/kana
    親しい/親しかった かしら/かな
    (I wonder if … is/was intimate)

(b) tekitō*/tekitō datta kashira/kana
    適当*/適当だった かしら/かな
    (I wonder if … is/was suitable)
    *Da だ drops.

The particles *kashira* and *kana* are used at the end of a sentence to express uncertainty. *Kashira* is mostly used by women and *kana* principally by men. When *kashira* or *kana* follows a negative adjective, it expresses the speaker's hope that someone or something is not, was not or will not be in some state (Example 3).

55

EXAMPLES:

1. Masako-san wa Kida-san to **shitashikatta** kashira.
   正子さんは木田さんと**親しかった**かしら。
   I wonder if Masako was intimate with Mr. Kida.

2. Kono purezento wa kanojo ni **tekitō** kana.
   このプレゼントは彼女に**適当**かな。
   I wonder if this present is suitable for her.

3. Kyō no kōgi wa **nagakunai** kashira.
   今日の講義は**長くない**かしら。
   I hope today's lecture won't be long.

3.12 | Adj pred + **sō da** そうだ | "I heard that ～"

(a) omoi/omokatta sō da   (I heard that ... is/was heavy/serious)
    重い/重かった そうだ

(b) kirai da/kirai datta sō da   (I heard that ... dislikes/disliked)
    嫌いだ/嫌いだった そうだ

Sō da is an auxiliary which expresses hearsay—what the speaker heard or obtained indirectly.

EXAMPLES:

1. Yamada-san no byōki wa totemo **omoi** sō da.
   山田さんの病気はとても**重い**そうだ。
   I heard that Mr. Yamada's illness is very serious.

2. Tomu wa seiseki ga **yokunakatta** sō da.
   トムは成績が**よくなかった**そうだ。

   I heard that Tom's grades were not good.

3. Midori-san wa neko ga **kirai datta** sō desu.
   緑さんはねこが**嫌いだった**そうです。

   I heard that Midori disliked cats.

PRACTICE 3 (3.7–3.12)

Fill in the blanks with the appropriate forms of the adjectives given in parentheses.

1. Buraun-san wa sakana ga _____ hazu desu. (kiraina)
   ブラウンさんは魚が _____ はずです。(嫌いな)

   I expect that Miss Brown dislikes fish.

2. Kore wa iro ga _____ dake da. Shitsu wa _____ nai.
   (kireina) (ii)
   これは色が _____ だけだ。質は _____ ない。(きれいな)
   (いい)

   This has a pretty color, that's all. The quality isn't good.

3. Ano umi wa _____ sō da. Kodomo ni wa _____ kana.
   (fukai) (kikenna)
   あの海は _____ そうだ。子供には _____ かな。(深い)
   (危険な)

   I heard that the ocean is deep. I wonder if it is dangerous for children.

4. Kono kōhī wa _____ bakari da. _____ nai. (nigai) (oishii)

このコーヒーは _____ ばかりだ。 _____ ない。（苦い）（おいしい）

This coffee is just plain bitter. It's not tasty.

5. Kinō kare wa _____ sō desu. Ashita wa _____ kashira. (isogashii) (himana)

昨日彼は _____ そうです。あしたは _____ かしら。（忙しい）（ひまな）

I heard that he was busy yesterday. I wonder if he is free tomorrow.

6. Kachō wa _____ keredomo _____ koto wa mina ga shitte iru. (genkakuna) (shinsetsuna)

課長は _____ けれども _____ ことは皆が知っている。（厳格な）（親切な）

Everybody knows that although he is strict, the section chief is kind.

7. Kono ko wa _____ ga _____ koto ga arimasu. (kashikoi) (sunaona)

この子は _____ が _____ ことがあります。（かしこい）（素直な）

This child is bright, but there are times when he is not obedient.

8. Hayashi-san no byōki ga _____ no wa _____ kashira. (omoi) (tashikana)

林さんの病気が _____ のは _____ かしら。（重い）（確かな）

I wonder if it is certain that Miss Hayashi's illness was not serious.

3.13 | Adj pred + **shi** し | "and what's more," "so," "moreover"

(a) yawarakai/yawarakakatta shi   (is/was soft and what's more)
柔かい/柔かかった し

(b) shizuka da/shizuka datta shi   (is/was quiet and what's more)
静かだ/静かだった し

The particle *shi* is used as a conjunction to link two or more states.

EXAMPLES:

1. Kono jaketto wa **yawarakai** shi, yasui desu.
このジャケットは**柔かい**し、安いです。
This jacket is soft, and what's more, it's inexpensive.

2. Koko wa eki kara **tōkunai** shi, tsūkin ni benri desu.
ここは駅から**遠くない**し、通勤に便利です。
This place is not far from the station, so it's convenient for commuting to work.

3. Sono shima wa **shizukadatta** shi, keshiki mo utsukushikatta.
その島は**静かだった**し、景色も美しかった。
That island was quiet, and moreover, the scenery was beautiful.

3.14 | Adj pred + **ka dō ka** かどうか | "whether or not"

(a) warui/warukatta ka dō ka   (whether or not ... is/was bad)
悪い/悪かった か ど う か

(b) kenkō*/kenkō datta ka dō ka   (whether or not ... is/was healthy)
健康*/健康だった か どう か   *Da だ drops.

The phrase *ka dō ka* indicates a question embedded in a sentence.

EXAMPLES:

1. Kono shōsetsu no yaku ga **warui** ka dō ka wakaranai.
   この小説の訳が**悪い**かどうか分からない。
   I can't tell whether the translation of this novel is bad or not.

2. Kyonen no natsu ga itsumo yori **atsukatta** ka dō ka oboete imasen.
   去年の夏がいつもより**暑かった**かどうか覚えていません。
   I don't remember whether last summer was hotter than usual or not.

3. Noda-san no akachan ga **kenkō** ka dō ka shirimasen.
   野田さんの赤ちゃんが**健康**かどうか知りません。
   I don't know whether Mrs. Noda's baby is healthy or not.

3.15 | **Adj pred + noni のに**   "although"

(a) itai/itakatta noni   (although ... is/was painful)
    痛い/痛かった のに

(b) anzenna*/anzen datta noni   (although is/was ... safe)
    安全な*/安全だった のに   *Da changes to *na* な.

The particle *noni*, when used as a conjunction, indicates a state that is followed by a result contrary to expectation. If the predicate of the main clause (the clause following *noni*) is in the past tense, the tense of the *noni* clause (the subordinate clause) may be either present or past (Example 3).

EXAMPLES:

1. Kare wa atama ga **itai** noni kusuri o nomanai.
   彼は頭が**痛いの**に薬を飲まない。
   Although he has a headache, he doesn't take medecine.

2. Sakana wa **atarashikatta** noni oishiku nakatta.
   魚は**新しかったの**においしくなかった。
   Although the fish was fresh, it didn't taste good.

3. Sono michi wa yoru demo **anzenna/anzen datta** noni dare mo tōranakatta.
   その道は夜でも**安全な/安全だった**のにだれも通らなかった。
   Although the street was safe even at night, no one passed along it.

PRACTICE 4 (3.13–3.15)

Fill in the blanks with the appropriate forms of the adjectives given in parentheses.

1. Umi no mizu wa _____ shi, nami mo _____ ta. (tsumetai) (takai)
   海の水は _____ し、波も _____ た。(冷たい)(高い)
   The ocean water was cold, and what's more, the waves were high, too.

2. Imōto wa watashi yori piano ga _____ ta ga, hitomae de hiku no ga _____ datta. (jōzuna) (kiraina)

妹は私よりピアノが _____ たが、人前で弾くのが _____ だった。（上手な）（嫌いな）

My younger sister was better at piano than me, but disliked to play in front of people.

3. Kare wa _____ ta ga, _____ ta ka dō ka shirimasen. (kashikoi) (shōjikina)

彼は _____ たが、_____ たかどうか知りません。（かしこい）（正直な）

He was bright, but whether or not he was honest, I don't know.

4. Koko wa natsu wa _____ shi, fuyu wa _____ shi, sumu noni _____ desu. (suzushii) (atatakai) (kaitekina)

ここは夏は _____ し、冬は _____ し、住むのに _____ です。（涼しい）（暖かい）（快適な）

Here it's cool in the summer, and what's more, it's warm in the winter, so it's a comfortable place to live.

5. Shiken wa _____ ta noni, kekka wa _____ ta. (kantanna) (ii)

試験は _____ たのに、結果は _____ た。（簡単な）（いい）

Although the exam was simple, the result wasn't good.

3.16 | Adj pred + **toki** 時 | "when"

(a) sabishii/sabishikatta toki (ni)　　　(when ... is/was lonely)
　　さびしい/さびしかった 時（に）

(b) taihenna*/taihen datta toki (ni)　　(when ... is/was difficult)
　　大変な*/大変だった 時（に）　　　 *Da だ changes to *na* な.

The pseudonoun *toki* is an indicator of time. The particle *ni* may follow it, but is optional. If the predicate of the main clause is in the past tense, the tense of the *toki* clause (the subordinate clause) may be either present or past (Examples 2, 3).

EXAMPLES:

1. **Sabishii** toki, tomodachi ni denwa shimasu.
　 さびしい時、友達に電話します。
　 When I'm lonely, I call my friends.

2. Bīru ga **yasui/yasukatta** toki ni, takusan katte oita.
　 ビールが**安い/安かった**時にたくさん買っておいた。
　 I bought a lot of beer when it was cheap.

3. Shigoto ga **taihenna/taihen datta** toki, dōryō ni tetsudatte moratta.
　 仕事が**大変な/大変だった**時、同僚に手伝ってもらった。
　 When the work was difficult, I had my colleagues help me.

3.17 | Adj pred + **uchi ni** うちに | "while"

(a) akarui uchi ni   (while … is/was light)
　　明るい うちに

(b) jōbuna* uchi ni   (while … is/was healthy/durable)
　　丈夫な* うちに   *Da だ changes to na な.

The phrase *uchi ni* is used as a conjunction. The *uchi ni* clause (the subordinate clause) denotes a period of time during which someone or something exists or existed in some state. The tense before *uchi ni* is always present, regardless of the tense of the main clause.

EXAMPLES:

1. **Akarui** uchi ni kaerimashō.
   明るいうちに帰りましょう。
   Let's go home while it is light.

2. **Atatakai** uchi ni tabete kudasai.
   温かいうちに食べてください。
   Please eat it while it is warm.

3. **Jōbuna** uchi ni dekiru dake hataraku tsumori datta.
   丈夫なうちに出来るだけ働くつもりだった。
   I intended to work as much as possible while I was healthy.

3.18 | Adj pred + **to** と | "if"

(a) chiisai to   (if ... is/was small)
    小さい と

(b) dame da to   (if ... is/was useless)
    駄目だ と

The particle *to* is used as a conjunction. The *to* clause (the subordinate clause) expresses a condition that entails an uncontrollable or unavoidable result. The tense before *to* must be present, regardless of the tense of the main clause.

EXAMPLES:

1. Mado ga **chiisai** to, heya wa kurai desu.
   窓が**小さい**と、部屋は暗いです。
   If the windows are small, the room will be dark.

2. Kono ryōri wa **karakunai** to, mazui desu ne.
   この料理は**辛くない**と、まずいですね。
   If it's not spicy, this dish won't taste good, will it?

3. Kono kikai ga **dame da** to, atarashii no o kawanakereba naranai.
   この機械が**駄目だ**と、新しいのを買わなければならない。
   If this machine is no good, we will have to buy a new one.

3.19 | Adj pred + **kara** から | "because," "so"

(a) kitanai/kitanakatta kara   (because … is/was dirty)
きたない/きたなかった から

(b) nesshin da/nesshin datta kara   (because … is/was enthusiastic)
熱心だ/熱心だった から

The particle *kara* is used as a conjunction. The *kara* clause (the subordinate clause) expresses a reason or cause as interpreted by the speaker. If the predicate of the main clause is in the past tense, the tense of the *kara* clause may be either present or past (Example 1). The plain style of speech is normally used in the subordinate clause, but the *masu* form may be used in very polite speech (Example 2).

EXAMPLES:

1. Heya ga **kitanai/kitanakatta** kara, sōji shimashita.
   部屋が**きたない/きたなかった**から、掃除しました。
   Because the room was dirty, I cleaned it.

2. Gogo wa **isogashiku arimasen** kara, asobi ni kite kudasai.
   午後は**忙しくありません**から、遊びに来てください。
   I am not busy in the afternoon, so please come visit me.

3. Kare wa gorufu ni **nesshin da** kara, mainichi renshū shite iru.
   彼はゴルフに**熱心だ**から、毎日練習している。
   He is enthusiastic about golf, so he practices every day.

3.20 | Adj pred + **node** ので | "because," "so"

(a) mezurashii/mezurashikatta node (because ... is/was rare)
珍しい/珍しかった ので

(b) jūdaina*/jūdai datta node (because ... is/was important)
重大な*/重大だった ので *Da だ changes to na な.

The particle *node* is used as a conjunction. The *node* clause (the subordinate clause) expresses a reason or cause that is more objective or reasonable to the listener than one introduced by *kara*. Unlike *kara*, *node* tends not to project the speaker's personal opinion. The *node* clause is usually not followed by a main clause involving the speaker's volition, opinion, command or invitation.

EXAMPLES:

1. Kono tokusanhin wa **mezurashii** node, kankōkyaku ni ninki ga arimasu.
   この特産品は**珍しい**ので、観光客に人気があります。
   This local product is rare, so it is popular with tourists.

2. Toshokan wa **shizukana/shizuka datta** node, yoku benkyō dekita.
   図書館は**静かな/静かだった**ので、よく勉強出来た。
   Because the library was quiet, I could study well.

3. Sono mondai wa **jūdaina** node, ima kaigi de tōgi shite iru.
   その問題は**重大な**ので、今会議で討議している。
   Because that problem is important, it is being discussed in the meeting now.

3.21 | Adj pred + **dake de naku** だけでなく

"not only ～ but also ～"

(a) nagai/nagakatta dake de naku
    長い/長かった だけでなく
    (is/was … not only long ～)

(b) ganjōna*/ganjō datta dake de naku
    頑丈な*/頑丈だった だけでなく
    (is/was … not only strong ～)
    *Da だ changes to na な.

Used after an adjective, the phrase *dake de naku* expresses two states in one sentence, with emphasis on the fact that the first is not the only. *Bakari de naku* may be used in place of *dake de naku* (Example 2).

EXAMPLES:

1. Kono inu wa ashi ga **nagai** dake de naku mimi mo nagai.
   この犬は足が**長い**だけでなく耳も長い。
   This dog has not only long legs, but also long ears.

2. Kanojo wa atama ga **yokatta** bakari de naku shigoto ni mo nesshin deshita.
   彼女は頭が**よかった**ばかりでなく仕事にも熱心でした。
   She was not only bright, but also intent on her work.

3. Kono kuruma wa **ganjōna** dake de naku sutairu mo kibatsu da.
   この車は**頑丈な**だけでなくスタイルも奇抜だ。
   Not only is this car durable, its style is also original.

3.22 | Adj pred + N | to make a relative clause

(a) kurai/kurakatta heya   (a room which is/was dark)
    暗い/暗かった 部屋

(b) azayakana*/azayaka datta iro   (a color which is/was bright)
    鮮やかな*/鮮やかだった 色   *Da だ changes to na な.

The relative clause is a modifying clause that is placed before the noun
to be modified. Japanese does not have relative pronouns such as
"who," "which," "that," nor relative adverbs like "when" or "where."
The tense of the relative clause must be in the present form if the
state presented there is concurrent with the action or state presented
in the main clause (Examples 2, 3).

EXAMPLES:

1. Sakki made **kurakatta** heya ni hi ga sashikonda.
   さっきまで**暗かった**部屋に日が差し込んだ。
   The sunlight streamed into the room, which had been dark until a
   while ago.

2. Uta ga **jōzuna** Mori-san wa itsumo pātī de utatte ita.
   歌が**上手な**森さんはいつもパーティーで歌っていた。
   Mr. Mori, who was good at singing, always sang at parties.

3. Michiko-san wa iro ga **azayakana** doresu ga suki deshita.
   道子さんは色が**鮮やかな**ドレスが好きでした。
   Michiko loved bright dresses.

Correct the mistakes in the following sentences.

1. Kono apāto wa semakatta dake de naku yachin mo takai.
   このアパートは狭かっただけでなく家賃も高い。
   Not only is this apartment small, its rent is also high.

2. Sakura no hana ga utsukushikatta uchi ni takusan shashin o
   torimashita.
   桜の花が美しかったうちにたくさん写真をとりました。
   I took a lot of pictures while the cherry blossoms were beautiful.

3. Sakki made aoi sora ga kyū ni kumotte kita.
   さっきまで青い空が急に曇ってきた。
   The sky, which had been blue a while ago, suddenly turned cloudy.

4. Tenjō ga hikui da to, heya ga kurai desu.
   天井が低いだと、部屋が暗いです。
   If the ceiling is low, the room will be dark.

5. Kono mondai wa fukuzatsuna kara, yoku kangaete kudasai.
   この問題は複雑なから、よく考えてください。
   This problem is complicated, so please think hard about it.

6. Kare wa shōjiki da node, mina ni shin'yō sarete imasu.
   彼は正直だので、皆に信用されています。
   Because he is honest, he is trusted by everybody.

7. Kōen de kubi ga nagakatta tori o mimashita.
   公園で首が長かった鳥を見ました。
   I saw a bird with a long neck in the park.

8. Hima datta toki, itsu demo kite kudasai.
   ひまだった時、いつでも来てください。
   Please come anytime you are free.

9. Pātī de Nihongo ga jōzu datta Amerikajin ni atta.
   パーティーで日本語が上手だったアメリカ人に会った。
   I met an American at the party who was good at Japanese.

4 Auxiliary Adjectives

Auxiliary adjectives are attached to adjectival predicates (Adj pred), the stems of adjectives (Adj stem) or the stems of the *masu* forms of verbs (V-(masu)). Auxiliary verbs may also be attached to the stems of adjectives.

4.1 | Adj pred + **kamoshirenai かもしれない** | "might"

(a) tsumaranai/tsumaranakatta kamoshirenai
    つまらない/つまらなかった かもしれない
    (might be/might have been boring)

(b) shinken*/shinken datta kamoshirenai
    真剣*/真剣だった かもしれない
    (might be/might have been serious)   *Da だ drops.

The auxiliary *i*-adjective *kamoshirenai* expresses the speaker's guess. *Kamoshiremasen* is the polite form.

EXAMPLES:

1. Ashita no pikunikku wa **tsumaranai** kamoshirenai.
   あしたのピクニックは**つまらない**かもしれない。
   Tomorrow's picnic might be boring.

2. Kare wa kondo no shigoto ni **shinken** kamoshirenai.
   彼は今度の仕事に**真剣**かもしれない。
   He might be serious about this new job.

3. Jimu wa Nihon no eiga ga **suki de wa nakatta** kamoshire-masen.
   ジムは日本の映画が**好きではなかった**かもしれません。
   Jim might not have liked Japanese movies.

4.2 | Adj pred + **ni chigainai** にちがいない | "must be," "no doubt"

(a) yasashii/yasashikatta ni chigainai   (is/was no doubt easy)
    易しい/易しかった にちがいない

(b) kōka*/kōka datta ni chigainai   (is/was no doubt expensive)
    高価*/高価だった にちがいない   *Da だ drops.

The auxiliary *i*-adjective *chigainai* preceded by *ni* expresses the speaker's conviction. *Chigaiarimasen* is the polite form.

EXAMPLES:

1. Wada-sensei no shiken wa **yasashii** ni chigainai.
   和田先生の試験は**易しい**にちがいない。
   Professor Wada's exam must be easy.

2. Tenrankai wa gakusei ni wa **omoshirokunakatta** ni chigaiarimasen.
   展覧会は学生には**面白くなかった**にちがいありません。
   The exhibition was no doubt uninteresting to the students.

3. Kono yubiwa wa **kōka** ni chigainai.
   この指輪は**高価**にちがいない。
   This ring must be expensive.

4.3 | Adj pred + **rashii** らしい | "seem," "look like"

(a) ōi/ōktatta rashii   (It seems that … is/was many/much)
    多い/多かった らしい

(b) fuben*/fuben datta rashii   (It seems that … is/was inconvenient)
    不便*/不便だった らしい   *Da だ drops.

The auxiliary *i*-adjective *rashii* expresses the speaker's conjecture based on what he has heard or read.

EXAMPLES:

1. Ano chihō wa ame ga **ōi** rashii desu.
   あの地方は雨が**多い**らしいです。
   It seems that region has much rain.

2. Soko e kuruma de iku no wa **fuben** rashii.
そこへ車で行くのは**不便**らしい。

It seems inconvenient to go there by car.

3. Kinō Ogawa-san wa **hima ja nakatta** rashii.
昨日小川さんは**ひまじゃなかった**らしい。

It seems that Mr. Ogawa was not free yesterday.

Used after a noun, *rashii* also carries the meaning, "is the epitome of." Since it is an *i*-adjective, it can modify any noun that follows it (Example 2).

1. Oda-san wa otoko **rashii**.
小田さんは男**らしい**。

Mr. Oda is manly. (lit. Mr. Oda is like the ideal model of a man.)

2. Kyō wa haru **rashii** hi desu ne.
今日は春**らしい**日ですね。

Today is a springlike day, isn't it?

4.4 | **Adj pred + yō da ようだ** | "seem," "look like"

(a) yowai/yowakatta yō da (It seems that ... is/was weak)
弱い/弱かった ようだ

(b) konnanna*/konnan datta yō da (It seems that ... is/was difficult)
困難な*/困難だった ようだ　　*Da だ changes to na な.

74

The auxiliary *na*-adjective *yō da* expresses the speaker's conjecture based on firsthand information. *Mitai da* may be used in casual conversation in place of *yō da* (Example 3).

EXAMPLES:

1. Kono kuruma wa batterī ga **yowai** yō da.
   この車はバッテリーが**弱い**ようだ。
   It seems that this car has a weak battery.

2. Sōnansha no kyūjo wa **konnanna** yō da.
   遭難者の救助は**困難な**ようだ。
   It seems that the rescue of the victims is difficult.

3. Hara-san no kega wa **karukatta** mitai da.
   原さんのけがは**軽かった**みたいだ。
   It seems that Miss Hara's injury was slight.

Yō da also expresses a likeness between two people or things. With *yō da*, the speaker is drawing a similarity based on the visual information available to him. Since *yō da* is a *na*-adjective, its prenominal form *yōna* can modify any noun that follows it (Example 2).

1. Ano gaikokujin wa marude Nihonjin no **yō**/Nihonjin **mitai da**.
   あの外国人はまるで日本人の**よう**/日本人**みたいだ**。
   That foreigner is just like a Japanese person.

2. Asoko ni Neruson-san no **yōna**/Neruson-san **mitaina** hito ga imasu.
   あそこにネルソンさんの**ような**/ネルソンさん**みたいな**人がいます。
   There is a man over there who looks like Mr. Nelson.

4.5 | Adj stem + **sō da** そうだ | "look," "look like"

(a) ureshi sō da   (look happy)
嬉し そうだ

(b) kōkyū sō da   (look high-class)
高級 そうだ

The auxiliary *na*-adjective *sō da* attaches to the stem of an adjective. It expresses the speaker's conjecture concerning the present state of someone or something based on the visual information available to him. The adjective *ii* (good) and the negative *nai* (not) change to *yosa* and *nasa* before *sō da* (Example 2).

EXAMPLES:

1. Kyō wa Yoshiko-san wa totemo **ureshi** sō da.
   今日は良子さんはとても**嬉し**そうだ。
   Yoshiko looks very happy today.

2. Kochira wa **yosa** sō da ga, sochira wa **atarashikunasa** sō da.
   こちらは**よさ**そうだが、そちらは**新しくなさ**そうだ。
   This one looks good, but that one doesn't look fresh.

3. Ano okujō no resutoran wa **kōkyū** sō da ne.
   あの屋上のレストランは**高級**そうだね。
   The restaurant on the roof (of that building) looks high-class, doesn't it?

Sōna, the prenominal form of *sō da*, is used to modify nouns.

1. Kore wa taka **sōna** kuruma desu ne.

   これは高**そうな**車ですね。

   This is an expensive-looking car, isn't it?

2. Ano mise ni wa shinsen **sōna** sakana ga takusan atta.

   あの店には新鮮**そうな**魚がたくさんあった。

   There were many fish that looked fresh in that store.

PRACTICE 6 (4.1–4.5)

Complete the following sentences with the auxiliary adjectives *kamo-shirenai, ni chigainai, rashii, yō da* or *sō da*, using the adjectives given in parentheses.

1. Kondo no kōchi wa mae no kōchi yori _____.
   (kibishii)

   今度のコーチは前のコーチより _____。（厳しい）

   The new coach might be stricter than the old one.

2. Kanojo ga kite iru jaketto wa _____. (atatakai)

   彼女が着ているジャケットは _____。（暖かい）

   The jacket she is wearing looks warm.

3. Noda-san no hanashi ni yoru to, sono tetsuzuki wa _____
   _____. (mendōna)

   野田さんの話によると、その手続きは _____。（面
   倒な）

   According to what Mrs. Noda said, the procedures seemed to be troublesome.

4. Kono apāto wa _____ ga, yachin ga _____. (ii)
   (takai)

   このアパートは _____ が、家賃が _____。 (いい)
   (高い)

   This apartment looks good, but the rent must be expensive.

5. Kono mizuumi wa _____ da. Mizu ga _____.
   (fukai) (tsumetai)

   この湖は _____ だ。水が _____。 (深い)(冷
   たい)

   This lake looks deep. The water might be cold.

6. Nando mo shirabeta ga, kono kikai wa mō _____.
   (damena)

   何度も調べたが、この機械はもう _____。 (駄目な)

   I checked it many times, but this machine seems no good now.

7. Sara wa _____ datta. Shiken no kekka ga _____.
   (kanashii) (warui)

   サラは _____ だった。試験の結果が _____。
   (悲しい)(悪い)

   Sarah looked sad. The result of the exam must have been bad.

4.6 | V(-masu) + **yasui やすい** | "easy to ～"

   yomi yasui/yasukatta   (is/was easy to read)
   読み やすい/やすかった

The auxiliary *i*-adjective *yasui* attaches to the stem of the *masu* form of a verb. It indicates that someone or something (usually the topic of the sentence) is easy to ～.

EXAMPLES:

1. Kono hon wa **yomi**yasui.
この本は**読み**やすい。
This book is easy to read.

2. Wada-san wa issho ni shigoto ga **shi**yasukatta.
和田さんは一緒に仕事が**し**やすかった。
Miss Wada was easy to work with.

3. **Aruki**yasui kutsu ga hoshii desu.
歩きやすいくつが欲しいです。
I want shoes that are easy to walk in.

4.7 | V(-masu) + **nikui にくい** | "hard to ～"

oboe nikui/nikukatta   (is/was hard to memorize)
覚え にくい/にくかった

The auxiliary *i*-adjective *nikui* attaches to the stem of the *masu* form of a verb. It indicates that someone or something (usually the topic of the sentence) is hard to ～.

EXAMPLES:

1. Kono kanji wa **oboe**nikui.
この漢字は**覚え**にくい。
This kanji is hard to memorize.

2. Kida-sensei wa **hanashi**nikutatta desu.

木田先生は**話し**にくかったです。

Professor Kida was hard to talk to.

3. Hashi de **tabe**nikui ryōri wa kirai desu.

はしで**食べ**にくい料理は嫌いです。

I dislike food that is hard to eat with chopsticks.

4.8 | V(-masu) + **tai たい** | "want to"

kai tai   (want to buy)

買い たい

The auxiliary *i*-adjective *tai* attaches to the stem of the *masu* form of a verb. It indicates someone's desire to do something, usually the speaker's if the sentence is declarative and someone else's if it is interrogative.

EXAMPLES:

1. Ano akai jaketto ga/o **kai**takatta.

あの赤いジャケットが/を**買い**たかった。

I wanted to buy that red jacket.

2. Konban donna eiga ga/o **mi**tai desu ka.

今晩どんな映画が/を**見**たいですか。

What kind of movie do you want to see tonight?

3. Kyō wa nani mo **shi**taku arimasen.

今日は何もしたくありません。

I don't want to do anything today.

Tai can also indicate someone else's desire to do something when it is used with the auxiliary *i*-adjective *rashii* or the auxiliary *na*-adjective *sō da*.

EXAMPLES:

1. Haruko-san wa Pari e ikitai **rashii**.
   春子さんはパリへ行きたい**らしい**。
   It seems that Haruko wants to go to Paris.

2. Yamada-san wa tenisu o shita **sō da**.
   山田さんはテニスをした**そうだ**。
   It looks like Mr. Yamada wants to play tennis.

4.9 | Adj stem + **garu** がる | "show signs of 〜"

(a) kowa garu   (show signs of being scared)
    こわ がる

(b) meiwaku garu   (show signs of being annoyed)
    迷惑 がる

The auxiliary verb *garu* attaches to the stems of adjectives expressing human emotion or sensation. It indicates that a person other than the speaker shows signs of being happy, sad or lonely, or that he feels pain, cold, hot, etc. *Garu* conjugates like a regular group-I verb: *kowagaranai, kowagarimasu, kowagaru, kowagatte, kowagatta*.

EXAMPLES:

1. Kono ko wa ōki inu o **kowa**garimasu.

   この子は大きい犬を**こわ**がります。

   This child fears big dogs. (lit. This child shows signs of being scared of big dogs.)

2. Akira wa ashi o **ita**gatte iru.

   明は足を**痛**がっている。

   Akira feels a pain in his leg. (lit. Akira shows signs of having a pain in his leg.)

3. Hara-san wa sono shōtai o **meiwaku**gatte ita.

   原さんはその招待を**迷惑**がっていた。

   Mr. Hara felt annoyed by that invitation. (lit. Mr. Hara showed signs of being annoyed by that invitation.)

Garu is also used with the *i*-adjective *hoshii* or the auxiliary *i*-adjective *tai* to indicate another person's desire to do something.

1. Otōto wa atarashii kuruma o **hoshi**gatte iru.

   弟は新しい車を**欲し**がっている。

   My younger brother wants a new car. (lit. My younger brother shows signs of wanting a new car.)

2. Hiroshi wa inu to **asobita**gatta.

   宏は犬と**遊びた**がった。

   Hiroshi wanted to play with the dog. (lit. Hiroshi showed signs of wanting to play with the dog.)

4.10 | Adj stem + **sugiru すぎる** | "too ～"

(a) kata sugiru   (too tough/hard)
かた すぎる

(b) zeitaku sugiru   (too extravagant)
ぜいたく すぎる

The verb *sugiru* (pass, go beyond a limit) is used as an auxiliary verb with the stem of an adjective to indicate that someone or something is in some state to an excessive degree. The adjective *ii* (good) changes to *yo* before *sugiru* (Example 2). *Sugiru* conjugates as a regular group-II verb: *suginai, sugimasu, sugiru, sugite, sugita*.

EXAMPLES:

1. Kono niku wa **kata**sugite taberarenai.
   この肉は**かた**すぎて食べられない。

   This beef is too tough to eat.

2. Kono sūtsu wa gakusei ni wa **yo**sugimasu.
   このスーツは学生には**よ**すぎます。

   This suit is too good for a student.

3. Ano apāto wa wakai fūfu ni wa **zeitaku** sugimasu ne.
   あのアパートは若い夫婦には**ぜいたく**すぎますね。

   That apartment is too extravagant for a young couple, isn't it?

Fill in the blanks with the appropriate forms of the adjectives or verbs given in parentheses, with proper auxiliaries if necessary.

1. kono hon wa kanji ga _____ kara, gakusei ni wa _____ nai. (ōi) (tekitōna)

   この本は漢字が _____ から、学生には _____ ない。
   （多い）（適当な）

   Because this book has too many kanji, it might not be appropriate for students.

2. Mizu ga _____ to, _____ desu. (asai) (oyogu)

   水が _____ と、 _____ です。（浅い）（泳ぐ）

   If the waters are too shallow, it is hard to swim.

3. Karui baggu wa _____ kara, ryokō ni _____ desu. (motsu) (benrina)

   軽いバッグは _____ から、旅行に _____ です。（持つ）
   （便利な）

   Light bags are easy to carry, so they are convenient for travel.

4. Kare wa chishiki wa _____ da ga, kono shoku ni wa _____ darō. (fukai) (wakai)

   彼は知識は _____ だが、この職には _____ だろう。（深い）
   （若い）

   His knowledge seems vast, but he is too young for this job.

5. Kore wa _____ da keredomo, _____ kara ima kaemasen. (hitsuyōna) (takai)

これは ＿＿＿＿＿＿ だけれども、＿＿＿＿＿＿ から今買えません。
（必要な）（高い）

Although this is necessary, it is too expensive, so I can't buy it now.

6. Soto ga ＿＿＿＿＿＿ ta node, kōgi ga ＿＿＿＿＿＿ ta. (sawagashii)
(kiku)

外が ＿＿＿＿＿＿ たので、講義が ＿＿＿＿＿＿ た。（さわがしい）（聞く）

Because it was noisy outside, it was hard to listen to the lecture.

7. Watashi wa inu ga ＿＿＿＿＿＿ ga, Masako-san wa neko o
＿＿＿＿＿＿ te iru. (hoshii)

私は犬が ＿＿＿＿＿＿ が、正子さんはねこを ＿＿＿＿＿＿ ている。
（欲しい）

I want a dog, but Masako wants a cat.

8. Watashi wa tenrankai ni ＿＿＿＿＿＿ ga, Toda-san wa ＿＿＿＿＿＿
nai rashii. (iku)

私は展覧会に ＿＿＿＿＿＿ が、戸田さんは ＿＿＿＿＿＿ ないらしい。
（行く）

I want to go to the exhibition, but it seems that Miss Toda doesn't want to go.

9. Kono ryōri wa ＿＿＿＿＿＿ node, dare mo ＿＿＿＿＿＿ nai yō desu.
(karai) (taberu)

この料理は ＿＿＿＿＿＿ ので、だれも ＿＿＿＿＿＿ ないようです。
（辛い）（食べる）

Because this food is too spicy, it seems that no one wants to eat it.

⑤ The Conjunctive (Adj conj) and *Te* (Adj te) Forms

The conjunctive form (*ku* form) of an *i*-adjective and the *te* form of an *i*- or a *na*-adjective are used in various ways as follows.

5.1 | Adj conj ～く | "and"

ao ku   (is blue and)
青 く

The conjunctive form (*ku* form) of an *i*-adjective is used to link adjectives or clauses.

EXAMPLES:

1. Sora wa **aoku**, kumo wa shiroi.
   空は**青く**、雲は白い。
   The sky is blue and clouds are white.

2. Kesa wa netsu ga **takaku**, nodo ga itakatta.
   今朝は熱が**高く**、のどが痛かった。
   This morning I had a high fever and a sore throat.

3. Kono mise wa **yasuku**, shinsenna yasai o utte iru.
   この店は**安く**、新鮮な野菜を売っている。
   This store sells inexpensive, fresh vegetables.

5.2 | Adj **te** ～て | "and"

(a) atsuku te   (is hot and)
     暑く て

(b) sunao de   (is obedient and)
     素直 で

The *te* form of an *i*- or a *na*-adjective is used to link adjectives or clauses. The state expressed by the first adjective is often the reason for the state or action that follows (Example 3).

EXAMPLES:

1. Kinō wa **atsukute**, iyana tenki datta.
   昨日は**暑くて**、嫌な天気だった。
   Yesterday was a hot, nasty day.

2. Koko wa natsu wa **suzushikute**, fuyu wa atatakai.
   ここは夏は**涼しくて**、冬は暖かい。
   Here it's cool in summer and warm in winter.

3. Yasuko wa sunao de, **kawaikute**, mina ni aisareta.
   安子は素直で、**かわいくて**、皆に愛された。
   Yasuko was obedient and cute and loved by everybody.

5.3 | Adj conj/Adj **te** + **nakute** ～く/で なくて

"is not ～, so ～," "because ～ is not ～"

(a) **tōku nakute**　　　　　　　(isn't far and ～)
　　遠く なくて

(b) **suki de (wa) nakute**　　　(doesn't like and ～)
　　好き で（は）なくて

Nakute, the *te* form of the negative *nai*, attaches to the conjunctive *ku* form of an *i*-adjective or the *te* form of a *na*-adjective. It indicates a reason or cause for a state or an action.

EXAMPLES:

1. Sūpā ga ie kara **tōkunakute** totemo benri desu.
　スーパーが家から**遠くなくて**、とても便利です。
　The supermarket isn't far from my house, so it is very convenient.

2. Eiga ga **omoshirokunakute** tochū de demashita.
　映画が**面白くなくて**途中で出ました。
　The movie wasn't interesting, so I left in the middle.

3. Nikuryōri ga **suki de nakute** Yōroppa no ryokōchū komari-mashita.
　肉料理が**好きでなくて**、ヨーロッパの旅行中困りました。
　Because I don't like meat dishes, I had trouble during my trip to Europe.

SPECIAL USAGE: The *ku* forms of *tōi* 遠い (far), *chikai* 近い (near) and *ōi* 多い (many/much) may be used as nouns. A noun plus *no* modifies the noun that follows it.

tōku no mori	遠くの森	distant woods
chikaku no hon'ya	近くの本屋	a nearby bookstore
ōku no gakusei	多くの学生	many students

5.4 | Adj conj/Adj **te** + **naku naru** 〜く/で なくなる |

"not 〜 anymore"

(a) takaku naku naru   (isn't expensive anymore)
高く なくなる

(b) mare de (wa) naku naru   (isn't rare anymore)
まれ で(は) なくなる

The phrase *naku naru* attached to the conjunctive *ku* form of an *i*-adjective, or to the *te* form of a *na*-adjective, indicates that the state expressed by the adjective no longer applies.

EXAMPLES:
1. Konpyūtā wa **takaku** nakunarimashita.
   コンピューターは**高く**なくなりました。
   Computers aren't expensive anymore.

2. Atarashii tomodachi ga dekite, Michiko wa mō **sabishiku** nakunatta.

新しい友達が出来て、道子はもう**さびしくなく**なった。

Michiko made new friends and is no longer lonely.

3. Amerika kara no yunyūhin wa mō **mare de** (wa) nakunatta.

アメリカからの輸入品はもう**まれで**（は）なくなった。

Imports from America are no longer rare.

5.5 | **Adj te + mo ～ても** | "even if"

(a) chikakute mo   (even if … is near)
    近くても

(b) muri de mo   (even if … is difficult/unreasonable)
    無理でも

The *te* form of an *i-* or a *na*-adjective followed by *mo* constitutes a conjunction that expresses a condition.

EXAMPLES:

1. Kare wa **chikakute** mo kuruma de ikimasu.

   彼は**近くても**車で行きます。

   Even if it is near, he goes by car.

2. Chichi wa tenki ga **yokunakute** mo tsuri ni dekakemasu.

   父は天気が**よくなくても**釣りに出かけます。

   Even if the weather isn't good, my father goes out fishing.

3. Watashi wa **muri de** mo kono purojekuto o tsuzuketai.
   私は**無理**でもこのプロジェクトを続けたい。

   Even if it is very difficult, I want to continue this project.

5.6 | Adj **te** + **mo ii** ～てもいい | "It is all right if"

(a) semakute mo ii   (It is all right if ... is small.)
    狭くて も いい

(b) hade de mo ii   (It is all right if ... is showy/loud.)
    派手 で も いい

The *te* form of an *i*- or a *na*-adjective followed by *mo ii* indicates some-one's conceding something.

EXAMPLES:

1. Heya wa **semakute** mo ii desu ka.
   部屋は**狭くて**もいいですか。

   Is it all right if the room is small?

2. Kono sūtsu ni wa nekutai wa **hade de** mo ii desu yo.
   このスーツにはネクタイは**派手で**もいいですよ。

   For this suit, it's all right if the tie is flashy, I tell you.

3. Tanjōbi no purezento wa **kōka de nakute** mo ii.
   誕生日のプレゼントは**高価でなくて**もいい。

   It's all right if the birthday present isn't expensive.

5.7 Adj conj/Adj te + mo ～ mo nai ～く/でも ～ く/でもない

"neither ～ nor ～"

(a) utsukushiku mo minikuku mo nai
美しく も みにくく も ない
(is neither beautiful nor ugly)

(b) shiawase de mo fushiawase de mo nai
幸せでも 不幸せでも ない
(is neither happy nor unhappy)

The phrase ~ *mo* ~ *mo nai* attached to the conjunctive *ku* form of an *i*-adjective, or to the *te* form of a *na*-adjective, expresses a state that is neither positive nor negative.

EXAMPLES:

1. Kanojo wa **utsukushiku** mo **minikuku** mo nai.
   彼女は**美しく**も**みにくく**もない。
   She is neither beautiful nor ugly.

2. Kare no isshō wa **shiawase de** mo **fushiawase de** mo nakatta.
   彼の一生は**幸せ**でも**不幸せ**でもなかった。
   His life was neither happy nor unhappy.

3. Kono tatemono wa **modan de** mo **rippa de** mo nai.
   この建物は**モダン**でも**立派**でもない。
   This building is neither modern nor magnificent.

5.8 | Adj conj/Adj **te** + **nakereba naranai** ~ く/で なければならない | "have to," "must"

(a) hiroku nakereba naranai   (has to be large/spacious)
広く なければならない

(b) kinben de nakereba naranai   (has to be industrious)
勤勉で なければならない

The phrase *nakereba naranai* attached to the conjunctive *ku* form of an *i*-adjective, or to the *te* form of a *na*-adjective, indicates that the state or condition expressed by the adjective is a necessity. *Nakereba narimasen* is the polite form.

EXAMPLES:

1. Kodomo no asobiba wa **hiroku** nakereba narimasen.
   子供の遊び場は**広く**なければなりません。
   The playground for children must be spacious.

2. Ii seiseki o toru tame ni wa gakusei wa **kinben de** nakereba naranai.
   いい成績をとるためには学生は**勤勉で**なければならない。
   In order to get good grades, students must be diligent.

3. Ji wa kirei de **yomiyasuku** nakereba naranai.
   字はきれいで**読みやすく**なければならない。
   Handwriting must be neat and easy to read.

5.9 | Adj **te** + **tamaranai** 〜 てたまらない

"unbearably," "extremely"

(a) kanashikute tamaranai   (is unbearably sad)
悲しくて たまらない

(b) yukai de tamaranai   (is extremely delightful)
愉快で たまらない

The phrase *tamaranai* attached to the *te* form of an *i-* or a *na*-adjective expresses the feeling of the speaker or of someone close to him that something is extreme or unendurable. *Tamarimasen* is the polite form.

EXAMPLES:

1. Koinu ga shinde, **kanashikute** tamarimasen.
   子犬が死んで、**悲しくて**たまりません。
   My puppy died, and I am very, very sad.

2. Tomodachi ga ōzei kite, pātī wa **yukai de** tamaranakkata.
   友達が大勢来て、パーティーは**愉快で**たまらなかった。
   Many of my friends came, and the party was extremely delightful.

3. Imōto wa ryōri ya sōji ga **iya de** tamaranai.
   妹は料理や掃除が**嫌で**たまらない。
   My younger sister just hates cooking and cleaning.

Fill in the blanks with the appropriate forms of the adjectives given in parentheses.

1. Kimira-san no ie wa _____ te _____ ta. (chiisai) (furui)

   木村さんの家は _____ て _____ た。(小さい)(古い)

   Mr. Kimura's house was small and old.

2. Kono hoteru wa _____ de _____ desu. (shizukana) (kaitekina)

   このホテルは _____ で _____ です。(静かな)(快適な)

   This hotel is quiet and comfortable.

3. Ano mise no ten'in wa _____ nakute _____ datta. (shinsetsuna) (fuyukaina)

   あの店の店員は _____ なくて _____ だった。(親切な)(不愉快な)

   The salesperson at that store was not kind—he was unpleasant.

4. Shingō ga dekite, ano michi wa mō _____ nakunatta. (abunai)

   信号が出来て、あの道はもう _____ なくなった。(危ない)

   A (traffic) signal was put up, so the road is no longer dangerous.

5. _____ demo Eberesuto-zan ni nobori _____ tama-ranai. (kikenna) (tai)

   _____ でもエベレスト山に登り _____ たまらない。(危険な)(たい)

   Even if it's dangerous, I really want to climb Mt. Everest.

6. Himo wa _____ nakute mo ii desu ka. Ee, _____ te mo
   ii desu. (nagai) (mijikai)

   ひもは _____ なくてもいいですか。ええ、_____ ても
   いいです。（長い）（短い）

   Is it all right if the cord isn't long? Yes, the cord may be short.

7. Ano sakka wa _____ mo _____ mo nai. (binbōna)
   (yūfukuna)

   あの作家は _____ も _____ もない。（貧乏な）（裕福な）

   That writer is neither poor nor rich.

8. Kion mo shitsudo mo _____ te _____ tamaranai. (takai)
   (mushiatsui)

   気温も湿度も _____ て _____ たまらない。（高い）（蒸し
   暑い）

   The temperature and humidity are both high, so it's unbearably sultry.

9. Tatemono wa _____ de _____ nakereba narimasen.
   (ganjōna) (anzenna)

   建物は _____ で _____ なければなりません。（頑丈な）
   （安全な）

   Buildings must be strong and safe.

The Adverbial Form (Adj adv)

Adjectives are used as adverbs to modify verbs, other adjectives and adverbs as well. For *i*-adjectives, the adverbial form is obtained by changing the final *i* to *ku*, and for *na*-adjectives, by adding *ni* to the stem.

6.1 | Adj adv ～く/に + V | "-ly"

(a) hayaku okiru   (get up early)
　　早く 起きる

(b) shinchō ni okonau   (act prudently)
　　慎重に 行う

The adverbial form of an *i*- or a *na*-adjective modifies the verb that follows it.

EXAMPLES:

1. Chichi wa maiasa **hayaku** okimasu.
   父は毎朝**早く**起きます。
   My father gets up early every morning.

2. Niwa ni hana ga **utsukushiku** saite ita.
   庭に花が**美しく**咲いていた。
   Flowers were blooming beautifully in the garden.

3. Kono koto wa taisetsu da kara, **shinchō ni** okonawanakereba naranai.

この事は大切だから、**慎重に**行わなければならない。

Because this matter is important, we must act prudently.

6.2 | Adj adv 〜く/に + Adj/Adv | "-ly"

(a) sugoku kireina   (extremely pretty)
    すごく きれいな

(b) mōretsu ni atsui   (terribly hot)
    猛烈に 暑い

The adverbial form of an *i-* or a *na*-adjective modifies other adjectives (Examples 1, 2) and adverbs (Example 3).

EXAMPLES:

1. Oda-san no okusan wa wakakute **sugoku** kireina hito desu.
   小田さんの奥さんは若くて**すごく**きれいな人です。
   Mr. Oda's wife is a young and extremely pretty woman.

2. Kotoshi no natsu wa **mōretsu ni** atsukatta.
   今年の夏は**猛烈に**暑かった。
   This past summer was terribly hot.

3. Kono sūtsukēsu wa **hidoku** ranbō ni atsukawareta rashii.
   このスーツケースは**ひどく**乱暴に扱われたらしい。
   It seems that this suitcase was handled very roughly.

6.3 | Adj adv + **naru** ～く/に なる | "become ～"

(a) akaku naru   (become red)
　　赤く なる

(b) yūmei ni naru   (become famous)
　　有名に なる

The adverbial form of an *i*- or a *na*-adjective followed by the verb *naru* indicates a change of state.

EXAMPLES:

1. Aki ni wa kono ki wa ha ga **akaku** narimasu.
　秋にはこの木は葉が**赤く**なります。
　In autumn, the leaves of this tree become red.

2. Kare wa besutoserā o kaite, **yūmei ni** natta.
　彼はベストセラーを書いて、**有名に**なった。
　He wrote a bestseller and became famous.

3. Nyūkoku no tetsuzuki ga **kantan ni** natta.
　入国の手続きが**簡単に**なった。
　The immigration procedures became simple.

6.4 | Adj adv + **suru** ～く/に する | "do ～"

(a) hikuku suru   (make low)
　　低く する

(b) kirei ni suru   (make clean)
きれいに する

The adverbial form of an *i*- or a *na*-adjective followed by the verb *suru* indicates someone's altering the state of something.

EXAMPLES:

1. Terebi no oto o **hikuku** shite kudasai.
テレビの音を**低く**してください。
Please lower the volume of the TV.

2. Denki o tsukete, heya o **akaruku** shimashita.
電気をつけて、部屋を**明るく**しました。
I turned on the lights and made the room bright.

3. Tomodachi ga kuru kara, ie o **kirei ni** shita.
友達が来るから、家を**きれいに**した。
Because my friend is coming, I cleaned the house.

PRACTICE 9 (6.1–6.4)

Fill in the blanks with the appropriate forms of the adjectives given in parentheses.

1. Saikin yoru ga _____ narimashita. (mijikai)
最近夜が _____ なりました。(短い)
Lately the nights have become shorter.

2. Undōjō de kodomo ga _____ asonde iru. (genkina)

運動場で子供が _____ 遊んでいる。（元気な）

Children are playing excitedly on the playground.

3. Kare wa itsumo gakkō ni _____ kimasu. (osoi)

彼はいつも学校に _____ 来ます。（遅い）

He always comes to school late.

4. Depāto ga dekite, kono hen wa _____ _____ natta. (sugoi) (benrina)

デパートが出来て、この辺は _____ _____ なった。（すごい）（便利な）

A department store was built, making this area very convenient.

5. Kokuban ni kanji o _____ kakimashita. (ōkii)

黒板に漢字を _____ 書きました。（大きい）

I wrote kanji big on the blackboard.

6. Senshū wa _____ ta ga getsuyōbi kara _____ natta. (isogashii) (himana)

先週は _____ たが月曜日から _____ なった。（忙しい）（ひまな）

I was busy last week, but I became free as of Monday.

7. Tomodachi ga gaikoku e itte, _____ _____ narimashita. (hidoi) (sabishii)

友達が外国へ行って、 _____ _____ なりました。（ひどい）（さびしい）

My friend went abroad, and I became very lonely.

8. Kono ita wa _____ sugiru kara, motto _____ shite kudasai. (atsui) (usui)

この板は _____ すぎるから、もっと _____ してください。（厚い）（薄い）

This board is too thick, so please make it a little thinner.

7 The Conditional (Adj cond) and *Tara* (Adj tara) Forms

For *i*-adjectives (including auxiliaries and the negative *nai*), the conditional form is obtained by adding *kereba* to the stem, and for *na*-adjectives, by adding *nara(ba)* or *de areba* to the stem. The *tara* form, which is a more colloquial conditional form, is obtained by adding *kattara* to the stem of an *i*-adjective and *dattara* to the stem of a *na*-adjective.

7.1 | Adj cond 〜ば | "if"

(a) **samukereba**   (if ... is cold)
    寒ければ

(b) **shinsetsu nara(ba)/shinsetsu de areba**   (if ... is kind)
    親切 なら（ば）/親切であれば

The conditional form of an *i*-adjective (the *ba* form) is used as a conjunction to express a condition. *Nara* used with a *na*-adjective is the simplified form of *naraba*, which is the conditional form of the copula *da.* (*Ba* is usually optional after *nara.*) The main clause may express the speaker's volition, hope, suggestion or command.

EXAMPLES:

1. **Samukereba** mado o shimete kudasai.
   寒ければ窓を閉めてください。
   If it's cold, please close the window.

2. Kono hon o/ga **yomitakereba** kashite agemasu.
   この本を/が読みたければ貸してあげます。
   If you want to read this book, I'll lend it to you.

3. Ten'in ga **shinsetsu nara/shinsetsu de areba**, mise wa yoku hayarimasu.
   店員が親切なら/親切であれば、店はよくはやります。
   If the salespeople are kind, the store becomes popular.

7.2 | Adj cond ～ **hodo/dake** ～ば ～ ほど/だけ |

"the more ～, the more ～"

(a) kuwashikereba kuwashii hodo/dake
   詳しければ 詳しい ほど/だけ
   (the more detailed, the more ～)

(b) shinsen nara(ba) shinsenna hodo/dake
   新鮮 なら(ば) 新鮮な ほど/だけ
   (the fresher, the more ～)

The conditional form of an *i-* or a *na-*adjective (the *ba* form) plus the same adjective in the prenominal form, followed by *hodo/dake*, expresses a proportional relationship between two states (Examples 1, 2) or between a state and an action (Example 3).

EXAMPLES:

1. Setsumei wa **kuwashikereba kuwashii** hodo wakari yasui desu.
   説明は**詳しければ詳しい**ほど分かりやすいです。
   The more detailed the explanation is, the easier it is to understand.

2. Kudamono wa **shinsen nara shinsenna** dake oishii desu.
   果物は**新鮮なら新鮮な**だけおいしいです。
   The fresher the fruit, the more delicious.

3. Shinamono wa **yasukereba yasui** hodo yoku ureru.
   品物は**安ければ安い**ほどよく売れる。
   The cheaper the articles are, the better they sell.

7.3 | Adj cond + **koso** 〜ばこそ | "because," "only because"

(a) tanoshikereba koso   (because … is enjoyable)
    楽しければ こそ

(b) daitan nara(ba)/daitan de areba koso   (because … is bold)
    大胆なら(ば)/大胆であれば こそ

The conditional form of an *i-* or a *na-*adjective (the *ba* form) plus *koso* puts emphasis on a reason or cause.

EXAMPLES:

1. **Tanoshikereba** koso sofu wa mainichi niwa de hatarakimasu.
   楽しければこそ祖父は毎日庭で働きます。
   Because it's enjoyable, my grandfather works in the yard every day.

2. Noda-san wa **daitan nara/daitan de areba** koso hitori de tozan shimasu.
   野田さんは**大胆なら/大胆であれば**こそひとりで登山します。
   Only because he is bold, Mr. Noda climbs mountains alone.

3. **Suki nara/suki de areba** koso heta demo gorufu ga yamer-arenai.
   好きなら/好きであればこそ下手でもゴルフがやめられない。
   Because I love golf, I can't give it up, even though I am poor at it.

7.4 | Adj **tara** 〜たら | "if"

(a) sukunakattara   (if … a few/little)
    少なかったら

(b) shinpai dattara   (if … uneasy/anxious)
    心配だったら

The *tara* form of an *i*- or a *na*-adjective is, compared to the *ba* form, a more colloquial way of expressing a condition.

EXAMPLES:

1. Sankasha ga **sukunakattara** kono tsuā wa kyanseru saremasu.

   参加者が**少なかったら**このツアーはキャンセルされます。

   If the participants are few, this tour will be canceled.

2. **Oishikattara** tabemasu ga, **oishikunakattara** tabemasen.

   おいしかったら食べますが、**おいしくなかったら**食べません。

   If it's delicious, I'll eat it, but if it's not, I won't.

3. Hitori de iku no ga **shinpai dattara**, watashi ga issho ni ikimasu yo.

   ひとりで行くのが、**心配だったら**私が一緒に行きますよ。

   If you're uneasy about going alone, I'll go with you.

PRACTICE 10 (7.1–7.4)

Fill in the blanks with the appropriate forms of the adjectives given in parentheses.

1. _____ ba aruite ikimashō. (chikai)

   _____ ば歩いて行きましょう。（近い）

   If it's near, let's walk.

2. Mizu ga _____ tara oyoganai hō ga ii desu yo. (tsumetai)

   水が _____ たら泳がない方がいいですよ。（冷たい）

   If the water is cold, you had better not swim.

3. _____ nara _____ temo kawanakereba naranai. (hitsuyōna) (takai)

106

_____ なら _____ ても買わなければならない。(必要な)
(高い)

If it's necessary, I will have to buy it, even if it's expensive.

4. _____ tara nokoshite kudasai. (kiraina)
   _____ たら残してください。(嫌いな)

   If you don't like it, please leave it.

5. Mondai wa _____ nara _____ hodo tokinikui desu.
   (fukuzatsuna)
   問題は _____ なら _____ ほど解きにくいです。(複雑な)

   The more complicated a problem, the harder it is to solve.

6. Kuruma wa _____ nara _____ dake _____ desu.
   (ganjōna) (anzenna)
   車は _____ なら _____ だけ _____ です。(頑丈な)
   (安全な)

   The more durable the car, the safer.

7. Kare wa _____ koso _____ kōdō shimasu. (wakai)
   (daitanna)
   彼は _____ こそ _____ 行動します。(若い)(大胆な)

   Because he is young, he acts boldly.

8. Hayashi-san wa _____ koso _____ kurasemasu.
   (yūfukuna) (zeitakuna)
   林さんは _____ こそ _____ 暮らせます。(裕福な)(ぜい
   たくな)

   Because Mrs. Hayashi is rich, she can live in luxury.

The *Tari* Form (Adj tari)

The *tari* form is obtained by adding *kattari* to the stem of an *i*-adjective or *dattari* to the stem of a *na*-adjective.

8.1 | Adj **tari** + Adj **tari suru** 〜 たり 〜 たりする |

"sometimes 〜 and sometimes 〜"

(a) **kibishikattari suru**　　　　　(is sometimes strict)
厳しかったり する

(b) **seikaku dattari suru**　　　　　(is sometimes accurate)
正確だったり する

The repeated use of the *tari* form of an *i*- or a *na*-adjective followed by the verb *suru* expresses an alternative or indefinite number of states in no particular sequence.

EXAMPLES:

1. Kida-sensei wa gakusei ni **kibishikattari yasashikattari** suru.
木田先生は学生に**厳しかったりやさしかったり**する。

Professor Kida is sometimes strict and sometimes gentle with his students.

2. Ano mise no hōsōshi wa **akakattari shirokattari aokattari** shimasu.
あの店の包装紙は**赤かったり白かったり青かったり**します。

The wrapping paper at that store is sometimes red, sometimes white, and sometimes blue.

3. Kono tokei wa **seikaku dattari fuseikaku dattari** suru.
   この時計は**正確だったり不正確だったり**する。

   This watch is sometimes accurate and sometimes inaccurate.

8.2 Adj **tari** + (Adj) **nakattari suru** 〜 たり 〜 なかったりする

"sometimes 〜 and sometimes not 〜"

(a) tadashikattari (tadashiku) nakattari suru
     正しかったり（正しく）なかったり する

     (sometimes … is correct and sometimes not (correct))

(b) sekkyokuteki dattari (sekkyokuteki de) nakattari suru
     積極的だったり（積極的で）なかったり する

     (sometimes … is positive and sometimes not (positive))

The use of the *tari* form of an *i-* or a *na*-adjective followed by the negative *tari* form of the same adjective, plus the verb *suru*, indicates that a pair of opposite states are at work.

EXAMPLES:

1. Kono reprōto no dēta wa **tadashikattari** (tadashiku)**nakattari** suru.
   このレポートのデータは**正しかったり**（正しく）**なかったり**する。

   The data in this report is sometimes correct and sometimes not (correct).

2. Kotoshi no haru wa **atatakakattari** (atatakaku)**nakattari** shita.

今年の春は**暖かかったり**（暖かく）**なかったり**した。

This past spring was at times warm and at times not (warm).

3. Kare no shigoto ni taisuru taido wa **sekkyokuteki dattari** (sekkyokuteki de) **nakattari** shimasu.

彼の仕事に対する態度は**積極的だったり**（積極的で）**なかったり**します。

His attitude toward his work is sometimes positive and sometimes not (positive).

PRACTICE 11 (8.1–8.2)

Fill in the blanks with the appropriate forms of the adjectives given in parentheses.

1. Oda-sensei no kōgi wa _____ tari _____ tari shimasu. (omoshiroi)

小田先生の講義は _____ たり _____ たりします。（面白い）

Professor Oda's lectures are sometimes interesting and sometimes not.

2. Senshū wa _____ tari _____ tari shita. (isogashii) (himana)

先週は _____ たり _____ たりした。（忙しい）（ひまな）

Last week I was sometimes busy and sometimes free.

3. Masao wa _____ tari _____ tari suru. (sunaona)

正夫は _____ たり _____ たりする。（素直な）

Masao is sometimes obedient and sometimes not.

4. Ano hito wa sakana ga _____ tari _____ tari shimasu.
   (sukina) (kiraina)

   あの人は魚が _____ たり _____ たりします。（好きな）
   （嫌いな）

   He sometimes likes fish and sometimes dislikes it.

5. Ane no ryōri wa _____ tari _____ tari shite, _____ nai.
   (amai) (karai) (oishii)

   姉の料理は _____ たり _____ たりして、_____ ない。
   （甘い）（辛い）（おいしい）

   The meals my older sister cooks are sometimes sweet and sometimes
   salty, and they are not good.

6. Pari no seikatsu wa _____ tari _____ tari shita. (kaitekina)

   パリの生活は _____ たり _____ たりした。（快適な）

   My life in Paris was sometimes comfortable and sometimes not.

9 Noun Forms

An adjective may be used as a noun by adding the suffix *sa* to the stem.
The suffix *mi* may also be used with a limited number of *i*-adjectives.

9.1 | Adj stem + **sa** さ | "-ness"

(a) shirosa   (whiteness)
     白さ

(b) rippasa   (fineness)
     立派さ

The suffix *sa* added to the stem of an *i*- or a *na*-adjective turns the adjective into a noun that expresses degree.

EXAMPLES:

1. Kabe no **shirosa** ga heya o akaruku shita.
   壁の**白さ**が部屋を明るくした。

   The whiteness of the walls brightened the room.

2. Kono ike no **fukasa** wa dono gurai desu ka.
   この池の**深さ**はどのぐらいですか。

   What is the approximate depth of this pond?

3. Kare no taido no **rippasa** ni kanshin shita.
   彼の態度の**立派さ**に感心した。

   I was impressed by his fine attitude (lit. the fineness of his attitude).

9.2　| Adj stem + **mi** み |　"-ness"

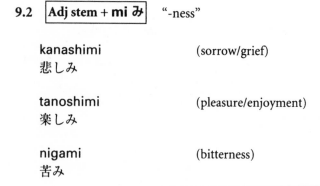

kanashimi   (sorrow/grief)
悲しみ

tanoshimi   (pleasure/enjoyment)
楽しみ

nigami   (bitterness)
苦み

The suffix *mi* added to the stem of a limited number of *i*-adjectives turns the adjective into a noun that expresses something emotive or tangible.

EXAMPLES:

1. Kanojo wa tomodachi no shi no shirase ni fukai **kanashimi** ni shizunda.
   彼女は友達の死の知らせに深い**悲しみ**に沈んだ。
   At the news of her friend's death, she yielded to a deep sorrow.

2. Ryokō wa watashi no ichiban no **tanoshim**i desu.
   旅行は私の一番の**楽しみ**です。
   Traveling is my number one pleasure.

3. Kono bīru wa **nigami** ga arimasu ne.
   このビールは**苦み**がありますね。
   This beer has a bitter taste, doesn't it?

PRACTICE 12 (9.1–9.2)

Fill in the blanks with the appropriate forms of the adjectives given in parentheses.

1. Kono kozutsumi no _____ o hakatte kudasai. (omoi)
   この小包の _____ を計ってください。（重い）
   Please weigh this package.

2. Kono ofisu no _____ wa chōdo ii desu. (hiroi)
   このオフィスの _____ は丁度いいです。（広い）
   The size of this office is just right.

3. Kodomo-tachi wa jiken no _____ ga wakaranai yō da. (jūdaina)

子供達は事件の _____ が分からないようだ。（重大な）

It seems that children do not understand the seriousness of the incident.

4. Kono kēki wa _____ ga tarimasen ne. (amai)

このケーキは _____ が足りませんね。（甘い）

This cake isn't sweet enough (lit. lacks sweetness), is it?

5. Watashi wa mune ni _____ o kanjita. (itai)

私は胸に _____ を感じた。（痛い）

I felt a pain in my chest.

6. Yamada-san no chōsho wa seikaku no _____ desu. (seiketsuna)

山田さんの長所は性格の _____ です。（清潔な）

Mr. Yamada's strong point is the pureness of his character.

7. _____ to kenkō ga kare no _____ desu. (wakai) (tsuyoi)

_____ と健康が彼の _____ です。（若い）（強い）

Youth and health are his strengths.

Polite Forms

Adjectives have polite forms. These include not only simple, polite expressions, but honorific and humble expressions as well.

10.1 | **o-/go- お-/ご- + Adj** | to make a polite expression

(a) o-isogashii   (busy)
お忙しい

o-yoroshii   (good)
およろしい

(b) go-shinsetsuna   (kind)
ご親切な

The prefix *o-* or *go-* added to an adjective expresses politeness. Basically, *o-* is used for Japanese-origin words and *go-* for Chinese-origin words. All *i*-adjectives are Japanese in origin, while most *na*-adjectives are Chinese in origin. Some Chinese-origin *na*-adjectives may take *o-* instead of *go-*.

EXAMPLES:
1. *i*-adjectives:
   o-atsui お暑い (hot), **o**-tsuyoi お強い (strong)

2. Chinese-origin *na*-adjectives:
   go-teineina ごていねいな (polite), **go**-shinsetsuna ご親切な (kind)

3. Japanese-origin *na*-adjectives:
   o-shizukana お静かな (quiet), **o**-sukina お好きな (favorite)

4. *na*-adjectives that take *o-*:
   o-jōzuna お上手な (skillful), **o**-genkina お元気な (healthy)

10.2 | Adj **te** + **irassharu** 〜 ていらっしゃる |

to make an honorific expression

(a) kashikokute irassharu   (is intelligent/bright)
    かしこくて いらっしゃる

(b) o-jōzu de irassharu   (is skillful)
    お上手で いらっしゃる

The *te* form of an *i-* or a *na*-adjective followed by the verb *irassharu* constitutes an honorific expression that shows respect to the person it is directed at—usually the speaker's superior (one who is older or of higher social status than the speaker). The respect conveyed by *irassharu* extends to the listener's family members as well. *Irasshaimasu* is the polite form of *irassharu*.

EXAMPLES:

1. Yano-san no okosan wa **kashikokute** irassharu.
   矢野さんのお子さんは**かしこくて**いらっしゃる。
   Mr. Yano's child is bright.

2. Shachō wa gorufu ga **o-jōzu de** irasshaimasu.
   社長はゴルフが**お上手で**いらっしゃいます。
   Our company president is good at golf.

3. O-kāsama wa **o-genki de** irasshaimasu ka.
   お母様は**お元気で**いらっしゃいますか。
   Is your mother well?

10.3 | Adj stem/Adj **te** + **gozaimasu** 〜う/で ございます |

to make a superpolite/humble expression

(a) 1. ai → ō chiisai → chiisō   **gozaimasu** (is small)
        小さい → 小そう   ございます

   oi → ō tsuyoi → tsuyō   **gozaimasu** (is strong)
        強い → 強う   ございます

2. ii → ū ureshii → ureshū   **gozaimasu** (is happy)
        うれしい → うれしゅう ございます

   ōkii   → ōkyū   **gozaimasu** (is big)
   大きい   → 大きゅう   ございます

3. ui → ū atsui   → atsū   **gozaimasu** (is hot)
        熱い   → 熱う   ございます

(b) zannen de   **gozaimasu** (is regrettable)
    残念で   ございます

The stem of an *i*-adjective or the *te* form of a *na*-adjective, followed by *gozaimasu*, is a superpolite form. It can also be a humble form if the subject of the sentence is the speaker or someone close to him. The stems of *i*-adjectives make the above changes before *gozaimasu*.

EXAMPLES:

1. Kochira wa **chiisō** gozaimasu ga, sochira yori **tsuyō** gozaimasu.

   こちらは**小そう**ございますが、そちらより**強う**ございます。

   This one is smaller but stronger than that one.

2. Haha ga genki de **ureshū** gozaimasu.

   母が元気で**うれしゅう**ございます。

   My mother is healthy and I am happy.

3. Waga chīmu ga makete **zannen de** gozaimashita.

   我がチームが負けて**残念で**ございました。

   It was regrettable that our team lost (the game).

GREETINGS: The superpolite forms of some adjectives are used as greetings.

arigatō	**gozaimasu**	(Thank you)
ありがとう	ございます	
omedetō	**gozaimasu**	(Congratulations)
おめでとう	ございます	
o-hayō	**gozaimasu**	(Good morning)
お早う	ございます	

o-atsū	gozaimasu	(It is hot)
お暑う	ございます	

o-samū	gozaimasu	(It is cold)
お寒う	ございます	

PRACTICE 13 (10.1–10.3)

A. Change the following sentences into honorific expressions.

1. **Mori-san no okosan wa kawaii desu.**
   森さんのお子さんはかわいいです。
   Mrs. Mori's child is lovely.

2. **Ano kata wa borantia no shigoto ni nesshin desu.**
   あの方はボランティアの仕事に熱心です。
   He is enthusiastic about his volunteer work.

3. **Shachō wa san-ji made isogashii desu.**
   社長は三時まで忙しいです。
   The company president is busy until three o'clock.

4. **Sumisu-san wa Nihon ryōri ga suki desu.**
   スミスさんは日本料理が好きです。
   Mr. Smith likes Japanese meals.

5. **Ogawa-sensei wa gakusei katsudō ni kyōryokuteki desu.**
   小川先生は学生活動に協力的です。
   Professor Ogawa is cooperative in students' activities.

B. Change the following sentences into polite/humble expressions.

1. Rainen wa Itaria e ikitai desu.
   来年はイタリアへ行きたいです。
   I want to go to Italy next year.

2. Chichi no byōki wa karukatta desu.
   父の病気は軽かったです。
   My father's illness was slight.

3. Kono hen de jūgatsu ni yuki ga furu no wa mezurashii desu.
   この辺で十月に雪が降るのは珍しいです。
   It rarely (lit. It is rare that it) snows in this area in October.

4. Tetsuzuki wa omotta yori mendō deshita.
   手続きは思ったより面倒でした。
   The procedure was more troublesome than expected.

5. Ano resutoran wa takai desu ne.
   あのレストランは高いですね。
   That restaurant is expensive, isn't it?

ADVERBS

INTRODUCTION

This section deals with some of the main features of Japanese adverbs. You are advised to read it carefully before moving on.

KINDS OF ADVERBS

Adverbs are non-conjugating words that modify other words. Japanese adverbs may be divided into two types according to usage: (a) those that modify verbs, adjectives, other adverbs and certain nouns, and (b) those used for special expressions involving negatives, interrogatives, conditionals, etc.

(a) Modify verbs, adjectives, other adverbs and certain nouns

Yukkuri arukimashita.   (verb)
ゆっくり歩きました。
I walked slowly.

Eiga wa **totemo omoshirokatta.   (adjective)
映画はとても面白かった。
The movie was very interesting.

Motto yukkuri hanashite kudasai.   (adverb)
もっとゆっくり話してください。
Please speak more slowly.

Motto mae ni susunde kudasai. (noun)

もっと前に進んでください。

Please move forward a bit more.

Soko wa machi no **kanari** kita desu. (noun)

そこは町の**かなり**北です。

That place is fairly north of the city.

(b) Used for special expressions

Ano hito wa **kesshite** sonna koto wa shimasen.

あの人は**決して**そんなことはしません。 (negative)

He/she would never do such a thing.

Yamada-san wa **tabun** konai darō. (conjecture)

山田さんは**多分**来ないだろう。

Mr. Yamada probably won't come.

WORD MODIFIERS

As mentioned above, Japanese adverbs are used as word modifiers. These modifiers may be grouped according to the concepts they express.

1. Kare wa **itsumo** rokuji ni okiru. (time)

   彼は**いつも**六時に起きる。

   He always gets up at six o'clock.

2. **Takusan** tabemashita. (quantity)

   たくさん食べました。

   I ate a lot.

3. Kono kabin wa **totemo** takai.   (degree)
   この花びんは**とても**高い。
   This flower vase is very expensive.

4. **Hakkiri** kotaenasai.   (circumstance)
   はっきり答えなさい。
   Answer clearly.

   Jiken ga **zokuzoku** okotta.   (circumstance)
   事件が**続々**起こった。
   Incidents occurred one after another.

ONOMATOPOEIC WORDS

Onomatopoeic words are words that imitate natural sounds (*giseigo*) or describe actions, manners or states (*gitaigo*). In Japanese, they are used as adverbs to describe circumstances.

1. *Giseigo* (sound-imitating words)

   Ame ga **zāzā** futte iru.   (sound of rain)
   雨が**ざあざあ**降っている。
   The rain is pouring down.

2. *Gitaigo* (words that describe actions, manners or states)

   Kodomo ga **nikoniko** waratte iru.   (manner of smiling)
   子供が**にこにこ**笑っている。
   The child is smiling cheerfully.

SPECIAL EXPRESSIONS

As mentioned earlier, some Japanese adverbs are used for special expressions. These expressions vary considerably but can be roughly grouped according to their functions or the notions they express.

1. Kono mondai wa **sappari** wakaranai.   (negative)
   この問題は**さっぱり**わからない。
   I don't understand this problem at all.

2. **Naze** tabenai no desu ka.   (interrogative)
   なぜ食べないのですか。
   Why don't you eat?

3. **Moshi** ame ga futtara ikimasen.   (conditional)
   もし雨が降ったら行きません。
   If it rains, I won't go.

4. **Zehi** ano kuruma o kaitai.   (desire)
   ぜひあの車を買いたい。
   I definitely want to buy that car.

5. Densha wa **tabun** okureru deshō.   (conjecture)
   電車は**多分**遅れるでしょう。
   The train will probably be delayed.

6. **Marude** haru no yō ni atatakai desu ne.   (resemblance)
   まるで春のように暖かいですね。
   It's so warm, it's like spring, isn't it?

ADVERBS USED AS VERBS

Some adverbs, particularly those that express manner of action or human emotion, combine with the verb *suru* to form verbs.

Onsen de ni-sannichi **yukkuri shimashita**.
温泉で二、三日**ゆっくりしました**。
We spent a few days leisurely at a hot spring.

Densha ga okurete **iraira shita**.
電車が遅れて**いらいらした**。
The train was late, so I got irritated.

ADVERBIAL POSITION

The position of an adverb in a sentence is relatively free as long as it is placed before the word it modifies.

Kaigi wa **mō sugu** hajimarimasu.
会議は**もうすぐ**始まります。
Mō sugu kaigi wa hajimarimasu.
もうすぐ会議は始まります。
The meeting will begin soon.

However, it is better placed near the word it modifies when the sentence is at all complex.

Jigyō ni shippai shite mo, kare wa **kesshite** kujikenai.
事業に失敗しても、彼は**決して**くじけない。 (correct)
Even if he fails in his work, he will never lose heart.

Kesshite jigyō ni shippai shite mo, kare wa kujikenai.
決して事業に失敗しても、彼はくじけない。　　(incorrect)

OTHER WORDS USED AS ADVERBS

There are a number of other kinds of words, besides those outlined above, which can be used as adverbs in Japanese. These include adjectives in the adverbial form, certain nouns that express time or number and verbs in the *te* form.

Kesa **hayaku** okita.　　　　　　　　　　　(*i*-adjective)
今朝早く起きた。
I got up early this morning.

Shizuka ni shite kudasai.　　　　　　　　　(*na*-adjective)
静かにしてください。
Please be quiet.

Kimura-san wa **ashita** Amerika kara kaerimasu.
木村さんは明日アメリカから帰ります。　　(noun)
Mr. Kimura will return from America tomorrow.

Ringo o **mittsu** kudasai.　　　　　　　　　(noun)
りんごを三つください。
Please give me three apples.

Gakusei ga **gonin** kita.　　　　　　　　　　(noun)
学生が五人来た。
Five students came.

Isoide hirugohan o tabeta. (verb)

急いで昼ご飯を食べた。

I ate lunch in a hurry.

Sofa ni nete hon o yomimasu. (verb)

ソファに寝て本を読みます。

Lying on a sofa, I read a book.

USAGE OF ADVERBS

As mentioned earlier, Japanese adverbs modify verbs, adjectives, other adverbs and certain nouns, and some adverbs are used to create special expressions. This section presents the most commonly used adverbs. They are grouped according to what they express and placed under such headings as time, quantity, degree, circumstance and so forth. Therefore, you can go straight to any heading that interests you. The adverbial usage of nouns, adjectives and verbs is not covered here.

 Adverbs Expressing Time

1.1 | **itsumo いつも** | "always," "habitually"

Itsumo indicates a habitual action or a constant state. It is primarily used in conversation.

EXAMPLES:

1. Chichi wa **itsumo** hachiji mae ni ie o demasu.
   父はいつも八時前に家を出ます。
   My father always leaves the house before eight o'clock.

2. Ano mise no pan wa **itsumo** atarashii desu ne.
   あの店のパンはいつも新しいですね。
   The bread at that store is always fresh, isn't it?

1.2 | **tsune ni 常に** | "always," "habitually"

Tsune ni indicates a habitual action or a constant state. It is primarily used in writing.

EXAMPLES:

1. Toda-san wa **tsune ni** tabemono ni chūi shite iru.
   戸田さんは**常に**食べ物に注意している。
   Miss Toda always pays attention to what she eats.

2. Hara-san no taido wa **tsune ni** sekkyokuteki da.
   原さんの態度は**常に**積極的だ。
   Mr. Hara's attitude is always positive.

1.3 | **taezu 絶えず** | "constantly," "incessantly," "consistently"

Taezu indicates a continuous action or a constant state.

EXAMPLES:

1. Yūbe kara **taezu** ame ga futte imasu.
   ゆうべから**絶えず**雨が降っています。
   It has been raining incessantly since last night.

2. Kono biru no mae o **taezu** kuruma ga tōtte iru.
   このビルの前を**絶えず**車が通っている。
   Cars are constantly passing in front of this building.

3. Jimu wa **taezu** doryoku shita kara, seiseki ga agatta.
   ジムは**絶えず**努力したから、成績が上がった。

   Jim made a consistent effort, so his grades went up.

1.4 | shikiri ni しきりに | "constantly," "strongly," "eagerly"

Shikiri ni indicates a continuous action or a constant state (Examples 1, 2). It can also express eagerness (Example 3).

EXAMPLES:

1. Tonari no denwa ga **shikiri ni** natte iru.
   隣の電話が**しきりに**鳴っている。

   The phone next door is ringing constantly.

2. Tomodachi ni kaigai ryokō o **shikiri ni** susumerareta.
   友達に海外旅行を**しきりに**勧められた。

   I was strongly advised by my friend to travel abroad.

3. Kare wa **shikiri ni** supōtsukā o kaitagatte iru.
   彼は**しきりに**スポーツカーを買いたがっている。

   He is eager to buy a sports car.

1.5 | tabitabi 度々 | "often," "frequently"

Tabitabi indicates repetition of an action or event. It is primarily used in casual conversation.

EXAMPLES:

1. Buchō wa shigoto de **tabitabi** Furansu e ikimasu.
   部長は仕事で**度々**フランスへ行きます。

   The head of our department often goes to France on business.

2. Sara wa byōki de **tabitabi** gakkō o yasunda.
   サラは病気で**度々**学校を休んだ。

   Sarah was frequently absent from school due to illness.

1.6 | **shibashiba しばしば** | "often," "frequently"

Shibashiba indicates repetition of an action or event. It is essentially interchangeable with *tabitabi*.

EXAMPLES:

1. Ano hōru de **shibashiba** konsāto ga okonawareru.
   あのホールで**しばしば**コンサートが行われる。

   Concerts are held frequently in that hall.

2. Kono atari wa **shibashiba** yuki ga furimasu.
   この辺りは**しばしば**雪が降ります。

   It often snows in this area.

1.7 | **tokidoki 時々** | "sometimes," "once in a while"

Tokidoki indicates that an action or state occurs or exists from time to time.

EXAMPLES:

1. **Tokidoki** kodomo o kōen e tsurete ikimasu.
時々子供を公園へ連れて行きます。

   Sometimes I take my children to the park.

2. Ano depāto no gyararī de **tokidoki** shashinten ga aru.
あのデパートのギャラリーで**時々**写真展がある。

   Photo exhibitions are sometimes held in the gallery of that department store.

1.8 | **tama ni たまに** | "occasionally," "once in a great while"

Tama ni indicates that an action or state occurs or exists only occasionally.

EXAMPLES:

1. Shokuba no dōryō to **tama ni** shokuji o shimasu.
職場の同僚と**たまに**食事をします。

   I occasionally have meals with my colleagues.

2. **Tama ni** asa hayaku okite sanpo ni iku koto ga aru.
たまに朝早く起きて散歩に行くことがある。

   Once in a great while I get up early in the morning and go for a walk.

Circle the correct adverb among the choices given in parentheses.

1. Ano hito wa (tokidoki/itsumo/tama ni) goji mae ni kaisha o
   deru.

   あの人は（時々/いつも/たまに）五時前に会社を出る。

   He leaves the office before five o'clock once in a while.

2. Kachō wa kaigi de (shikiri ni/tsune ni/tama ni) jibun no iken
   o shuchō suru.

   課長は会議で（しきりに/常に/たまに）自分の意見を主張する。

   The section chief always asserts his opinions at meetings.

3. Yūbe tonari no inu ga (tokidoki/shikiri ni/itsumo) naite yoku
   nemurenakkata.

   ゆうべ隣の犬が（時々/しきりに/いつも）ないてよく眠れなか
   った。

   Last night the constant barking of the dog next door kept me awake.

4. Kotoshi wa sekai kakuchi de (shibashiba/taezu/tsune ni)
   jishin ga atta.

   今年は世界各地で（しばしば/絶えず/常に）地震があった。

   This year there were often earthquakes in various parts of the world.

5. Mainichi isogashii ga, (tabitabi/itsumo/tama ni) shachō to
   gorufu o suru.

   毎日忙しいが、（度々/いつも/たまに）社長とゴルフをする。

   I'm busy every day, but once in a great while I play golf with the
   company president.

6. Kinō wa asa kara (taezu/tsune ni/shibashiba) tsuyoi kaze ga
   fuite ita.

   昨日は朝から（絶えず/常に/しばしば）強い風が吹いていた。

   Yesterday, strong winds blew constantly from morning on.

1.9 | shibaraku しばらく | "for a while," "for a long time"

Shibaraku indicates that an action or event occurs for a short or long
period, depending on context (Examples 1, 2). It is also used as a
greeting (Example 3).

EXAMPLES:

1. Koko de **shibaraku** o-machi kudasai.

   ここで**しばらく**お待ちください。

   Please wait here for a while.

2. **Shibaraku** Nihongo o hanasanakatta node, heta ni natta.

   しばらく日本語を話さなかったので、下手になった。

   Because I didn't speak Japanese for a long time, I became bad at it.

3. **Shibaraku** desu ne. O-genki desu ka.

   しばらくですね。お元気ですか。

   It's been quite some time since I last saw you. How have you been?

1.10 | shūshi 終始 | "from beginning to end," "throughout"

Shūshi indicates that an action or a state continues to occur or exist
with little variance throughout a period.

EXAMPLES:

1. Kōgi no aida Biru wa **shūshi** nōto o totte ita.

講義の間ビルは**終始**ノートをとっていた。

Bill was taking notes throughout the lecture.

2. Kinō no kaigi de Ono-san no kotoba wa **shūshi** odayaka datta.

昨日の会議で小野さんの言葉は**終始**おだやかだった。

At yesterday's meeting, Mr. Ono's words were amicable from beginning to end.

1.11 | **zutto** ずっと | "throughout," "all the time," "all the way"

Zutto indicates that an action or a state continues to occur or exist for a long period or is constant throughout a limited period.

EXAMPLES:

1. Kyūkachū **zutto** ryōshin no ie ni imashita.

休暇中**ずっと**両親の家にいました。

I stayed at my parents' house throughout the holidays.

2. Sumisu-san wa Nihon e kite kara, **zutto** kono ie ni sunde iru.

スミスさんは日本に来てから、**ずっと**この家に住んでいる。

Mr. Smith has lived in this house ever since he came to Japan.

3. Kare wa Shinkansen no naka de Ōsaka kara Tōkyō made **zutto** nete ita.

彼は新幹線の中で大阪から東京まで**ずっと**寝ていた。

He was sleeping in the bullet train all the way from Osaka to Tokyo.

1.12 | sugu (ni) すぐ (に) | "right away"

Sugu (ni) indicates someone's doing something without delay.

EXAMPLES:

1. **Sugu** kite kudasai.
   すぐ来てください。
   Please come right away.

2. Hoteru ni tsuite **sugu ni** shawā o abita.
   ホテルに着いて**すぐに**シャワーを浴びた。
   I arrived at the hotel and took a shower right away.

1.13 | sassoku 早速 | "immediately"

Sassoku indicates someone's doing something without delay. It is more formal than *sugu (ni)*.

EXAMPLES:

1. Bōnasu o moratta node, **sassoku** atarashii konpyūtā o kai-mashita.
   ボーナスをもらったので、**早速**新しいコンピューターを買いました。
   Since I received a bonus, I bought a new computer immediately.

2. Shinamono wa **sassoku** o-todoke itashimasu.
   品物は**早速**お届けいたします。
   We will deliver the article immediately.

1.14 | tadachi ni ただちに | "immediately," "at once"

Tadachi ni indicates someone's doing something immediately in response to some event. It suggests urgency and is used, for example, when an emergency occurs.

EXAMPLES:

1. Hayashi-san ga taoreta node, **tadachi ni** kyūkyūsha o yonda.

   林さんが倒れたので、**ただちに**救急車を呼んだ。

   Mr. Hayashi collapsed, so we called for an ambulance immediately.

2. Kasai keihō de gakusei wa **tadachi ni** tatemono no soto ni deta.

   火災警報で学生は**ただちに**建物の外に出た。

   At the (sound of the) fire alarm, the students immediately got out of the building.

1.15 | tachimachi たちまち | "at once," "in no time," "suddenly"

Tachimachi indicates that something happens quickly or abruptly. It is not used when the speaker's volition is involved.

EXAMPLES:

1. Ano rokku shingā no konsāto no kippu wa **tachimachi** uri-kireta.

   あのロックシンガーのコンサートの切符は**たちまち**売り切れた。

   Tickets to that rock star's concert sold out in no time.

2. Sono kusuri o nomu to, **tachimachi** zutsū ga naotta.
   その薬を飲むと、**たちまち**頭痛が治った。

   When I took the medicine, my headache went away at once.

3. Kuroi kumo ga **tachimachi** sora ni hirogatta.
   黒い雲が**たちまち**空に広がった。

   Dark clouds suddenly spread across the sky.

1.16 | sono uchi (ni) そのうち(に)

"soon," "one of these days," "before long"

Sono uchi (ni) expresses the speaker's expectation that an action or event will occur before long (Examples 1, 2). When the final verb of the sentence is in the past tense, it simply means "before long," with reference to some past occurrance (Example 3).

EXAMPLES:

1. **Sono uchi** kōen no sakura mo saku deshō.
   そのうち公園の桜も咲くでしょう。

   The cherry blossoms in the park will probably be out soon.

2. Kare kara **sono uchi ni** renraku ga aru to omou.
   彼から**そのうちに**連絡があると思う。

   I think that he will contact me one of these days.

3. **Sono uchi** kanojo ni wa kare no seikaku ga wakatte kita.
   そのうち彼女には彼の性格がわかってきた。

   His personality revealed itself to her before long.

1.17 izure いずれ "soon," "one of these days," "before long"

Izure expresses the speaker's expectation that an action or event will occur eventually. It is more formal than *sono uchi (ni)*.

EXAMPLES:

1. **Izure** Noda-sensei o o-tazune suru tsumori desu.
   いずれ野田先生をお訪ねするつもりです。
   I intend to visit Professor Noda one of these days.

2. **Izure** mata o-ai shimashō.
   いずれまたお会いしましょう。
   Let's meet again soon.

1.18 mō sugu もうすぐ "soon," "before long"

Mō sugu expresses the speaker's expectation that an action or event will occur shortly.

EXAMPLES:

1. **Mō sugu** natsu desu ne.
   もうすぐ夏ですね。
   Summer is just around the corner, isn't it?

2. Kono densha wa **mō sugu** Yokohama ni tsukimasu.
   この電車はもうすぐ横浜に着きます。
   This train will soon arrive in Yokohama.

1.19 | yagate やがて

"soon," "before long," "at (long) last," "in the end"

Yagate expresses the speaker's expectation that an action or event will occur eventually (Examples 1, 2). When the final verb of the sentence is in the past tense, it means "at (long) last" or "in the end" (Example 3). *Yagate* is more formal than *sono uchi (ni)* and can also express a stronger sense of cause and effect.

EXAMPLES:

1. Waga kuni no keizai wa **yagate** kaifuku suru darō.
   我が国の経済は**やがて**回復するだろう。
   The economy of our country will probably recover before long.

2. **Yagate** kaimaku ni narimasu kara, o-isogi kudasai.
   やがて開幕になりますから、お急ぎください。
   The curtains will soon rise, so please hurry.

3. **Yagate** jiken wa kaiketsu shita.
   やがて事件は解決した。
   At last the case was solved.

1.20 | mamonaku 間もなく   "soon," "shortly," "before long"

Mamonaku indicates that an action or event will occur shortly or that it has occurred not long after some other action or event.

EXAMPLES:

1. **Mamonaku** Kyōto-yuki ga hassha shimasu.

間もなく京都行きが発車します。

The train bound for Kyoto will depart shortly.

2. Nihon de wa **mamonaku** sōsenkyo ga okonawareru rashii.

日本では**間もなく**総選挙が行われるらしい。

It seems that a general election will soon be held in Japan.

3. Futari wa kekkon shite, **mamonaku** rikon shita

二人は結婚して**間もなく**離婚した。

The two got a divorce not long after getting married.

PRACTICE 2 (1.9–1.20)

Circle the correct adverb among the choices given in parentheses.

1. Gakkō ga owatta node, (sono uchi/mamonaku/sugu ni) ryokō ni iku tsumoi desu.

学校が終わったので、(そのうち/間もなく/すぐに) 旅行に行くつもりです。

School has ended, so I will soon be going on a trip.

2. Waga chīmu wa (sugu/sassoku/shūshi) yoku tatakatta.

我がチームは (すぐ/早速/終始) よく戦った。

Our team fought well all the way.

3. Kachō ga kuru to, (sugu ni/yagate/shibaraku) kaigi ga haji-matta.

課長が来ると、(すぐに/やがて/しばらく) 会議が始まった。

The meeting started as soon as the section chief showed up.

4. Kare wa kaijō no jumbi ga dekiru made, (shibaraku/mō sugu/zutto) rōka ni tatte ita.

彼は会場の準備が出来るまで、（しばらく/もうすぐ/ずっと）廊下に立っていた。

He was standing in the hallway the whole time until the assembly hall was ready.

5. Densha wa (mamonaku/shibaraku/izure) Ōsaka eki ni teisha shita.

電車は（間もなく/しばらく/いずれ）大阪駅に停車した。

The train stopped for a while at Osaka Station.

6. Watashi wa jiko no shirase de (yagate/tadachi ni/tachimachi) genba ni kaketsuketa.

私は事故の知らせで（やがて/ただちに/たちまち）現場にかけつけた。

At the news of the accident, I rushed to the scene.

7. Parēdo ga (shibaraku/mamonaku/sassoku) kono michi o tōrimasu.

パレードが（しばらく/間もなく/早速）この道を通ります。

The parade will soon pass along this street.

8. Mizu o yaru to, puranto ga (yagata/tachimachi/izure) ikikaetta.

水をやると、プラントが（やがて/たちまち/いずれ）生き返った。

When I watered the plant, it revived immediately.

9. Sensei ni hon o itadaita node, (yagate/sassoku/tachimachi) o-rei no tegami o kaita.

先生に本を頂いたので、（やがて/早速/たちまち）お礼の手紙を書いた。

I received a book from my teacher, so I immediately wrote him a thank-you note.

1.21 | sakki さっき | "a (little) while ago"

Sakki refers to a moment in the immediate past. It is primarily used in casual conversation.

EXAMPLES:
1. Kare wa **sakki** uchi e kaerimashita.
   彼はさっきうちへ帰りました。
   He went home a little while ago.

2. **Sakki** Rondon no shisha kara fakkusu ga haitta.
   さっきロンドンの支社からファックスが入った。
   A fax came in from the branch office in London just a little while ago.

1.22 | sakihodo 先ほど | "a (little) while ago"

Sakihodo refers to a moment in the immediate past. It is primarily used in formal conversation and in writing.

EXAMPLES:
1. Sotsugyōshiki wa **sakihodo** shūryō shimashita.
   卒業式は先ほど終了しました。
   The graduation ceremony ended just a little while ago.

2. Honda-sensei wa **sakihodo** made ofisu ni irasshaimashita.
   本田先生は先ほどまでオフィスにいらっしゃいました。
   Professor Honda was in his office until a little while ago.

1.23 **tatta ima たった今**   "just now," "a moment ago"

Tatta ima refers to a moment in the immediate past that is generally closer to the present than an event expressed by *sakki* or *sakihodo*.

EXAMPLES:

1. **Tatta ima** okita tokoro desu.
   たった今起きたところです。
   I got up just a moment ago.

2. Yoshida-san wa **tatta ima** shokuji ni demashita.
   吉田さんはたった今食事に出ました。
   Mr. Yoshida has just left for lunch.

1.24 **sudeni すでに**   "already"

Sudeni indicates that an action or event has been completed by the time some other action or event occurs.

EXAMPLES:

1. Kūkō ni tsuita toki, hikōki wa **sudeni** deteita.
   空港に着いた時、飛行機はすでに出ていた。
   When I arrived at the airport, the plane had already taken off.

2. Hoteru ni denwa shitara, kare wa **sudeni** chekkuauto shite ita.
   ホテルに電話したら、彼はすでにチェックアウトしていた。
   When I called him at the hotel, he had already checked out.

1.25 | kanete かねて | "before," "previously," "for some time"

Kanete indicates that an action or a state has continued from some point in the past up to the present.

EXAMPLES:

1. Sono uwasa wa **kanete** kiite imashita.
   その噂はかねて聞いていました。
   I had heard the rumor before.

2. Kore wa **kanete** hoshikatta mono desu.
   これはかねて欲しかった物です。
   This is something I've wanted for some time.

3. Kanojo wa **kanete** renshū shite ita kyoku o hīta.
   彼女はかねて練習していた曲を弾いた。
   She played the piece (of music) that she had been practicing for some time.

1.26 | hajimete 初めて | "for the first time"

Hajimete indicates that an action or event is the first of its kind.

EXAMPLES:

1. Kare wa kyonen **hajimete** Fuji-san ni nobotta.
   彼は去年初めて富士山に登った。
   He climbed Mt. Fuji last year for the first time (in his life).

2. Watashi wa hatachi no toki **hajimete** kuruma o unten shita.

私は二十歳の時、**初めて**車を運転した。

I drove a car for the first time at the age of twenty.

1.27 | mazu 先ず | "first"

Mazu indicates that the action it modifies is a priority.

EXAMPLES:

1. Kyōto ni tsuite **mazu** Tanabe-san ni denwa shita.

京都に着いて**先ず**田辺さんに電話した。

On arriving in Kyoto, I phoned Mrs. Tanabe first (before doing anything else).

2. **Mazu** kono shigoto o katazukete kara, tsugi no shigoto ni kakarimashō.

先ずこの仕事を片付けてから、次の仕事にかかりましょう。

Let's finish this job first and then move on to the next.

1.28 | mata また | "again," "once more"

Mata indicates the recurrence of an action or event.

EXAMPLES:

1. Kyūshū ni **mata** taifū ga kuru rashii.

九州に**また**台風が来るらしい。

It seems that a typhoon will hit Kyushu again.

2. Tsugi no shiai de **mata** ano chīmu o makashitai.

次の試合で**また**あのチームを負かしたい。

We want to beat that team again in the next game.

PRACTICE 3 (1.21–1.28)

Circle the correct adverb among the choices given in parentheses.

1. Jimu wa Nihonjin no tomodachi ni sasowarete (sakki/ hajimete/mazu) sumō o mini itta.

ジムは日本人の友達に誘われて（さっき/初めて/先ず）すもうを見に行った。

Having been invited by his Japanese friend, Jim went to see sumo for the first time.

2. Kozutsumi wa (mazu/tatta ima/sudeni) todoita bakaride, mada akete imasen.

小包は（先ず/たった今/すでに）届いたばかりで、まだ開けていません。

The package has just arrived and I haven't opened it yet.

3. Kanji no kuizu de (mata/sudeni/hajimete) onaji machigai o shita.

漢字のクイズで（また/すでに/始めて）同じ間違いをした。

I made the same mistake again on the kanji quiz.

4. Kyōto kenbutsu wa (mazu/mata/hajimete) doko kara hajimemashō ka.

京都見物は（先ず/また/初めて）どこから始めましょうか。

Where shall we start when sightseeing in Kyoto?

5. (Sudeni/sakki/kanete) byōki datta Kida-san wa kesa hayaku nakunarimashita.

（すでに/さっき/かねて）病気だった木田さんは今朝早く亡くなりました。

Mr. Kida, who had been ill for some time, passed away early this morning.

6. Tomodachi no hanashi ni yoru to, Minami-san wa (mata/sudeni/sakihodo) shinbunsha o yamete, ima shōsetsu o kaite iru sō da.

友達の話によると、南さんは（また/すでに/先ほど）新聞社を辞めて、今小説を書いているそうだ。

According to what my friend said, Mr. Minami has already quit the newspaper company and is writing a novel now.

1.29 | ato de 後で | "later," "afterward"

Ato de refers to a point in the near future.

EXAMPLES:

1. Sono koto wa mata **ato de** hanashiaimashō.

そのことはまた**後で**話し合いましょう。

Let's talk about that matter again later.

2. Ima isogashii kara, kono shigoto wa **ato de** shimasu.

今忙しいから、この仕事は**後で**します。

I'm busy now, so I'll do this work later.

1.30 | **nochihodo 後ほど** | "later," "afterward"

Nochihodo refers to a point in the near future. It is more formal than *ato de.*

EXAMPLES:

1. **Nochihodo** o-ukagai shimasu.
   後ほどお伺いします。
   I will call on you later.

2. Enkai no basho ni tsuite wa **nochihodo** o-shirase shimasu.
   宴会の場所については後ほどお知らせします。
   As for the location of the banquet, we'll let you know later.

1.31 | **saki ni 先に** | "before," "ahead of," "first"

Saki ni indicates that an action or event occurs prior to some other action or event.

EXAMPLES:

1. Kono mondai o **saki ni** kaiketsu shinakereba naranai.
   この問題を先に解決しなければならない。
   We must solve this problem first.

2. Maiku wa mina yori **saki ni** shiken o sumasete dete itta.
   マイクは皆より先に試験を済ませて出て行った。
   Mike finished the exam ahead of others and left (the classroom).

1.32 | **maemotte 前もって** | "beforehand," "in advance"

Maemotte indicates someone's doing something ahead of time in preparation for a future event.

EXAMPLES:

1. Kesseki no baai wa **maemotte** shirasete kudasai.
   欠席の場合は**前もって**知らせてください。
   Should you not attend, please let me know in advance.

2. Kono purojekuto ni wa **maemotte** sensei no shōdaku o emashita.
   このプロジェクトには**前もって**先生の承諾を得ました。
   For this project, we obtained our teacher's consent beforehand.

1.33 | **arakajime あらかじめ** | "beforehand," "in advance"

Arakajime indicates someone's doing something ahead of time in preparation for a future event. It is more formal than *maemotte*.

EXAMPLES:

1. Sono koto wa **arakajime** kachō to sōdan shite oita.
   そのことは**あらかじめ**課長と相談しておいた。
   I consulted with the section chief concerning that matter beforehand.

2. Konban no pātī ni wa bīru o **arakajime** yōi shite oite kudasai.
   今晩のパーティーにはビールを**あらかじめ**用意しておいてください。
   Please have beer ready in advance for tonight's party.

1.34 | **gūzen 偶然** | "unexpectedly," "by chance"

Gūzen indicates that something has occurred unexpectedly or by chance.

EXAMPLES:

1. Ginza de **gūzen** Yamada-san no okusan ni atta.
   銀座で**偶然**山田さんの奥さんに会った。

   I met Mr. Yamada's wife unexpectedly in Ginza.

2. Kanda no furuhon'ya de **gūzen** kono jisho o mitsuketa.
   神田の古本屋で**偶然**この辞書を見付けた。

   I found this dictionary by chance at a secondhand bookstore in Kanda.

1.35 | **ichiō 一応** | "once," "briefly," "for the time being"

Ichiō indicates someone's doing something in a brief or offhand manner, often for some future purpose. It may imply a lack of thoroughness.

EXAMPLES:

1. Kono repōto ni wa **ichiō** me o tōshimashita.
   このレポートには**一応**目を通しました。

   I glanced through this report once.

2. Mihon wa **ichiō** misete moraimashita.
   見本は**一応**見せてもらいました。

   I had him show me the sample briefly.

3. Kurejitto kādo dake de naku, **ichiō** genkin mo motte ikimasu.
   クレジットカードだけでなく**一応**現金も持っていきます。

   I'll take some cash as well as my credit card—just in case.

151

1.36 | **ittan** いったん |　　"once," "temporarily"

Ittan indicates someone's doing something temporarily.

EXAMPLES:

1. Buraun-san wa **ittan** kikoku shite Igirisu e itta sō da.
   ブラウンさんは**いったん**帰国してイギリスへ行ったそうだ。
   I hear that Mr. Brown returned to his country once and then went to England.

2. Kare wa daigaku o sotsugyō shite **ittan** ryōshin no ie ni ochitsuita.
   彼は大学を卒業して**いったん**両親の家に落ち着いた。
   He graduated from college and settled in temporarily at his parents' house.

1.37 | **tōtō** とうとう |　　"at last," "finally," "after all," "in the end"

Tōtō indicates that an expected situation has come about after a considerable amount of time has passsed.

EXAMPLES:

1. Matte ita tegami wa **tōtō** konakatta.
   待っていた手紙は**とうとう**来なかった。
   The letter that I had been waiting for didn't come after all.

2. Kanojo wa karō to shinpai no tame, **tōtō** byōki ni natta.
   彼女は過労と心配のため、**とうとう**病気になった。
   Due to overwork and anxiety, she finally fell ill.

1.38 | **tsui ni ついに** | "at last," "finally," "after all"

Tsui ni indicates that an anticipated result has been achieved after considerable time and effort has been spent.

EXAMPLES:

1. Ano futari wa **tsui ni** kekkon suru koto ga dekita.
   あの二人はついに結婚することが出来た。
   The two were able to get married at last.

2. Sūkai no shippai no ato, kare wa **tsui ni** jigyō ni seikō shita.
   数回の失敗の後、彼はついに事業に成功した。
   After several failures, he finally succeeded in his enterprise.

1.39 | **yatto やっと** | "at last," "finally," "barely"

Yatto indicates that a desirable result has been achieved at last and with great difficulty.

EXAMPLES:

1. Kanojo no pianisuto ni naru yume wa **yatto** jitsugen shita.
   彼女のピアニストになる夢はやっと実現した。
   Her dream of becoming a pianist came true at last.

2. Biru wa **yatto** shiken ni gōkau shimashita.
   ビルはやっと試験に合格しました。
   Bill finally managed to pass the exam.

1.40 | yōyaku ようやく | "at last," "finally," "barely"

Yōyaku indicates that a desirable result has been achieved at last and with great difficulty. It is more formal than *yatto*.

EXAMPLES:

1. **Yōyaku** rainendo no yosan ga kettei shita.
   ようやく来年度の予算が決定した。

   The budget for the next fiscal year has finally been settled.

2. Sono kaisha wa **yōyaku** tōsan o manukareta rashii.
   その会社はようやく倒産を免れたらしい。

   It seems that company has finally managed to escape bankruptcy.

PRACTICE 4 (1.29–1.40)

Circle the correct adverb among the choices given in parentheses.

1. Watashi wa mada shigoto ga aru kara, (ichiō/maemotte/saki ni) itte kudasai.
   私はまだ仕事があるから、（一応/前もって/先に）行ってくだ さい。

   I still have work to do, so please go ahead.

2. Yūbe no enkai de (gūzen/nochihodo/tsui ni) mukashi no dōsōsei no tonari ni suwatta.
   ゆうべの宴会で（偶然/後ほど/ついに）昔の同窓生の隣に座った。

   I happened to sit next to my old classmate at last night's banquet.

154

3. Teate no kai naku koinu wa kesa (yatto/tōtō/yōyaku) shinde
   shimatta.

   手当ての甲斐なく小犬は今朝（やっと/とうとう/ようやく）死
   んでしまった。

   The treatment had no effect, and my puppy ended up dying this morning.

4. (Saki ni/ittan/ato de) hoteru ni modotte, kikaete kara yūshoku
   ni demasu.

   （先に/いったん/後で）ホテルに戻って、着替えてから夕食に
   出ます。

   I'll return to the hotel for a bit, change my clothes, and go out for dinner.

5. Jikan no henkō ni tsuite wa (arakajime/yatto/ittan) tsūchi ga
   atta.

   時間の変更については（あらかじめ/やっと/いったん）通知が
   あった。

   I had advance notice of the change of the time.

6. Nando mo hanashiatte (gūzen/tōtō/yōyaku) kare no kimochi
   ga wakatta.

   何度も話し合って（偶然/とうとう/ようやく）彼の気持ちが分
   かった。

   After talking with him many times, I finally understood his feelings.

7. Kono dēta wa kaigi no mae ni Toda-san ni (yatto/ichiō/tsui ni)
   shirabete moraimasu.

   このデータは会議の前に戸田さんに（やっと/一応/ついに）調
   べてもらいます。

   I'll have Miss Toda check this data once before the meeting.

8. Rokuji made matta noni, kare wa (ittan/yatto/tsui ni) araware-nakatta.

六時まで待ったのに、彼は（いったん/やっと/ついに）現れなかった。

Although I waited for him until six o'clock, he didn't show up after all.

 2 **Adverbs Expressing Quantity**

Most of the adverbs below express quantity. However, some may, depending on context, also express time or degree.

2.1 | minna/mina みんな/みな | "all"

Minna or *mina* indicates a total number or an entire amount. *Mina* is primarily used in writing, whereas *minna* is colloquial.

EXAMPLES:

1. Kono ka no kanji wa **minna** oboeta.

この課の漢字は**みんな**覚えた。

I learned all the kanji in this chapter.

2. Kono bazā no uriage wa **mina** kyōkai ni kifu shimasu.

このバザーの売り上げは**みな**教会に寄付します。

We will donate all the proceeds from this bazaar to the church.

2.2 | subete すべて | "all"

Subete indicates a total number or an entire amount. It is often used in writing and is usually interchangeable with *mina*.

EXAMPLES:

1. Kare wa sono hikōki jiko de kazoku o **subete** ushinatta.
   彼はその飛行機事故で家族を**すべて**失った。
   He lost his entire family in that plane crash.

2. Ryokōchū ni genkin o **subete** nusumareta.
   旅行中に現金を**すべて**盗まれた。
   I had all my cash stolen during the trip.

2.3 | takusan たくさん | "many," "much," "enough"

Takusan indicates a number or an amount that is large or excessive.

EXAMPLES:

1. Kono tōri ni wa gifuto shoppu ga **takusan** arimasu.
   この通りにはギフトショップが**たくさん**あります。
   There are many gift shops on this street.

2. Kotoshi wa ame ga **takusan** futta.
   今年は雨が**たくさん**降った。
   We had much rain this year.

3. Sono taido wa mō **takusan** da.
   その態度はもう**たくさん**だ。
   Enough of that attitude!

2.4 jūbun (ni) 十分 (に)   "enough," "fully"

Jūbun (ni) indicates a quantity or degree that is plentiful or sufficient.

EXAMPLES:

1. O-cha o mō ippai ikaga desu ka. Iie, mō **jūbun ni** itadaki-mashita.
   お茶をもう一杯いかがですか。いいえ、もう**十分**に頂きました。
   How about another cup of tea? No, thanks, I've had enough.

2. Eiga ga hajimaru made ni, mada **jūbun** jikan ga aru.
   映画が始まるまでに、まだ**十分**時間がある。
   There is still plenty of time before the movie starts.

3. Hawai de Kurisumasu kyūka o **jūbun** tanoshinda.
   ハワイでクリスマス休暇を**十分**楽しんだ。
   We thoroughly enjoyed our Christmas vacation in Hawaii.

2.5 tappuri たっぷり   "full"

Tappuri indicates an ample number or amount.

EXAMPLES:

1. Asoko made aruite **tappuri** nijuppun kakarimasu.
   あそこまで歩いて**たっぷり**二十分かかります。
   It takes a full twenty minutes to get there on foot.

2. Kodomo wa pankēki ni shiroppu o **tappuri** kakete tabeta.
   子供はパンケーキにシロップを**たっぷり**かけて食べた。
   The child poured plenty of syrup over the pancakes and ate them.

2.6 | ippai いっぱい | "full"

Ippai indicates that something is full.

EXAMPLES:

1. Kinō no ame de ike no mizu ga **ippai** ni natta.
   昨日の雨で池の水が**いっぱい**になった。
   Due to yesterday's rain, the pond filled up.

2. Ano kissaten wa itsumo wakai hito ga **ippai** iru.
   あの喫茶店はいつも若い人が**いっぱい**いる。
   That coffee shop is always full of young people.

2.7 | hotondo ほとんど | "almost," "nearly"

Hotondo indicates a quantity that is slightly less than all, or a degree that is very near complete.

EXAMPLES:

1. Haha ga okutte kureta kukkī wa **hotondo** tabete shimatta.
   母が送ってくれたクッキーは**ほとんど**食べてしまった。
   I ate up almost all the cookies my mother had sent me.

2. Watashi no hakase ronbun wa **hotondo** kansei shita.
   私の博士論文は**ほとんど**完成した。
   My doctoral thesis was nearly complete.

2.8 | mitchiri みっちり | "thoroughly"

Mitchiri indicates an exhaustive quantity or degree.

EXAMPLES:

1. Pari de **mitchiri** e no benkyō o shitai.
   パリで**みっちり**絵の勉強をしたい。

   I want to study paintings in Paris (and learn everything there is to know about them).

2. Yamada-sensei ni **mitchiri** kanji o narawaserareta.
   山田先生に**みっちり**漢字を習わせられた。

   We were made to learn kanji (so thoroughly that we would not forget them) by Professor Yamada.

2.9 | sukunakarazu 少なからず | "not a few," "not a little"

Sukunakarazu is a kind of double negative. It indicates a quantity or degree that the speaker does not consider to be small.

EXAMPLES:

1. Kankyaku no naka ni wa **sukunakarazu** wakai josei ga ita.
   観客の中には**少なからず**若い女性がいた。

   There were more than a few young women in the audience.

2. Shachō no totsuzen no intai ni shain wa **sukunakarazu** odoroita.
   社長の突然の引退に社員は**少なからず**驚いた。

   The company employees were not a little surprised at the sudden retirement of their president.

Circle the correct adverb among the choices given in parentheses.

1. Pātī no junbi wa (subete/hotondo/sukunakarazu) kanryō shimashita.

   パーティーの準備は（すべて/ほとんど/少なからず）完了しました。

   All the preparations for the party have been made.

2. Kare no jimanbanashi wa mō (jūbun/subete/takusan) da.

   彼の自慢話はもう（十分/すべて/たくさん）だ。

   I've had enough of his bragging.

3. Ano mibōjin wa zaisan o (minna/tappuri/ippai) bokō ni kifu shita.

   あの未亡人は財産を（みんな/たっぷり/いっぱい）母校に寄付した。

   That widow donated her estate entirely to her alma mater.

4. Sono ken wa (takusan/ippai/jūbun) chōsa suru tsumori da.

   その件は（たくさん/いっぱい/十分）調査するつもりだ。

   We intend to investigate that matter fully.

5. Nihon ni iru aida ni, Nihongo bakari de naku Nihon bunka mo (sukunakarazu/mitchiri/hotondo) benkyō shitai.

   日本にいる間に、日本語ばかりでなく日本文化も（少なからず/みっちり/ほとんど）勉強したい。

   While in Japan, I wish to study not only the Japanese language but also Japanese culture thoroughly.

6. Tomu wa daigaku o sotsugyō suru noni (takusan/sukuna-karazu/tappuri) doryoku shita.

トムは大学を卒業するのに（たくさん/少なからず/たっぷり）努力した。

Tom made more than a little effort to graduate from college.

7. Fumiko-san ni karita shōsetsu wa (ippai/jūbun/hotondo) yonde shimatta.

文子さんに借りた小説は（いっぱい/十分/ほとんど）読んでしまった。

I have almost finished reading the novel I borrowed from Fumiko.

2.10 | sukoshi 少し | "a little," "a bit"

Sukoshi indicates a small quantity or degree.

EXAMPLES:

1. Sono posutā wa mō **sukoshi** migi ni hatte kudasai.

そのポスターはもう少し右に張ってください。

Please put that poster a little bit to the right.

2. Saikin **sukoshi** samuku narimashita ne.

最近少し寒くなりましたね。

It has become a bit cold lately, hasn't it?

2.11 | chotto ちょっと | "a little," "a bit"

Chotto indicates a small quantity or degree. It is more colloquial than *sukoshi*.

EXAMPLES:

1. **Chotto** ue o goran.
   ちょっと上をごらん。
   Look up a bit.

2. Achira e **chotto** iku to, hiroi michi ni demasu.
   あちらへ**ちょっと**行くと、広い道に出ます。
   If you go a little that way, you'll come out on a wide street.

2.12 | **wazuka わずか** | "a little," "only"

Wazuka indicates a quantity or degree that is so small that the speaker considers it insignificant. In certain cases it may be interchangeable with *sukoshi* or *chotto* (Example 1, not 2), but, in any case, it carries slightly more emphasis than either.

EXAMPLES:

1. Kion ga **wazuka** agarimashita.
   気温が**わずか**上がりました。
   The temperature went up a little.

2. Kare wa kega ga karukatta node, **wazuka** itsuka de taiin dekita.
   彼は怪我が軽かったので、**わずか**五日で退院出来た。
   Because his injury wasn't serious, he was able to get out of the hospital in only five days.

2.13 | tsui つい | "just," "only"

Tsui emphasizes closeness in time or space.

EXAMPLES:

1. Hayashi-san wa **tsui** sakki kaerimashita.
   林さんは**つい**さっき帰りました。
   Miss Hayashi went home only a moment ago.

2. Wada-sensei no ie wa gakkō no **tsui** saki desu.
   和田先生の家は学校の**つい**先です。
   Professor Wada's house is just down the street from the school.

2.14 | seizei せいぜい | "at most"

Seizei indicates an estimate unlikely to be exceeded.

EXAMPLES:

1. Kyūka o totte mo **seizei** isshūkan desu.
   休暇をとっても**せいぜい**一週間です。
   Even if I take a vacation, it will be one week at most.

2. Kono shina wa **seizei** goman-en gurai deshō.
   この品は**せいぜい**五万円ぐらいでしょう。
   The item would cost about 50,000 yen at most.

2.15 | sukunakutomo 少なくとも | "at least"

Sukunakutomo indicates a conservative estimate.

EXAMPLES:

1. Ronbun no shiryō o atsumeru noni **sukunakutomo** sūkagetsu wa kakaru.

   論文の資料を集めるのに**少なくとも**数か月はかかる。

   It takes at least several months to collect materials for a thesis.

2. Kūkō kara machi no chūshinbu made **sukunakutomo** nijū-mairu wa aru.

   空港から町の中心部まで**少なくとも**二十マイルはある。

   It is at least twenty miles from the airport to the city center.

2.16 | tatta たった | "only"

Tatta emphasizes the smallness of a number or an amount.

EXAMPLES:

1. Kare wa jogingu o hajimeta ga **tatta** mikka de yamete shimatta.

   彼はジョギングを始めたが**たった**三日でやめてしまった。

   He started jogging but quit in only three days.

2. Kanojo wa **tatta** hitori de tabi ni deta.

   彼女は**たった**一人で旅に出た。

   She went on a trip all alone.

2.17 | tada ただ | "only," "merely"

Like *tatta*, *tada* emphasizes the smallness of a number or an amount (Example 1). Unlike *tatta*, however, it often appears together with *dake* or *bakari* to indicate that someone or something is limited to some action or state (Examples 2, 3).

EXAMPLES:

1. Suzuki giin wa **tada** hitori sono hōan ni sansei shita.
   鈴木議員はただ一人その法案に賛成した。
   Representative Suzuki was the only person (in the Diet) to approve the bill.

2. Ono-san wa **tada** hataraku bakari de tanoshimu koto o shiranai.
   小野さんはただ働くばかりで楽しむことを知らない。
   Mr. Ono does nothing but work and doesn't know how to have fun.

3. Ano kōchō wa **tada** gakkō no hyōban o ki ni shite iru dake da.
   あの校長はただ学校の評判を気にしているだけだ。
   That principal is concerned about nothing but the school's reputation.

2.18 | tan ni 単に | "only," "merely"

Like *tada*, *tan ni* often appears together with *dake* or *bakari* to indicate that someone or something is limited to some action or state. When it is used in a negative expression, it means "not only" or "not merely." *Tan ni* is also more formal than *tada*.

EXAMPLES:

1. Kono e wa **tan ni** Mone no e o mohō shita dake da.

この絵は**単に**モネの絵を模倣しただけだ。

This painting is a mere imitation of Monet's.

2. Kore wa **tan ni** kono kuni no mondai dake de naku sekai zen-tai no mondai da.

これは**単に**この国の問題だけでなく世界全体の問題だ。

This is not only this country's problem, but a problem shared by the whole world.

PRACTICE 6 (2.10–2.18)

Circle the correct adverb among the choices given in parentheses.

1. Kyūkō de ikeba, soko made (sukunakutomo/wazuka/sukoshi) ichijikan de ikeru.

急行で行けば、そこまで（少なくとも/わずか/少し）一時間で行ける。

If you take an express train, you can get there in only one hour.

2. Kare wa (tan ni/seizei/tatta) isshūkan de sono shigoto o shi-ageta.

彼は（単に/せいぜい/たった）一週間でその仕事を仕上げた。

He completed that work in only one week.

3. Shōjo wa (tada/tatta/tsui) naku bakari de shitsumon ni kotae-nakatta.

少女は（ただ/たった/つい）泣くばかりで質問に答えなかった。

The girl did nothing but cry and she didn't answer the questions.

4. **Pātī wa rokuji kara desu ga (tsui/chotto/sukunakutomo) ha-yaku iku yō ni shimasu.**

パーティーは六時からですが（つい/ちょっと/少なくとも）早く行くようにします。

Even though the party starts at six o'clock, I'll try to go a little earlier.

5. **Kono biru no shūzen wa (seizei/sukunakutomo/tan ni) rokka-getsu wa kakaru darō.**

このビルの修繕は（せいぜい/少なくとも/単に）六か月はかかるだろう。

The renovation of this building would take at least six months.

6. **Kimura-san to wa (tsui/chotto/tada) senjitsu denwa de hana-shimashita.**

木村さんとは（つい/ちょっと/ただ）先日電話で話しました。

I talked with Mrs. Kimura over the phone only the other day.

7. **Jon wa (wazuka/tan ni/seizei) seiseki ga ii dake de naku sha-kai hōshi mo shite iru.**

ジョンは（わずか/単に/せいぜい）成績がいいだけでなく社会奉仕もしている。

John not only gets good grades, but also does social services.

2.19 | **yaku 約** | "about," "approximately"

Yaku indicates that what follows is an approximation.

EXAMPLES:

1. Bungakubu no gakusei no **yaku** rokujū pāsento wa joshi gakusei desu.

   文学部の学生の**約**六十パーセントは女子学生です。

   About sixty percent of the students in the literature department are female.

2. Kuruma no shūzen ni **yaku** isshūkan kakatta.

   車の修繕に**約**一週間かかった。

   It took about a week for my car to be repaired.

2.20 | **oyoso/ōyoso およそ／おおよそ** | "about," "roughly"

Oyoso or *ōyoso* indicates that what follows is an approximation. In certain cases (Example 1, not 2) it may be interchangeable with *yaku*.

EXAMPLES:

1. Kono machi no jinkō wa **oyoso** gomannin desu.

   この町の人口は**およそ**五万人です。

   The population of this city is about 50,000.

2. Kono kozutsumi no omosa wa **ōyoso** dono gurai desu ka.

   この小包の重さは**おおよそ**どのぐらいですか。

   What is the approximate weight of this package?

2.21 | zatto ざっと | "about," "roughly"

Zatto indicates that what follows is an approximation. In certain cases it may be interchangeable with *yaku, oyoso* or *ōyoso*.

EXAMPLES:

1. Hara-san no okusan wa **zatto** yonjussai gurai desu.
   原さんの奥さんはざっと四十歳ぐらいです。
   Mr. Hara's wife is somewhere around forty.

2. Nyūjōsha wa **zatto** sanjūnin no mikomi desu.
   入場者はざっと三十人の見込みです。
   The audience is estimated to be roughly thirty (people).

2.22 | hobo ほぼ | "almost," "nearly"

Hobo indicates that, all details considered, something is close to completion or perfection.

EXAMPLES:

1. Shi no dōro kōji wa **hobo** kansei shita.
   市の道路工事はほぼ完成した。
   The city's road construction was nearly completed.

2. Gakuchō no kōnin wa **hobo** kettei shita sō desu.
   学長の後任はほぼ決定したそうです。
   I hear that the university president's replacement has almost been decided.

2.23 | daitai 大体 | "almost," "roughly"

Daitai indicates that something is close to completion or perfection in a general way.

EXAMPLES:

1. Ashita no shiken no junbi wa **daitai** dekita.
   明日の試験の準備は**大体**出来た。
   The preparations for tomorrow's exam are just about done.

2. Gaido no setsumei de kono shiro no rekishi ga **daitai** wakatta.
   ガイドの説明でこの城の歴史が**大体**分かった。
   Thanks to the guide's explanation, I roughly understood the history of this castle.

2.24 | taitei たいてい | "usually," "mostly"

Taitei indicates that an action or state occurs or exists in most cases, but not in all.

EXAMPLES:

1. Kare wa **taitei** asagohan o tabemasen.
   彼はたいてい朝ご飯を食べません。
   He usually doesn't eat breakfast.

2. Fureba **taitei** doshaburi da.
   降ればたいていどしゃ降りだ。
   When it rains, it usually pours.

Circle the correct adverb among the choices given in parentheses.

1. Kongetsu no uriage wa (hobo/yaku) mokuhyō ni tasshita.
   今月の売り上げは（ほぼ/約）目標に達した。
   The sales for this month almost reached our goal.

2. Hako no naka ni ringo ga (taitei/zatto) jukko nokotte imasu.
   箱の中にりんごが（たいてい/ざっと）十個残っています。
   There are about ten apples left in the box.

3. Sara wa (hobo/taitei) hachiji mae ni gakkō e kimasu.
   サラは（ほぼ/たいてい）八時前に学校へ来ます。
   Sarah usually comes to school before eight o'clock.

4. Ie no sōji wa (taitei/daitai) owatta.
   家の掃除は（たいてい/大体）終わった。
   The housework was almost finished.

5. Jikken no kekka wa sono dēta kara (ōyoso/yaku) hanmei suru darō.
   実験の結果はそのデータから（おおよそ/約）判明するだろう。
   The results of the experiment may be roughly determined from the data.

③ Adverbs Expressing Degree

The following adverbs express degree or extent. See also ADVERBS EXPRESSING QUANTITY, as the two categories overlap.

3.1 | **taihen 大変** | "very," "extremely"

Taihen emphasizes degree.

EXAMPLES:

1. Eiga wa **taihen** omoshirokatta.
   映画は**大変**面白かった。
   The movie was very interesting.

2. Subarashii shirase ni kanojo wa **taihen** yorokonda.
   素晴らしい知らせに彼女は**大変**喜んだ。
   She was extremely delighted at the wonderful news.

3.2 | **zuibun ずいぶん** | "very," "awfully"

Zuibun emphasizes degree. It is primarily used in casual conversation.

EXAMPLES:

1. **Zuibun** samui desu ne.
   ずいぶん寒いですね。
   It's awfully cold, isn't it?

2. Kyō wa **zuibun** shigoto ga hakadotta.
今日はずいぶん仕事がはかどった。

My work went very well today.

3.3 | totemo とても | "very," "terribly"

Totemo emphasizes degree. In certain cases it may be interchangeable with *zuibun*.

EXAMPLES:

1. Kaigan zoi no keshiki wa **totemo** utsukushikatta.
海岸沿いの景色はとても美しかった。

The view along the coast was very beautiful.

2. Saikin, kono hen no apāto no yachin ga **totemo** takaku natta.
最近、この辺のアパートの家賃がとても高くなった。

Lately, rents for the apartments in this area have risen a lot.

3.4 | ōini 大いに | "very much," "greatly," "largely"

Ōini emphasizes degree, particularly of someone's involvement in something.

EXAMPLES:

1. Watashi wa kare no iken ni **ōini** sansei desu.
私は彼の意見に大いに賛成です。

I largely agree with his opinion.

2. Kongakki wa **ōini** benkyō suru tsumori da.

今学期は**大いに**勉強するつもりだ。

I intend to study very hard this term.

3.5 | **jitsu ni 実に** | "truly," "indeed"

Jitsu ni expresses the speaker's surprise or awe.

EXAMPLES:

1. Masako-san wa **jitsu ni** ryōri ga jōzu desu.

正子さんは**実に**料理が上手です。

Masako is indeed good at cooking.

2. Kare wa **jitsu ni** rippana seijika datta.

彼は**実に**立派な政治家だった。

He was truly a fine statesman.

3.6 | **kiwamete 極めて** | "very," "extremely"

Kiwamete expresses a degree that is exceedingly great. It is primarily used in writing.

EXAMPLES:

1. Kore wa kokubōjō **kiwamete** jūdaina mondai da.

これは国防上**極めて**重大な問題だ。

This is an extremely important problem for national defense.

2. Kono kikai wa **kiwamete** seikaku ni dēta o kiroku suru koto ga dekiru.

この機械は**極めて**正確にデータを記録することが出来る。

This machine can record data extremely accurately.

3.7 | kanari かなり | "fairly," "considerably"

Kanari expresses a degree that is greater than normal, but not exceedingly great.

EXAMPLES:

1. Kyō no shiken wa **kanari** muzukashikatta.

今日の試験は**かなり**難しかった。

Today's exam was fairly difficult.

2. Ano kuni wa **kanari** sangyō ga hattatsu shite iru.

あの国は**かなり**産業が発達している。

Industry is considerably developed in that country.

3.8 | sōtō 相当 | "fairly," "considerably"

Sōtō expresses a degree that is greater than normal, but not exceedingly great. It is interchangeable with *kanari*.

EXAMPLES:

1. Yasuko-san wa saka de koronde **sōtō** hidoi kega o shita.

安子さんは坂で転んで**相当**ひどい怪我をした。

Yasuko fell on the slope and suffered fairly severe injuries.

2. Neruson-san wa **sōtō** Nihongo ga jōzu ni natta.
ネルソンさんは**相当**日本語が上手になった。
Mr. Nelson became fairly competent in Japanese.

3.9 | daibu 大分 | "fairly," "quite"

Daibu expresses a degree that is greater than normal, but not exceedingly great. It is more colloquial than *kanari* or *sōtō*.

EXAMPLES:

1. Kyō wa **daibu** kibun ga ii desu.
今日は**大分**気分がいいです。
I feel quite well today.

2. Bijutsukan wa eki kara **daibu** tōi desu.
美術館は駅から**大分**遠いです。
The art museum is fairly far from the train station.

3.10 | nakanaka なかなか | "quite," "fairly," "considerably"

Nakanaka expresses a degree that is considerable, notable or exceeds the speaker's expectation.

EXAMPLES:

1. Kono sakubun wa ichinensei ni shite wa **nakanaka** yoku kakete iru.
この作文は一年生にしては**なかなか**よく書けている。
This composition is quite well written for a freshman student.

2. Kono shigoto o hikiuketa ga **nakanaka** mendō da.

この仕事を引き受けたが**なかなか**面倒だ。

I took this task upon myself, but I find it quite complicated.

PRACTICE 8 (3.1–3.10)

Circle the correct adverb among the choices given in parentheses.

1. Kono chihō de yuki ga furu no wa (sōtō/daibu/kiwamete) mezurashii.

この地方で雪が降るのは（相当/大分/極めて）珍しい。

It is extremely rare for it to snow in these parts.

2. Kare wa kabu de (totemo/jitsu ni/sōtō) mōketa rashii.

彼は株で（とても/実に/相当）もうけたらしい。

It seems he made a considerable amount of money in stocks.

3. Byōin de (daibu/jitsu ni/kiwamete) matasaremashita.

病院で（大分/実に/極めて）待たされました。

I was made to wait for quite a long time at the hospital.

4. Pātī de nondari, utattari, odottari shite, (nakanaka/daibu/ōini) tanoshinda.

パーティーで飲んだり、歌ったり、踊ったりして、（なかなか/大分/大いに）楽しんだ。

We greatly enjoyed drinking, singing, dancing and doing other things at the party.

5. Musume ga yoru osoku made kaeranakute, (taihen/nakanaka/kanari) shinpai shimashita.

娘が夜遅くまで帰らなくて、（大変/なかなか/かなり）心配しました。

My daughter didn't return home until late at night, so I was very worried.

6. Wakai baiorinisuto no debyū konsāto wa (kanari/jitsu ni/daibu) daiseikō datta.

若いバイオリニストのデビューコンサートは（かなり/実に/大分）大成功だった。

The young violinist's debut concert was a great success indeed.

7. Kono sōjiki wa tsukatte miru to (ōini/nakanaka/sōtō) benri desu.

この掃除機は使ってみると（大いに/なかなか/相当）便利です。

When I tried this vacuum cleaner, I found it quite convenient.

3.11 | isso いっそう | "more," "all the more"

Issō indicates an intensification of degree. It implies a contrast between two states or conditions.

EXAMPLES:

1. Hachigatsu ni wa atsusa ga **issō** kibishiku naru.

八月には暑さが**いっそう**厳しくなる。

In August the heat becomes even more severe.

2. Sono jiken ga ryōkoku no kankei o **issō** akka saseta.

その事件が両国の関係を**いっそう**悪化させた。

That incident worsened the relations between the two countries even more.

3.12 | masumasu ますます | "more and more," "increasingly"

Masumasu indicates an intensification of degree. It implies a contrast between a present and past state or condition, and thus its usage is more restricted than that of *issō*.

EXAMPLES:

1. Chichi wa jogingu o hajimete kara, **masumasu** wakagaetta.
   父はジョギングを始めてから、**ますます**若返った。

   Since he started jogging, my father has become more and more young-looking.

2. Damu kensetsu ni taisuru hantai no koe ga **masumasu** takamatta.
   ダム建設に対する反対の声が**ますます**高まった。

   Opposition to the construction of a dam became increasingly vocal.

3.13 | sara ni 更に | "even more," "further"

Sara ni indicates an intensification of degree or an increase in quantity or level. It is more formal than *issō* or *masumasu*.

EXAMPLES:

1. Fukeiki no tame kaisha no un'ei wa **sara ni** muzukashiku natta.
   不景気のため会社の運営は**更に**難しくなった。

   Due to the recession, managing the company became even more difficult.

2. Rainen kara **sara ni** gakusei no kazu ga fueru kamoshirenai.
来年から**更に**学生の数が増えるかもしれない。

Next year, the number of students may increase even more.

3.14 | motto もっと | "more," "-er"

Motto expresses the comparative form of an adjective.

EXAMPLES:

1. **Motto** yoku renshū shinakereba jōtatsu shimasen.
もっと良く練習しなければ上達しません。

Unless you practice harder, you won't improve.

2. **Motto** kantanna hōhō o oshiete kudasai.
もっと簡単な方法を教えてください。

Please tell me a simpler way.

3.15 | mottomo 最も | "most," "-est"

Mottomo expresses the superlative form of an adjective.

EXAMPLES:

1. Keiki kaifuku no tame ni **mottomo** taisetsuna koto wa nan desu ka.
景気回復のために**最も**大切なことは何ですか。

What is most important for the recovery of the economy?

2. Kanojo wa kaimono o shite iru toki ga **mottomo** tanoshii.

彼女は買い物をしている時が**最も**楽しい。

She enjoys herself the most when she is shopping.

3.16 | ichiban 一番 | "most," "-est"

Ichiban expresses the superlative form of an adjective. It is more colloquial than *mottomo*.

EXAMPLES:

1. Sono naka de **ichiban** ōkii no o moratta.

その中で**一番**大きいのをもらった。

I got the biggest one among them.

2. Anata no **ichiban** sukina sakkyokuka wa dare desu ka.

あなたの**一番**好きな作曲家はだれですか。

Who is your favorite composer?

3.17 | zutto ずっと | "by far," "far more"

Zutto indicates a great degree of difference between two states or conditions.

EXAMPLES:

1. Atarashi shachō wa buchō yori **zutto** wakai.

新しい社長は部長より**ずっと**若い。

Our new company president is much younger than the division manager.

2. Kono mise wa sūpā yori **zutto** sābisu ga ii.

この店はスーパーより**ずっと**サービスがいい。

This store provides far better services than supermarkets.

3.18 | **toku ni 特に** | "specially," "especially"

Toku ni expresses a degree that surpasses what is common.

EXAMPLES:

1. Nihon ryōri no naka de **toku ni** tenpura ga suki desu.

日本料理の中で**特に**てんぷらが好きです。

Of all the Japanese dishes, he especially likes tempura.

2. Nonaka-sensei wa **toku ni** Tōmasu Hādi no kenkyū de shirarete iru.

野中先生は**特に**トーマス・ハーディの研究で知られている。

Professor Nonaka is especially known for his studies of Thomas Hardy.

PRACTICE 9 (3.11–3.18)

Circle the correct adverb among the choices given in parentheses.

1. Kore yori (sara ni/motto/issō) yasui no o misete kudasai.

これより（更に/もっと/いっそう）安いのを見せてください。

Please show me a cheaper one than this.

2. Kono kyōkasho wa mae no kyōkasho yori (toku ni/zutto/masumasu) muzukashii.

この教科書は前の教科書より（特に/ずっと/ますます）難しい。

This textbook is far more difficult than the previous one.

3. Kare wa sūkakokugo ga hanaseru ga (motto/toku ni/issō) Kankokugo ga tokui da.

彼は数か国語が話せるが（もっと/特に/いっそう）韓国語が得意だ。

He is able to speak several languages, but he is especially fluent in Korean.

4. Yo ga fukeru to, (sara ni/mottomo/ichiban) kaze ga tsuyoku natta.

夜がふけると、（更に/最も/一番）風が強くなった。

When it grew late, the wind became even stronger.

5. Fuji-san wa Nihon de (motto/issō/mottomo) utsukushii yama desu.

富士山は日本で（もっと/いっそう/最も）美しい山です。

Mt. Fuji is the most beautiful mountain in Japan.

6. Biru wa sensei ni homerarete (toku ni/masumasu/zutto) benkyō shita.

ビルは先生に褒められて（特に/ますます/ずっと）勉強した。

Having been commended by his teacher, Bill worked harder than ever.

7. Sensei no naka de Ono-sensei ga (zutto/ichiban/sara ni) gakusei ni ninki ga aru.

先生の中で小野先生が（ずっと/一番/更に）学生に人気がある。

Of all the teachers, Professor Ono is the most popular with the students.

Adverbs Expressing Circumstance

The following adverbs express manners of action, human emotions, states or situations. Some of the adverbs that express manners or emotions optionally take the particles *to*, e.g., *yukkuri (to)* (leisurely), or *ni*, e.g., *tsugitsugi (ni)* (one after another), and may be combined with the verb *suru* to form verbs.

4.1 | **yukkuri ゆっくり** | "slowly," "leisurely"

Yukkuri indicates a leisurely manner.

EXAMPLES:

1. Motto **yukkuri** (to) hanashite kudasai.
   もっと**ゆっくり**（と）話してください。
   Please speak more slowly.

2. Shūmatsu wa taitei uchi de **yukkuri** shimasu.
   週末はたいていうちで**ゆっくり**します。
   I usually relax at home on weekends.

4.2 | **sassato さっさと** | "quickly," "hurriedly"

Sassato indicates a hasty or expeditious manner.

EXAMPLES:

1. Kanojo wa shigoto ga owaru to, **sassato** ie ni kaeru.
   彼女は仕事が終わると、**さっさと**家に帰る。
   When she finishes work, she hurries home.

2. Sono shigoto wa **sassato** katazukete kochira o tetsudatte kudasai.

その仕事は**さっさと**片付けてこちらを手伝ってください。

Please finish up that work quickly and help me with this.

4.3 | **hakkiri はっきり** | "clearly"

Hakkiri indicates a clear or unambiguous manner or state.

EXAMPLES:

1. Kare ga kangaete iru koto wa **hakkiri** (to) wakarimasu.

彼が考えていることは**はっきり**（と）分かります。

I understand clearly what he is thinking.

2. Kanojo wa kotoba o **hakkiri** (to) hatsuon shinai kara, wakarinikui desu.

彼女は言葉を**はっきり**（と）発音しないから、分かりにくいです。

Because she doesn't pronounce her words clearly, it is difficult to understand her.

3. Iesu ka nō ka, **hakkiri** shiro.

イエスかノーか、**はっきり**しろ。

Yes or no? Be clear!

4.4 **kippari きっぱり** "flatly," "once and for all"

Kippari indicates resolution.

EXAMPLES:

1. Kanojo wa kare no puropōzu o **kippari** (to) kotowatta.
   彼女は彼のプロポーズを**きっぱり**（と）断った。
   She flatly declined his proposal of marriage.

2. Kono ken wa tsugi no kaigi de **kippari** (to) kimetai.
   この件は次の会議で**きっぱり**（と）決めたい。
   I want to decide on this matter once and for all at the next meeting.

4.5 **kichinto きちんと** "regularly," "neatly"

Kichinto indicates orderliness.

EXAMPLES:

1. Kare wa rōn o **kichinto** shiharatte imasu.
   彼はローンを**きちんと**支払っています。
   He pays the loans regularly.

2. Kodomo ga asobi ni deta ato de, heya o **kichinto** katazuketa.
   子供が遊びに出た後で、部屋を**きちんと**片付けた。
   After my children went out to play, I tidied up the room.

4.6 | **kossori こっそり** | "quietly," "stealthily," "secretly"

Kossori indicates a secretive or sly manner.

EXAMPLES:

1. Jimu wa kōgi no tochū de **kossori** (to) kōdō o deta.
   ジムは講義の途中で**こっそり**（と）講堂を出た。
   Jim slipped out of the auditorium in the middle of the lecture.

2. Otto wa **kossori** (to) sono josei ni atte imashita.
   夫は**こっそり**（と）その女性に会っていました。
   My husband was meeting with the woman in secret.

4.7 | **sotto そっと** | "quietly," "softly"

Sotto indicates a quiet, gentle manner.

EXAMPLES:

1. Kanojo wa wain gurasu o **sotto** tēburu no ue ni oita.
   彼女はワイングラスを**そっと**テーブルの上に置いた。
   She placed a wine glass softly on the table.

2. Watashi-tachi ga hanashite iru toki, dareka **sotto** doa o akete haitte kita.
   私達が話している時、だれか**そっと**ドアを開けて入ってきた。
   As we were talking, someone quietly opened the door and walked in.

4.8 | **shikkari** しっかり | "steadily," "firmly"

Shikkari indicates a firm or steady manner or state.

EXAMPLES:

1. Daigaku ni hairitakereba **shikkari** (to) benkyō shinasai.
   大学に入りたければ、**しっかり** (と)勉強しなさい。
   If you want to get into college, study hard.

2. Rōpu ni **shikkari** (to) tsukamatta.
   ロープに**しっかり** (と)つかまった。
   I held on fast to the rope.

4.9 | **sesseto** せっせと | "diligently," "laboriously"

Sesseto indicates a diligent manner.

EXAMPLES:

1. Kida-san wa **sesseto** hataraite rippana ie o katta.
   木田さんは**せっせと**働いて立派な家を買った。
   Mr. Kida worked hard and bought a fine house.

2. Kon'yaku shita Nobuko-san wa **sesseto** ryōri kyōshitsu ni
   kayotte imasu.
   婚約した信子さんは**せっせと**料理教室に通っています。
   Nobuko, who is engaged, is diligently attending cooking classes.

4.10 | **narubeku なるべく** | "as ... as possible," "if possible"

Narubeku expresses the speaker's desire to do something or see something done if circumstances permit.

EXAMPLES:

1. Kono shina wa **narubeku** yasuku uru tsumori desu.
   この品は**なるべく**安く売るつもりです。
   We intend to sell this item as cheaply as possible.

2. Doyōbi no pikunikku ni wa **narubeku** sanka suru yō ni shimasu.
   土曜日のピクニックには**なるべく**参加するようにします。
   I'll try my best to come to the picnic on Saturday.

4.11 | **tonikaku とにかく** | "at any rate" "anyway"

Tonikaku introduces a decision or suggestion made without regard to, or in spite of, other considerations.

EXAMPLES:

1. Kimeru mae ni **tonikaku** mō ichido hanashiaimashō.
   決める前に**とにかく**もう一度話し合いましょう。
   At any rate, let's talk about it once more before we make a decision.

2. Saikin karada no guai ga warui node ashita **tonikaku** byōin e itte mimasu.
   最近体の具合が悪いので、明日**とにかく**病院へ行ってみます。
   I haven't been feeling well recently, so I think I'll just go to the hospital tomorrow.

4.12 | **sekkaku せっかく** | "with effort," "kindly," "especially"

Sekkaku expresses the speaker's regret over what he views as a wasted opportunity (Examples 1, 2). It also expresses his appreciation for trouble taken on his account (Example 3).

EXAMPLES:

1. Takashi wa **sekkaku** ii kaisha ni shūshoku shita noni, ichinen de yamete shimatta.
   孝は**せっかく**いい会社に就職したのに、一年で辞めてしまった。
   Although Takashi succeeded in finding work with a good company, he quit after only a year.

2. **Sekkaku** Ginza ni iru'n dakara, yukkuri shite ikimashō.
   せっかく銀座にいるんだから、ゆっくりしていきましょう。
   As long as we're in Ginza, let's relax and enjoy ourselves.

3. Kono doresu wa ane ga **sekkaku** kureta kara, konsāto ni kite iku tsumori desu.
   このドレスは姉が**せっかく**くれたから、コンサートに着て行くつもりです。
   I intend to wear this dress to the concert since my older sister went to the trouble of giving it to me.

4.13 | **wazawaza わざわざ** | "expressly," "specially"

Wazawaza indicates someone's taking time or trouble to do something on someone else's account.

EXAMPLES:

1. Tomodachi ga kuru node, **wazawaza** kēki o kai ni itta.

   友達が来るので、**わざわざ**ケーキを買いに行った。

   Because my friends are coming, I went out specially to buy some cakes.

2. Yukiko-san wa **wazawaza** watashi no ie made hana o motte kite kureta.

   雪子さんは**わざわざ**私の家まで花を持って来てくれた。

   Yukiko took the trouble of bringing flowers to my house.

4.14 | tsuide ni ついでに

"while (I am/you are at it)," "at the same time"

Tsuide ni indicates someone's taking advantage of a situation to do something additional and usually of secondary importance.

EXAMPLES:

1. Shigoto de Kyōto e kita **tsuide ni** kenbutsu mo shimashita.

   仕事で京都へ来た**ついでに**見物もしました。

   While I was in Kyoto on business, I did some sightseeing.

2. Kono heya ga sundara, **tsuide ni** tonari no heya mo sōji shite kudasai.

   この部屋が済んだら、**ついでに**隣の部屋も掃除してください。

   When this room is done, please clean the room next to it as well, as long as you're at it.

Circle the correct adverb among the choices given in parentheses.

1. Minna ga wakaru yō ni (hakkiri/kippari/sesseto) hanashinasai.

   みんなが分かるように（はっきり/きっぱり/せっせと）話しなさい。

   Speak clearly so that everybody understands you.

2. Kanojo wa daigaku o deru to (kichinto/sassato/hakkiri) bōi-furendo to kekkon shita.

   彼女は大学を出ると（きちんと/さっさと/はっきり）ボーイフレンドと結婚した。

   As soon as she got out of college, she hurried to marry her boyfriend.

3. Kare wa (narubeku/sekkaku/kippari) jōshi no iken ni hantai shinai yō ni shite iru.

   彼は（なるべく/せっかく/きっぱり）上司の意見に反対しないようにしている。

   He tries as much as possible not to oppose the opinions of his boss.

4. Kyonen wa totemo isogashikatta node, kotoshi wa (kichinto/yukkuri/hakkiri) shitai.

   去年はとても忙しかったので、今年は（きちんと/ゆっくり/はっきり）したい。

   I was very busy last year, so I want to relax this year.

5. Yūbinkyoku e iku no nara, (wazawaza/tsuide ni/kossori) kono tegami mo dashite kudasai.

   郵便局へ行くのなら、（わざわざ/ついでに/こっそり）この手紙も出してください。

   If you are going to the post office, please mail this letter at the same time.

6. Kuwashii koto wa wakaranai ga, (narubeku/tsuide ni/ toni-kaku) genba e itte miyō.

詳しいことは分からないが（なるべく/ついでに/とにかく）現場へ行ってみよう。

We may not know the details, but let's go to the scene anyway and see (what there is to see).

7. Akachan ga okinai yō ni (kossori/sotto/sassato) doa o shime-mashita.

赤ちゃんが起きないように（こっそり/そっと/さっさと）ドアを閉めました。

I closed the door quietly so that the baby wouldn't wake up.

8. Kono shōtaijō ni wa (kichinto/wazawaza/hakkiri) henji o da-sanakute mo ii desu yo.

この招待状には（きちんと/わざわざ/はっきり）返事を出さなくてもいいですよ。

You need not take the trouble to answer this invitation.

9. (Sekkaku/tsuide ni/sesseto) itta noni resutoran wa rinji kyū-gyō datta.

（せっかく/ついでに/せっせと）行ったのにレストランは臨時休業だった。

Although we went all the way to the restaurant, it was temporarily closed.

10. Kanojo wa (sesseto/kossori/narubeku) byōin ni chiryō ni kayotte iru.

彼女は（せっせと/こっそり/なるべく）病院に治療に通っている。

She is going to the hospital secretly for the treatment.

4.15 | **hotto** ほっと | "be relieved"

Hotto expresses relief that a worrisome situation is over.

EXAMPLES:

1. Yoi shirase ni watashi wa **hotto** shimashita.
   良い知らせに私は**ほっと**しました。
   I felt relieved at the good news.

2. Kōshō ga matomatta node, kankeisha wa **hotto** shiteiru.
   交渉がまとまったので、関係者は**ほっと**している。
   Since the negotiations have been squared away, the parties involved
   are breathing sighs of relief.

4.16 | **uttori** うっとり | "absorbedly," "in a trance"

Uttori expresses the feeling of being absorbed in something beautiful.

EXAMPLES:

1. Kanojo wa yūyakezora o **uttori** (to) nagameta.
   彼女は夕焼け空を**うっとり**（と）眺めた。
   She gazed fixedly at the sky aglow with the setting sun.

2. Meikyoku ni **uttori** shite jikan no tatsu no mo wasureta.
   名曲に**うっとり**して時間の経つのも忘れた。
   Entranced by the beautiful music, I was unaware of the passage of time.

4.17 | bonyari ぼんやり | "vacantly," "absentmindedly"

Bonyari indicates a spacey manner.

EXAMPLES:

1. Kare wa tori ga tonde iku no o **bonyari** nagamete ita.
   彼は鳥が飛んで行くのを**ぼんやり**眺めていた。
   He was looking vacantly at the birds flying away.

2. Saikin Sachiko-san wa konpyūtā no mae de yoku **bonyari** shite iru.
   最近幸子さんはコンピューターの前でよく**ぼんやり**している。
   Lately, Sachiko has been doing a lot of daydreaming in front of the computer.

4.18 | shonbori しょんぼり | "dejectedly"

Shonbori indicates a lonely or depressed manner.

EXAMPLES:

1. Ishidan ni otoko no ko ga **shonbori** suwatte iru.
   石段に男の子が**しょんぼり**座っている。
   A boy is sitting dejectedly on the stone stairway.

2. Ano rōjin wa inu ga inaku natte kara itsumo **shonbori** shite iru.
   あの老人は犬がいなくなってからいつも**しょんぼり**している。
   Ever since his dog disappeared, that old man has been depressed.

4.19 | sukkiri すっきり | "feel fine," "feel refreshed"

Sukkiri indicates a cheerful mood or a refreshing feeling due to a change in fortune or circumstances.

EXAMPLES:

1. Shakkin o minna haratte shimatte **sukkiri** shita.
   借金をみんな払ってしまって**すっきり**した。
   I paid off all my debts, and I feel great.

2. Iitai koto o itte kimochi ga **sukkiri** shita.
   言いたいことを言って気持ちが**すっきり**した。
   I said what I wanted to say and got it off my chest.

4.20 | sappari さっぱり | "feel refreshed," "feel relieved"

Sappari indicates a refreshing feeling or relief in general. It is usually interchangeable with *sukkiri*.

EXAMPLES:

1. Undō no ato de shawā o abite **sappari** shimashita.
   運動の後でシャワーを浴びて**さっぱり**しました。
   I took a shower after exercising and felt refreshed.

2. Kare to no kon'yaku o kaishō shite **sappari** shita.
   彼との婚約を解消して**さっぱり**した。
   I have broken off my engagement with him, so I feel relieved.

4.21 | gakkari がっかり | "be disappointed," "be discouraged"

Gakkari indicates a feeling of unhappiness due to the failure of hope.

EXAMPLES:

1. Kare wa kanojo ga dēto o kotowatta node **gakkari** shite iru.
   彼は彼女がデートを断ったので**がっかり**している。

   He is disappointed because she turned down a date with him.

2. Biru wa yoku benkyō shita noni shiken ni shippai shite **gakkari** shita.
   ビルはよく勉強したのに試験に失敗して**がっかり**した。

   Bill was discouraged because he failed the exam in spite of having studied hard for it.

4.22 | mutto むっと | "get angry," "be offended"

Mutto indicates a feeling of anger or hostility.

EXAMPLES:

1. Watashi wa Kihara-san no shitsureina kotoba ni **mutto** shita.
   私は木原さんの失礼な言葉に**むっと**した。

   I was offended by Mr. Kihara's rude remark.

2. Tomu wa kesa kara zutto **mutto** shite imasu.
   トムは今朝からずっと**むっと**しています。

   Tom has been scowling all morning.

4.23 | **hatto はっと** | "be startled," "be taken aback"

Hatto indicates a feeling of surprise or alarm.

EXAMPLES:

1. Surudoi tori no nakigoe ni **hatto** shita.

鋭い鳥の鳴き声に**はっと**した。

I was startled by the sharp cry of a bird.

2. Kuruma no mae ni kojika ga tobidashita toki, watashi wa **hatto** shite burēki o kaketa.

車の前に子鹿が飛び出した時、私は**はっと**してブレーキをかけた。

When a fawn rushed out in front of the car, I got startled and slammed on the brakes.

PRACTICE 11 (4.15-4.23)

Circle the correct adverb among the choices given in parentheses.

1. Ame de pikunikku ga chūshi sareta node, (sappari/sukkiri/gakkari) shimashita.

雨でピクニックが中止されたので、（さっぱり/すっきり/がっかり）しました。

We were disappointed because the picnic was called off due to the rain.

2. O-furo ni haitte kami o aratte kikaetara, jitsu ni (bonyari/sappari/uttori) shita.

お風呂に入って髪を洗って着替えたら、実に（ぼんやり/さっぱり/うっとり）した。

199

Once I took a bath, washed my hair and changed my clothes, I felt truly refreshed.

3. **Akira wa tomodachi ga Nagoya e iten shita node (shonbori/uttori/sukkiri) shite iru.**

明は友達が名古屋へ移転したので（しょんぼり/うっとり/すっきり）している。

Since his friend moved to Nagoya, Akira has been lonely.

4. **Purojekuto ga kigenmae ni kansei shite minna (sukkiri/hotto/hatto) shite imasu.**

プロジェクトが期限前に完成してみんな（すっきり/ほっと/はっと）しています。

Our project was completed on time, so we all feel relieved.

5. **Hayashi-san wa watashi ga dēta no machigai o shiteki suru to (shonbori/gakkari/mutto) shimashita.**

林さんは私がデータの間違いを指摘すると（しょんぼり/がっかり/むっと）しました。

Miss Hayashi scowled when I pointed out to her the mistakes in the data.

6. **Haha ga nyūinchū, watashi wa denwa ga naru to (hatto/hotto/mutto) shita.**

母が入院中、私は電話が鳴ると（はっと/ほっと/むっと）した。

During the period my mother was in the hospital, the sound of the phone ringing never failed to startle me.

4.24 | kitchiri きっちり | "exactly," "perfectly"

Kitchiri indicates an exact or perfect state or manner of events.

EXAMPLES:

1. Kono jaketto wa watashi ni **kitchiri** (to) aimasu.
   このジャケットは私に**きっちり**（と）合います。
   This jacket fits me perfectly.

2. Kaigi wa **kitchiri** (to) sanji ni hajimarimashita.
   会議は**きっちり**（と）三時に始まりました。
   The meeting began exactly at three o'clock.

4.25 | pittari ぴったり | "exactly," "perfectly"

Pittari indicates an exact or perfect state or manner of events. In certain cases (Example 2, not 1) it may be interchangeable with *kitchiri*.

EXAMPLES:

1. Kono keisan wa **pittari** (to) atte imasu.
   この計算は**ぴったり**（と）合っています。
   This calculation is perfectly correct.

2. Hikōki wa **pittari** (to) teikoku ni tōchaku shita.
   飛行機は**ぴったり**（と）定刻に到着した。
   The airplane arrived right on schedule.

4.26　chōdo ちょうど　"just," "right," "exactly"

Chōdo indicates that a time, size, number or amount conforms to a certain standard or expectation.

EXAMPLES:

1. Soko made densha de **chōdo** ichijikan kakaru.
   そこまで電車で**ちょうど**一時間かかる。
   It takes exactly an hour to get there by train.

2. Raishū no kayōbi nara **chōdo** tsugō ga ii desu.
   来週の火曜日なら**ちょうど**都合がいいです。
   Next Tuesday would suit my schedule very nicely.

4.27　yuttari ゆったり　"be spacious," "be loose"

Yuttari indicates ampleness in terms of size or space.

EXAMPLES:

1. Watashi no atarashii apāto wa mae no apāto yori kanari **yuttari** shite iru.
   私の新しいアパートは前のアパートよりかなり**ゆったり**している。
   My new apartment is quite a bit more spacious than my previous one.

2. Kono gaun wa **yuttari** shite kigokochi ga ii desu.
   このガウンは**ゆったり**して着心地がいいです。
   This gown is loose and comfortable to wear.

4.28 | **hissori ひっそり** | "quietly," "still"

Hissori indicates stillness, tranquility or a quiet state of isolation.

EXAMPLES:

1. Gogo hachiji sugiru to kono machi wa **hissori** suru.
   午後八時過ぎるとこの町は**ひっそり**する。
   This town becomes quiet after eight o'clock p.m.

2. Mori no naka ni marutagoya ga **hissori** (to) tatte iru.
   森の中に丸太小屋が**ひっそり**（と）立っている。
   A log cabin stands quietly isolated in the woods.

4.29 | **tsugitsugi 次々** | "one after another" "in succession"

Tsugitsugi indicates the continual occurrence of an action or event.

EXAMPLES:

1. Ii kangae ga **tsugitsugi** (ni) mune ni ukanda.
   いい考えが**次々**（に）胸に浮かんだ。
   Good ideas came to mind one after another.

2. Kono shina wa hyōban ga yoku **tsugitsugi** (ni) chūmon ga
   kuru.
   この品は評判が良く**次々**（に）注文が来る。
   This product is popular and orders keep coming in.

4.30 | zokuzoku 続々 | "one after another," "in succession"

Zokuzoku indicates the perpetual occurrence of an action or event. In certain cases it may be interchangeable with *tsugitsugi*. However, the frequency expressed by *zokuzoku* is usually greater than that of *tsugitsugi*, and it often implies accumulation.

EXAMPLES:

1. Sono jiken no ato de fushigina dekigoto ga **zokuzoku** (to) okotta.
   その事件の後で不思議な出来事が**続々**（と）起こった。
   After that incident, strange events occurred one after another.

2. Hanami no jiki ni wa kono kōen ni kankōkyaku ga **zokuzoku** (to) otozureru.
   花見の時期にはこの公園に観光客が**続々**（と）訪れる。
   During cherry blossom season, tourists come flocking to this park.

4.31 | chakuchaku 着々 | "steadily," "step by step"

Chakuchaku indicates steady progression.

EXAMPLES:

1. Idenshi no kenkyū wa **chakuchaku** (to) susunde iru.
   遺伝子の研究は**着々**（と）進んでいる。
   Genetic research has been making steady progress.

2. Kare wa ikoku de **chakuchaku** (to) Kirisutokyō o hirometa.
   彼は異国で**着々**（と）キリスト教を広めた。

   He steadily spread Christianity in foreign countries.

4.32 | jojo ni じょじょに | "gradually," "slowly"

Jojo ni indicates slow, gentle change. Its emphasis is on the quality of change rather than the direction.

EXAMPLES:

1. Tenki wa **jojo ni** kaifuku suru deshō.
   天気は**じょじょに**回復するでしょう。

   The weather will gradually clear up.

2. Kion wa **jojo ni** jōshō shi, sesshi yonjūdo o koeta.
   気温は**じょじょに**上昇し、摂氏四十度を越えた。

   The temperature went up gradually, exceeding forty degrees Celsius.

4.33 | dandan だんだん | "gradually," "slowly"

Dandan indicates gradual change. Its emphasis is on the direction of the change rather than the quality.

EXAMPLES:

1. Hikōki no oto ga **dandan** kikoenaku natta.
   飛行機の音が**だんだん**聞こえなくなった。

   The sound of the airplane gradually died away.

2. Kono chiiki no kankyō ga **dandan** yokunatta.

この地域の環境が**だんだん**良くなった。

The environment in this area has shown gradual improvement.

PRACTICE 12 (4.24–4.33)

Circle the correct adverb among the choices given in parentheses.

1. Ima ga hanami ni wa (kitchiri/yuttari/chōdo) ii jiki desu.

今が花見には（きっちり/ゆったり/ちょうど）いい時期です。

Now is just the right time for cherry-blossom viewing.

2. Kore kara (dandan/tsugitsugi/hissori) samuku natte kimasu yo.

これから（だんだん/次々/ひっそり）寒くなってきますよ。

It will gradually start to get colder, I tell you.

3. Ressha wa jikan dōri (chōdo/kitchiri/yuttari) hassha shsita.

列車は時間通り（ちょうど/きっちり/ゆったり）発車した。

The train departed exactly on time.

4. Kono mise ni wa watashi ni (pittari/yuttari/hissori) au saizu ga nai.

この店には私に（ぴったり/ゆったり/ひっそり）合うサイズがない。

This store does not carry any size that fits me perfectly.

5. Kare no jigyō wa (jojo ni/chakuchaku to/zokuzoku to) yoi jisseki o agete iru.

彼の事業は（じょじょに/着々と/続々と）良い実績を上げている。

His business is steadily showing positive results.

6. Ano resutoran wa kyaku ga sukunaku itsumo (kitchiri/yuttari/hissori) shite iru.
   あのレストランは客が少なくいつも（きっちり/ゆったり/ひっそり）している。
   That restaurant has few customers and is always quiet.

7. Kuruma ga (zokuzoku/jojo ni/dandan) kite michi ga watarenai.
   車が（続々/じょじょに/だんだん）来て道が渡れない。
   Cars are coming one after another, so I can't cross the street.

4.34 | **kitto きっと** | "surely," "certainly," "without fail"

Kitto expresses the speaker's confidence or strong belief.

EXAMPLES:

1. Kono hon wa **kitto** yaku ni tatsu to omoimasu.
   この本は**きっと**役に立つと思います。
   I am sure this book will be helpful.

2. Watashi ga kuruma o arau to, **kitto** ame ga furu.
   私が車を洗うと、**きっと**雨が降る。
   When I wash my car, it rains without fail.

4.35 | **kanarazu 必ず** | "surely," "certainly," "without fail"

Kanarazu expresses the speaker's conviction. It is more formal than *kitto*.

EXAMPLES:

1. Kono shigoto wa **kanarazu** getsumatsu made ni kansei shimasu.

   この仕事は**必ず**月末までに完成します。

   This work will surely be completed by the end of the month.

2. Kōtsū kisoku wa **kanarazu** mamoranakereba naranai.

   交通規則は**必ず**守らなければならない。

   You must obey traffic regulations no matter what.

| 4.36 | **mochiron もちろん** | "of course," "no doubt" |

Mochiron expresses the speaker's certainty about something.

EXAMPLES:

1. Akiko-san ga ikanai no nara, **mochiron** watashi mo ikimasen.

   秋子さんが行かないのなら、**もちろん**私も行きません。

   If Akiko doesn't go, I won't go either, of course.

2. Taifū ga kureba, **mochiron** fune wa demasen.

   台風が来れば、**もちろん**船は出ません。

   If a typhoon comes, the ship is certain not to set sail.

| 4.37 | **yahari/yappari やはり/やっぱり** | "as expected," "after all" |

Yahari or *yappari* indicates that something has turned out the way it
was expected to. *Yappari* is more colloquial than *yahari* and, in some
cases, more emphatic.

EXAMPLES:

1. **Yahari** watashi no suisoku wa tadashikatta.
   やはり私の推測は正しかった。

   I was right in my conjecture after all.

2. Ano kaisha wa **yappari** tōsan shita sō da.
   あの会社は**やっぱり**倒産したそうだ。

   I hear that company went bankrupt, as predicted.

4.38 | kekkyoku 結局 | "after all," "finally," "in the end"

Kekkyoku emphasizes the fact that a conclusion has been reached regardless of whatever decisions or circumstances led to it.

EXAMPLES:

1. Yoku kangaeta ue de, **kekkyoku** sono ginkō ni tsutomeru koto ni shita.
   良く考えた上で、**結局**その銀行に勤めることにした。

   Upon careful consideration, I finally decided to work for the bank.

2. Nando mo hanashiatta ga **kekkyoku** ketsuron wa denakatta.
   何度も話し合ったが、**結局**結論は出なかった。

   Although we discussed the issue many times, in the end we never reached a conclusion.

3. Karera wa sanzan kenka o shite ita kedo **kekkyoku** kekkon shita.
   彼らはさんざんけんかをしていたけど、**結局**結婚した。

   They bickered a lot, but in the end, they got married.

4.39 | tsumari つまり | "in brief," "in other words," "that is to say"

Tsumari is used to summarize or rephrase what has been said.

EXAMPLES:

1. Kore wa imōto no musuko, **tsumari**, watashi no oi no shashin desu.

   これは妹の息子、**つまり**私の甥の写真です。

   This is a picture of my younger sister's son, that is, my nephew.

2. Ano sūtsu wa takakute kaenai. **Tsumari** o-kane ga nai to iu koto desu.

   あのスーツは高くて買えない。**つまり**お金がないということです。

   That suit is too expensive. In other words, I haven't got the money for it.

4.40 | tatoeba 例えば | "for instance"

Tatoeba is used to give an example.

EXAMPLES:

1. Nihon no shōsetsu, **tatoeba** Kawabata ya Mishima no sakuhin o yonda koto ga arimasu ka.

   日本の小説、例えば川端や三島の作品を読んだことがありますか。

   Have you ever read any Japanese novels—works by Kawabata or Mishima, for example?

2. Natsuyasumi ni iroirona koto o shita. **Tatoeba** umi de oyoi-
   dari, sakana o tsuttari, kyanpu ni ittari shita.
   夏休みに色々なことをした。**例えば**、海で泳いだり、魚を釣っ
   たり、キャンプに行ったりした。
   We did a lot of things over summer vacation—swam in the ocean, went
   fishing, went camping…

4.41 | aikawarazu 相変わらず | "as usual," "as always"

Aikawarazu indicates that an action or state is ongoing.

EXAMPLES:

1. Yoshida-san wa **aikawarazu** ganko desu ne.
   吉田さんは**相変わらず**頑固ですね。
   Mr. Yoshida is being his usual stubborn self, isn't he?

2. Kare wa **aikawarazu** asonde bakari imasu.
   彼は**相変わらず**遊んでばかりいます。
   He does nothing but fool around, as always.

4.42 | kaette かえって | "on the contrary"

Kaette introduces a result that is contrary to expectation.

EXAMPLES:

1. Homerareru dokoro ka, **kaette** shikarareta.
   褒められるどころか、**かえって**叱られた。
   Far from being praised, I was scolded.

2. Hirune o shite **kaette** zutsū ga hidoku natta.
昼寝をして**かえって**頭痛がひどくなった。

I took a nap and woke up with a worse headache.

4.43 | saiwai 幸い | "fortunately"

Saiwai indicates a favorable situation.

EXAMPLES:

1. Ono-san no ofisu ni yottara, **saiwai** kare wa hima datta.
小野さんのオフィスに寄ったら、**幸い**彼はひまだった。

When I stopped by Mr. Ono's office, he was, fortunately, not busy.

2. Pikunikku no hi wa **saiwai** ichinichijū tenki ga yokatta.
ピクニックの日は**幸い**一日中天気が良かった。

Fortunately, on the day of the picnic, the weather was good all day long.

4.44 | ainiku あいにく | "unfortunately"

Ainiku indicates an unfavorable situation.

EXAMPLES:

1. Sore o kaitakatta ga **ainiku** kurejitto kādo o motte inakatta.
それを買いたかったが**あいにく**クレジットカードを持っていなかった。

I wanted to buy it, but unfortunately I didn't have my credit card with me.

2. **Ainiku** kaze o hiite enkai ni shusseki dekinakatta.

あいにくかぜを引いて宴会に出席出来なかった。

Unfortunately, I got a cold and couldn't attend the banquet.

PRACTICE 13 (4.34–4.44)

Circle the correct adverb among the choices given in parentheses.

1. Raigetsu no kurasukai ni wa (kitto/yahari/kekkyoku) kite kudasai ne.

来月のクラス会には（きっと/やはり/結局）来てくださいね。

Please be sure to come to the class reunion next month.

2. Yosan ga nai kara kono purojekuto wa (tsumari/yahari/ainiku) dekinai sō desu.

予算がないからこのプロジェクトは（つまり/やはり/あいにく）出来ないそうです。

I heard that this project cannot be carried out as expected for lack of budget.

3. Watashi wa yakusoku shita koto wa (saiwai/kaette/mochiron) jikkō shimasu.

私は約束したことは（幸い/かえって/もちろん）実行します。

I will of course carry out what I promised to do.

4. Sofu wa (kanarazu/tatoeba/aikawarazu) chōshokumae ni sanpo ni dekakeru.

祖父は（必ず/例えば/相変わらず）朝食前に散歩に出かける。

My grandfather goes out for a walk before breakfast as usual.

5. Jimu wa (tsumari/kekkyoku/ainiku) gakkō o yamete shimatta.

ジムは（つまり/結局/あいにく）学校を辞めてしまった。

Jim quit school after all, to my regret.

6. Yamada-san wa (ainiku/saiwai/mochiron) sono ochita hikōki ni notte inakatta.

山田さんは（あいにく/幸い/もちろん）その落ちた飛行機に乗っていなかった。

Fortunately, Mr. Yamada wasn't on the airplane that had gone down.

7. Kanojo wa kōkana mono bakari kau sō desu ga, (tsumari/tatoeba/yahari) donna mono desu ka.

彼女は高価な物ばかり買うそうですが、（つまり/例えば/やはり）どんな物ですか。

I hear she buys nothing but expensive things, but what things does she buy, for example?

8. Tenchi shitara (yahari/kitto/kaette) taichō ga waruku natta.

転地したら（やはり/きっと/かえって）体調が悪くなった。

I went for a change of air, but became more ill.

 5 Onomatopoeic Words

Onomatopoeic words are adverbs that imitate sounds (*giseigo*) or describe actions, manners or states (*gitaigo*). Some onomatopoeic words may optionally be followed by the particles *to* or *ni*, and can combine with the verb *suru* to form verbs.

English has onomatopoeic words too, but they tend to be verbs rather than adverbs, e.g., "murmur," "scuttle," "screech," etc. This tendency is evident in the entries below, where some words are translated as verbs. Such translations are intended to be conceptual.

5.1 | **nikoniko にこにこ** | "with a smile," "happily"

Nikoniko describes a smile that conveys happiness, pleasure, friendliness or kindness.

EXAMPLES:

1. Akachan ga watashi o mite **nikoniko** waraimashita.
   赤ちゃんが私を見てにこにこ笑いました。
   The baby smiled happily at me.

2. Otōto wa tanjōbi ni kamera o moratte **nikoniko** shite iru.
   弟は誕生日にカメラをもらってにこにこしている。
   My little brother got a camera for his birthday and is all smiles.

5.2 | **niyaniya にやにや** | "with a grin," "with a smirk"

Niyaniya describes a grin, smirk or knowing smile.

EXAMPLES:

1. Shiranai otoko no hito ga **niyaniya** warainagara watashi ni chikazuita.
   知らない男の人がにやにや笑いながら私に近づいた。
   A strange man approached me with a sly grin.

2. Kare ga **niyaniya** shite iru toki ni wa kanarazu nanika taku-
   rande iru.

   彼がにやにやしている時には必ず何か企んでいる。

   When he grins, you know he is up to something.

5.3 | **kusukusu くすくす** | "giggle," "chuckle"

Kusukusu describes a giggle or a chuckle.

EXAMPLES:

1. Shōjo-tachi wa rōjin no okashina kakkō o mite **kusukusu**
   waratta.

   少女達は老人のおかしな格好を見てくすくす笑った。

   The girls giggled at the old man's odd appearance.

2. Hito ga majime ni hanashite iru toki **kusukusu** warau no wa
   shitsurei da.

   人がまじめに話している時くすくす笑うのは失礼だ。

   It's rude to giggle when someone is speaking seriously.

5.4 | **geragera げらげら** | "(laugh) loudly"

Geragera describes the sound of someone exploding with laughter.

EXAMPLES:

1. Kanshū wa shikaisha no jōdan ni **geragera** waratta.

   観衆は司会者の冗談にげらげら笑った。

   The audience roared with laughter at the MC's jokes.

2. Nan de mo nai koto ni **geragera** warau hito wa kirai desu.

   何でもないことに**げらげら**笑う人は嫌いです。

   I don't like people who laugh loudly at nothing.

5.5　| **shikushiku しくしく** |　"sob," "weep"

Shikushiku describes the sound of someone quietly sobbing (Examples 1, 2). It also describes a slight pain, as in the stomach (Example 3).

EXAMPLES:

1. Shoppingu mōru de maigo ni natta onna no ko ga **shiku-shiku** naite iru.

   ショッピングモールで迷子になった女の子が**しくしく**泣いている。

   The girl who is lost in the shopping mall is weeping sadly.

2. Haha wa chichi no sōshiki no aida **shikushiku** naite ita.

   母は父の葬式の間**しくしく**泣いていた。

   Mother sobbed throughout Father's funeral.

3. Kesa kara hara ga **shikushiku** suru.

   今朝から腹が**しくしく**する。

   I've had a stomachache since this morning.

5.6　| **wāwā わあわあ** |　"(weep) loudly," "wail," "cheer"

Wāwā describes the sound of someone wailing or cheering loudly.

EXAMPLES:

1. Subette koronda kodomo wa **wāwā** nakidashita.

   滑って転んだ子供は**わあわあ**泣き出した。

   The child who had slipped and fallen started to cry loudly.

2. Kanojo wa sono kanashii shirase ni hitomae de **wāwā** naita.

   彼女はその悲しい知らせに人前で**わあわあ**泣いた。

   Hearing the sad news, she started bawling in front of everyone.

3. Sakkā fan ga **wāwā** sawaide ita.

   サッカーファンが**わあわあ**騒いでいた。

   The soccer fans were cheering loudly.

5.7 | **poroporo ぽろぽろ** | "(shed tears) in large drops"

Poroporo describes the manner in which tears trickle down the face.

EXAMPLES:

1. Kanojo wa yūzai no hanketsu ni **poroporo** namida o koboshita.

   彼女は有罪の判決に**ぽろぽろ**涙をこぼした。

   She shed tears at the verdict of "guilty."

2. Watashi wa namida ga **poroporo** kanojo no hoho o koboreru no o mita.

   私は涙が**ぽろぽろ**彼女の頬をこぼれるのを見た。

   I saw tears trickle down her cheeks.

5.8 | kankan (ni) かんかん (に)

"(fume) with anger," "(shine) hot"

Kankan describes boiling anger or intense heat.

EXAMPLES:

1. Watashi ga mudan de kaigi ni kesseki shita node, kachō wa **kankan (ni)** okotte iru.

   私が無断で会議に欠席したので、課長は**かんかん（に）**怒っている。

   The section chief was furious because I missed the meeting without permission.

2. Musume wa hahaoya ni bōifurendo no tegami o yomarete **kankan ni** natta.

   娘は母親にボーイフレンドの手紙を読まれて**かんかん**になった。

   The daughter was furious because the letter from her boyfriend was read by her mother.

3. Hi ga **kankan** (ni) tette iru kara, bōshi o kabutte ikinasai.

   日が**かんかん**（に）照っているから、帽子をかぶって行きなさい。

   The sun is shining hot, so go out with your hat on.

5.9 | punpun ぷんぷん

"in anger," "in a huff"

Punpun describes indiscriminate anger.

EXAMPLES:

1. Jōkyaku wa kūkō de nanjikan mo matasarete **punpun** okotte ita.

   乗客は空港で何時間も待たされて**ぷんぷん**怒っていた。

   The passengers were very angry because they were made to wait for many hours at the airport.

2. Watashi dake pātī ni sasowareta no o shitte Michiko-san wa **punpun** shite imasu.

   私だけパーティーに誘われたのを知って道子さんは**ぷんぷん**しています。

   Michiko knows that only I was invited to the party, and she is in a huff because of it.

5.10 | **gamigami がみがみ** | "(snap at someone) angrily"

Gamigami describes the manner in which someone who is angry lashes out at another.

EXAMPLES:

1. Tonari no okusan wa asa kara ban made kodomo o **gamigami** shikatte iru.

   隣の奥さんは朝から晩まで子供を**がみがみ**叱っている。

   The woman nextdoor scolds her children harshly from morning till night.

2. Noda-san wa jōshi ni **gamigami** iwarete repōto o kaki-naoshite iru.

野田さんは上司に**がみがみ**言われてレポートを書き直している。

Miss Noda was yelled at by her boss, so she is rewriting the report.

PRACTICE 14 (5.1–5.10)

Circle the correct adverb among the choices given in parentheses.

1. Chikagoro Ishida-san wa (gamigami/niyaniya/punpun) shite
   chikazukinikui.

   近頃石田さんは　（がみがみ/にやにや/ぷんぷん）して近づきに
   くい。

   Lately, Ms. Ishida has been in such an angry mood that it is difficult
   to approach her.

2. Yano-san wa atarashii jitensha o nusumarete (wāwā/gami-
   gami/kankan ni) okotte iru.

   矢野さんは新しい自転車を盗まれて　（わあわあ/がみがみ/かん
   かんに）怒っている。

   Mr. Yano is furious that his new bicycle has been stolen.

3. Kurai eigakan no ushiro no seki de dareka (geragera/kusu-
   kusu/niyaniya) waratte ita.

   暗い映画館の後ろの席でだれか（げらげら/くすくす/にやにや）
   笑っていた。

   Someone was giggling in a rear seat in the dark movie theater.

4. Erebētā o oriru to, Wada-san ga (nikoniko/kusukusu/gera-
   gera) shite tatte ita.

   エレベーターを降りると、和田さんが（にこにこ/くすくす/げ
   らげら）して立っていた。

When I got off the elevator, Mr. Wada was standing there (in front of me) with a broad smile.

5. Densha no naka de osanai kodomo ga (shikushiku/boro-boro/wāwā) naite hahaoya o komaraseta.
電車の中で幼い子供が（しくしく/ぼろぼろ/わあわあ）泣いて母親を困らせた。
A young child cried loudly in the train, embarrassing his mother.

6. Watashi ga heya ni haitta toki, Ono-san wa (niyaniya/kusu-kusu/punpun) shinagara zasshi o mite ita.
私が部屋に入った時、小野さんは（にやにや/くすくす/ぷんぷん）しながら雑誌を見ていた。
When I entered the room, Mr. Ono was looking at a magazine and grinning.

7. Ano ko wa (kankan ni/gamigami/punpun) itte mo terebi o mite bakari imasu.
あの子は（かんかんに/がみがみ/ぷんぷん）言ってもテレビを見てばかりいます。
Even if I scold him harshly, that child does nothing but watch TV.

5.11 | gatsugatsu がつがつ

"hungrily," "gluttonously," "(eat) like a pig"

Gatsugatsu describes the manner in which a very hungry person eats. It carries negative connotations.

1. Mikka mo tabenakatta node, dasareta tabemono o **gatsug-atsu** tabeta.

   三日も食べなかったので、出された食べ物を**がつがつ**食べた。

   Because I hadn't eaten for three days, I wolfed down the food that was served.

2. Kare wa ōkii sutēki ni **gatsugatsu** shite iru.

   彼は大きいステーキに**がつがつ**している。

   He is hungry for a big steak.

5.12 | morimori もりもり

"(eat) like a horse," "have a hearty appetite"

Morimori describes the manner in which a person with a good appetite eats heartily.

1. Senshu-tachi wa shiai no ato de yūshoku o **morimori** tabeta.

   選手達は試合の後で夕食を**もりもり**食べた。

   After the game, the players wolfed down their dinner.

2. Byōki ga hobo kaifuku shita node, **morimori** taberareru yō ni natta.

   病気がほぼ回復したので、**もりもり**食べられるようになった。

   Having recovered almost fully from my illness, I'm able to eat like a horse again.

5.13 | poripori ぽりぽり | "munch"

Poripori describes the sound of someone eating crackers or other crunchy treats.

EXAMPLES:

1. Otoko no ko ga futari kōen no benchi ni suwatte poteto chippu o **poripori** tabete iru.

   男の子が二人公園のベンチに座ってポテトチップを**ぽりぽり**食べている。

   Two boys are sitting on a bench in the park and munching on potato chips.

2. Eigakan de tonari no hito ga poppukōn o **poripori** tabete urusakute tamaranakatta.

   映画館で隣の人がポップコーンを**ぽりぽり**食べてうるさくてたまらなかった。

   The person sitting next to me in the movie theater was munching on popcorn, and it was extremely irritating.

5.14 | pekopeko ぺこぺこ

"on an empty stomach," "with one's head bowed"

Pekopeko describes the sound of someone's stomach growling for food (Examples 1, 2). It also describes a groveling, obsequious manner (Example 3).

EXAMPLES:

1. Hashitta kara onaka ga **pekopeko** desu.
   走ったからおなかがぺこぺこです。
   I ran, so I'm awfully hungry.

2. Onaka ga **pekopeko** de taore sō da.
   おなかがぺこぺこで倒れそうだ。
   I'm so hungry I feel like I'm going to collapse.

3. Kare wa itsu de mo jōshi ni **pekopeko** shite imasu.
   彼はいつでも上司にぺこぺこしています。
   He's always playing up to his boss.

5.15 | **gabugabu がぶがぶ** | "quaff," "(drink) thirstily,"

Gabugabu describes the manner in which someone guzzles something.

EXAMPLES:

1. Nodo ga kawaita kara mizu o **gabugabu** nonda.
   のどが渇いたから水をがぶがぶ飲んだ。
   Because I was thirsty, I drank a lot of water.

2. Kida-san wa bīru o **gabugabu** nomu kara, saikin futotte kita.
   木田さんはビールをがぶがぶ飲むから、最近太ってきた。
   Mr. Kida drinks a lot of beer, and that's why he has recently gained weight.

5.16 | chibichibi ちびちび | "(sip) little by little," "in sips"

Chibichibi describes the manner in which someone sips something.

EXAMPLES:

1. Kare wa bā de hitori uisukī o **chibichibi** nonde iru.
   彼はバーでひとりウイスキーを**ちびちび**飲んでいる。
   He is sipping whiskey alone at the bar.

2. Yoshiko-san wa wain o susumerarete, **chibichibi** nonde ita.
   良子さんはワインを勧められて、**ちびちび**飲んでいた。
   Having been offered a glass of wine, Yoshiko (accepted it and) drank it in sips.

5.17 | perapera ぺらぺら | "fluently," "rapidly"

Perapera describes the manner in which someone speaks fluently in a foreign language or rapidly in general.

EXAMPLES:

1. Sumisu-san wa sannen de Nihongo ga **perapera** ni nari-mashita.
   スミスさんは三年で日本語が**ぺらぺら**になりました。
   Mr. Smith became fluent in Japanese in three years.

2. Sensei ga Nihongo de **perapera** hanashita node, nani mo wakaranakatta.

先生が日本語で**べらべら**話したので、何も分からなかった。

Because the teacher spoke rapidly in Japanese, I understood nothing.

5.18 | berabera べらべら | "(talk) on and on," "blab"

Berabera describes the manner in which someone talks on and on without stopping, often about something that he should not be talking about.

EXAMPLES:

1. Kanojo wa hito no hanashi o kikazu hitori de **berabera** shaberu.

   彼女は人の話を聞かず一人で**べらべら**しゃべる。

   She talks on and on without listening to others.

2. Ano hito wa nan demo **berabera** hanasu kara, ki o tsuketa hō ga ii desu yo.

   あの人は何でも**べらべら**話すから、気を付けたほうがいいですよ。

   He blabs about everything, so you had better be careful about what you say.

5.19 | pechakucha ぺちゃくちゃ | "(talk) noisily," "chatter"

Pechakucha describes the manner in which someone talks noisily without stopping.

1. Kanojo ga kuru to itsumade mo **pechakucha** shaberu kara, shigoto ga dekinai.

   彼女が来るといつまでも**ぺちゃくちゃ**しゃべるから、仕事が出来ない。

   Whenever she comes over, she chatters on and on, so I can't get my work done.

2. Kissaten de wakai josei ga o-cha o nominagara, **pechakucha** shabette ita.

   喫茶店で若い女性がお茶を飲みながら、**ぺちゃくちゃ**しゃべっていた。

   Some young women were chattering away while having tea in the coffee shop.

5.20 | hakihaki はきはき | "clearly," "unambiguously"

Hakihaki describes the manner in which someone speaks clearly and/or with conviction.

EXAMPLES:

1. Sono ko wa keikan no shitsumon ni otona no yō ni **hakihaki** kotaeta.

   その子は警官の質問に大人のように**はきはき**答えた。

   That child answered the policeman's questions clearly, like an adult.

2. Ono-san wa taido ga **hakihaki** shinai kara, gokai sareru koto ga aru.

小野さんは態度が**はきはき**しないから、誤解されることがある。

Because Mr. Ono's attitude is ambiguous, there are times when he is misunderstood.

5.21 | hisohiso ひそひそ | "in whispers"

Hisohiso describes the manner in which someone speaks in a low voice so as not to be heard by others.

EXAMPLES:

1. Ano futari wa itsumo heya no sumi de **hisohiso** hanashite imasu.

   あの二人はいつも部屋の隅で**ひそひそ**話しています。

   Those two are always talking in whispers in the corner of the room.

2. Jugyōchū **hisohiso** hanashite sensei ni shikarareta.

   授業中**ひそひそ**話して先生に叱られた。

   We whispered during class and got scolded by the teacher.

PRACTICE 15 (5.11–5.21)

Circle the correct adverb among the choices given in parentheses.

1. Gaikoku de mizu o (chibichibi/gabugabu/gatsugatsu) nonde geri o shita.

   外国で水を（ちびちび/がぶがぶ/がつがつ）飲んで下痢をした。

   I drank a lot of water while abroad and had diarrhea.

2. Kesa kara nani mo tabete inai kara, onaka ga (gatsugatsu/
   morimori/pekopeko) da.

   今朝から何も食べていないから、おなかが（がつがつ/もりも
   り/ぺこぺこ）だ。

   I haven't eaten anything since this morning, so I am starving.

3. Hara-san wa Pari de umare Pari de sodatta kara, furansugo
   ga (hakihaki/perapera/berabera) desu.

   原さんはパリで生まれパリで育ったから、フランス語が（は
   きはき/ぺらぺら/べらべら）です。

   Miss Hara was born and raised in Paris, so she is fluent in French.

4. Hondana no mukō de futari no josei ga (hisohiso/hakihaki/
   pechakucha) shabette iru no ga yoku kikoeru.

   本棚の向こうで二人の女性が（ひそひそ/はきはき/ぺちゃくち
   ゃ）しゃべっているのがよく聞こえる。

   I can clearly hear the two women chattering behind the bookshelf.

5. Hayaku genki ni natte mae no yō ni (morimori/gatsugatsu/
   poripori) tabete kudasai.

   早く元気になって前のように（もりもり/がつがつ/ぽりぽり）
   食べてください。

   Please get well soon and regain your hearty appetite.

6. Mada kimatte inai noni, Yoshida-san wa tsugi no purojekuto no koto o (berabera/hakihaki/pekopeko) hanashite ita.

   まだ決まっていないのに、吉田さんは次のプロジェクトのこ
   とを（べらべら/はきはき/ぺこぺこ）話していた。

   In spite of the fact that it hasn't been decided yet, Mr. Yoshida was
   blabbing about our next project.

7. Kodomo ga kurakkā o (gatsugatsu/poripori/pekopeko) tabe-
   nagara ehon o mite iru.
   子供がクラッカーを （がつがつ/ぽりぽり/ぺこぺこ） 食べなが
   ら絵本を見ている。
   The child is looking at a picture book while munching on crackers.

5.22 | burabura ぶらぶら | "leisurely," "idly"

Burabura describes the manner in which someone dangles something
(Example 1) or the way something dangles. It also describes leisurely
movement that is without purpose (Example 2), or the manner in
which someone idles his time away (Example 3).

EXAMPLES:

1. Sono onna no ko wa isu ni swatte ashi o **burabura** sasete ita.
   その女の子はいすに座って脚を**ぶらぶら**させていた。

   The girl was sitting on the chair, dangling her feet.

2. Kōen o **burabura** arukimashita.
   公園を**ぶらぶら**歩きました。

   I went for a leisurely walk in the park.

3. Kare wa shitsugyō shite kara **burabura** hi o okutte iru.
   彼は失業してから**ぶらぶら**日を送っている。

   Since he lost his job, he has been leading an idle life.

5.23 | zorozoro ぞろぞろ | "in succession," "in streams"

Zorozoro describes the comings and goings of crowds of people.

EXAMPLES:

1. Tenrankai no kaijō ni hito ga **zorozoro** haitte kita.

   展覧会の会場に人が**ぞろぞろ**入ってきた。

   People streamed into the exhibition hall.

2. Sensei ni insotsu sarete, shōgakusei ga **zorozoro** michi o watatte iru.

   先生に引率されて、小学生が**ぞろぞろ**道を渡っている。

   Led by a teacher, a crowd of schoolchildren is crossing the street.

5.24 | tobotobo とぼとぼ | "trudge"

Tobotobo describes a slow, heavy gait.

EXAMPLES:

1. Yūhi o se ni shite nōfu ga inakamichi o **tobotobo** aruite itta.

   夕日を背にして農夫が田舎道を**とぼとぼ**歩いて行った。

   With his back against the setting sun, a peasant trudged along the country road.

2. Watashi wa kachō ga rōjin no yō ni **tobotobo** aruku no o mita.

   私は課長が老人のように**とぼとぼ**歩くのを見た。

   I saw our section chief trudging along wearily like an old man.

5.25 | yoroyoro よろよろ | "stagger"

Yoroyoro describes an unsteady gait due to drunkenness, handicap or physical weakness.

EXAMPLES:

1. Yopparai ga kurai roji o **yoroyoro** aruite itta.
   酔っ払いが暗い路地を**よろよろ**歩いていった。
   A drunken man staggered along the dark alley.

2. Yuka ni taoreta otoko wa **yoroyoro** tachiagatta.
   床に倒れた男は**よろよろ**立ち上がった。
   The man who had fallen to the floor staggered to his feet.

5.26 | urouro うろうろ | "wander about," "hang about"

Urouro describes the manner in which someone loiters or wanders about aimlessly in a limited area.

EXAMPLES:

1. Hen na otoko ga ie no mae o **urouro** shite imasu.
   変な男が家の前を**うろうろ**しています。
   A strange man is wandering about in front of my house.

2. Isogashii toki ni kono heya no naka o **urouro** shinai de hoshii.
   忙しい時にこの部屋の中を**うろうろ**しないでほしい。
   When I'm busy, I don't want you to hang about in this room.

5.27 utouto うとうと   "drowse," "doze"

Utouto describes the manner in which someone falls into a light sleep unintentionally.

EXAMPLES:

1. Sensei no setsumei o kikinagara Rinda wa **utouto** shite ita.
先生の説明を聞きながらリンダは**うとうと**していた。
Linda dozed off while listening to the teacher's explanation.

2. **Utouto** shite iru aida ni terebi no bangumi wa owatte ita.
うとうとしている間にテレビの番組は終わっていた。
While I was dozing, the TV program ended.

5.28 suyasuya すやすや   "(sleep) calmly," "(sleep) peacefully"

Suyasuya describes the manner in which someone sleeps peacefully without any disturbance.

EXAMPLES:

1. Akachan ga ubaguruma no naka de **suyasuya** nemutte iru.
赤ちゃんが乳母車の中で**すやすや**眠っている。
The baby is sleeping peacefully in the baby carriage.

2. Byōnin wa kusuri o nonda ato de nanjikan mo **suyasuya** nemuritsuzuketa.
病人は薬を飲んだ後で何時間も**すやすや**眠り続けた。
After taking the medicine, the sick person continued to sleep peacefully for hours.

5.29 | gūgū ぐうぐう | "z-z-z," "(sleep) soundly," "snore"

Gūgū describes the manner in which someone sleeps soundly. It also describes the sound of a snore.

EXAMPLES:

1. Shujin wa gaikoku ryokō kara kaeru to, shawā o abite **gūgū** nete shimatta.

   主人は外国旅行から帰ると、シャワーを浴びて**ぐうぐう**寝てしまった。

   When my husband came home from abroad, he took a shower and fell soundly asleep.

2. Hoteru no tonari no heya de dareka **gūgū** ibiki o kaite ita.

   ホテルの隣の部屋でだれか**ぐうぐう**いびきをかいていた。

   Someone was snoring loudly in the hotel room next door.

PRACTICE 16 (5.22–5.29)

Circle the correct adverb among the choices given in parentheses.

1. Kankōkyaku ga gaido no ato kara (burabura/yoroyoro/zoro-zoro) tsuite ikimasu.

   観光客がガイドの後から（ぶらぶら/よろよろ/ぞろぞろ）ついて行きます。

   The sightseers are closely following the guide in a crowd.

2. Koko o (utouto/urouro/yoroyoro) shinai de sassato shigoto o katazukenasai.

ここを（うとうと/うろうろ/よろよろ）しないでさっさと仕事を片付けなさい。

Don't hang around here. Finish up your work quickly.

3. Tenki ga yoi kara kōen demo (burabura/tobotobo/zorozoro) arukimashō ka.

天気が良いから、公園でも（ぶらぶら/とぼとぼ/ぞろぞろ）歩きましょうか。

Since the weather is good, shall we take a stroll in the park?

4. Densha no naka de (suyasuya/utouto/yoroyoro) shite eki o norikoshita.

電車の中で（すやすや/うとうと/よろよろ）して駅を乗り越した。

I dozed off on the train and rode past the station.

5. Eki no hōmu o (tobotobo/yoroyoro/zorozoro) aruite ita otoko ga watashi ni butsukatta.

駅のホームを（とぼとぼ/よろよろ/ぞろぞろ）歩いていた男が私にぶつかった。

The man staggering along the station platform bumped into me.

6. Kare wa tomodachi ni sake o nomasarete sofa no ue de (urouro/utouto/gūgū) nete shimatta.

彼は友達に酒を飲まされてソファの上で（うろうろ/うとうと/ぐうぐう）寝てしまった。

He was made to drink sake by his friends and fell fast asleep on the sofa.

5.30 | furafura ふらふら | "feel dizzy," "be unsteady"

Furafura describes a dizzy or lightheaded feeling. It also describes someone who is shakey or unsteady.

EXAMPLES:

1. Kesa okiru to atama ga **furafura** shita.
   今朝起きると頭がふらふらした。
   When I got up this morning, I felt dizzy.

2. Haha wa taiin shimashita ga mada ashi ga **furafura** shite imasu.
   母は退院しましたがまだ足がふらふらしています。
   Although my mother is out of the hospital, her legs are still unsteady.

5.31 | gangan がんがん |

   "have a splitting headache," "hear a ringing in one's ears"

Gangan describes a splitting headache or a ringing in the ears.

EXAMPLES:

1. Kaze o hiite atama ga **gangan** shite imasu.
   かぜを引いて頭ががんがんしています。
   I have a cold and my head aches.

2. Hikōki ga chakuriku suru toki mimi ga **gangan** natta.
   飛行機が着陸する時耳ががんがん鳴った。
   I had a terrible ringing in my ears as the airplane landed.

5.32 | fūfū ふうふう | "puffing and panting," "gasping for breath"

Fūfū describes the sound of hard breathing or blowing.

EXAMPLES:

1. Kare wa hashitte kita node **fūfū** itte iru.
   彼は走って来たのでふうふういっている。
   Because he came running, he is panting.

2. Kanojo wa **fūfū** iinagara shiken benkyo o shite iru.
   彼女はふうふういいながら試験勉強をしている。
   She is wearing herself out studying for the exam.

5.33 | zokuzoku ぞくぞく | "feel excited," "shiver"

Zokuzoku describes tingling joy or excitement, or a chill due to fear, a fever or cold weather.

EXAMPLES:

1. Ichirō no fainpurē ni **zokuzoku** suru hodo kōfun shita.
   イチローのファインプレーにぞくぞくするほど興奮した。
   Ichiro's fine play sent shivers down my spine.

2. Yo ga fukeru to, samusa de karada ga **zokuzoku** shi hajimeta.
   夜がふけると、寒さで体がぞくぞくし始めた。
   As night wore on, I began to shiver from the cold.

3. Kare wa kōnetsu de karadajū ga **zokuzoku** shita.

   彼は高熱で体中が**ぞくぞく**した。

   Due to his high fever, he felt chills throughout his entire body.

5.34 | gatagata がたがた | "rattle," "tremble"

Gatagata describes a rattling sound or the manner in which the body trembles.

EXAMPLES:

1. Kaze de doa ga **gatagata** shi hajimeta.

   風でドアが**がたがた**し始めた。

   The door began to rattle in the wind.

2. Kawa kara tasukeagerareta kodomo wa samusa de **gata-gata** furuete ita.

   川から助け上げられた子供は寒さで**がたがた**震えていた。

   The child rescued from the river was trembling from the cold.

3. Yama de kuma ga arawareta toki, osoroshisa de hiza ga **gatagata** furueta.

   山で熊が現れた時、恐ろしさでひざが**がたがた**震えた。

   When a bear appeared in the mountains, my knees trembled with fear.

5.35 | kirikiri きりきり | "have a sharp pain"

Kirikiri describes a sharp pain.

EXAMPLES:

1. Atama ga **kirikiri** itamu node asupirin o nonda.
   頭が**きりきり**痛むのでアスピリンを飲んだ。

   I have a piercing headache, so I have taken some aspirin.

2. Tanaka-san wa sutoresu de i ga **kirikiri** suru to itte iru.
   田中さんはストレスで胃が**きりきり**すると言っている。

   Mr. Tanaka says that stress causes him an acute stomachache.

5.36 | **zukizuki ずきずき** |　　"sting," "throb"

Zukizuki describes a sharp, throbbing pain.

EXAMPLES:

1. Yūbe ha ga **zukizuki** itande yoku nemurenakatta.
   ゆうべ歯が**ずきずき**痛んでよく眠れなかった。

   Last night I had a toothache and couldn't sleep well.

2. Yubi no kirikizu ga **zukizuki** suru.
   指の切り傷が**ずきずき**する。

   The cut in my finger throbs with pain.

5.37 | **pinpin ぴんぴん** |　　"be lively," "be full of life"

Pinpin describes a healthy state.

EXAMPLES:

1. Sobo wa shi no zenjitsu made genki de **pinpin** shite ita.

祖母は死の前日まで元気で**ぴんぴん**していた。

My grandmother was well and full of energy until the day before her death.

2. Mori-san wa ikkagetsu mae ni ōkega o shita noni mō **pin-pin** shite iru.

森さんは一か月前に大怪我をしたのにもう**ぴんぴん**している。

Although Mr. Mori was badly hurt a month ago, he is already full of life again.

PRACTICE 17 (5.30–5.37)

Circle the correct adverb among the choices given in parentheses.

1. Ha ga (zukizuki/gatagata/gangan) itamu node nani mo tabe-rarenai.

歯が（ずきずき/がたがた/がんがん）痛むので何も食べられない。

Because my tooth aches, I can't eat anything.

2. Yūbe karada ga (furafura/zukizuki/zokuzoku) shita node, atsui o-furo ni haitte neta.

ゆうべ体が（ふらふら/ずきずき/ぞくぞく）したので、熱いお風呂に入って寝た。

Last night I had the chills, so I took a hot bath and went to bed.

241

3. Kinō made (kirikiri/pinpin/furafura) shite ita Hayashi-san ga
   kyū ni nakunatta.

   昨日まで（きりきり/ぴんぴん/ふらふら）していた林さんが急
   に亡くなった。

   Miss Hayashi, who was full of life until yesterday, passed away suddenly.

4. Hajimete disuko ni itta toki, sōon de mimi ga (gangan/zoku-
   zoku/zukizuki) shita.

   初めてディスコに行った時、騒音で耳が（がんがん/ぞくぞく/
   ずきずき）した。

   The first time I went to a disco, the loud noise caused a ringing in my
   ears.

5. Kare wa ōisogi de kita node,heya ni haitta toki (furafura/
   fūfū/gatagata) itte ita.

   彼は大急ぎで来たので、部屋に入った時（ふらふら/ふうふう/
   がたがた）いっていた。

   Since he came in a big hurry, he was puffing and panting when he
   entered the room.

6. Jūsei o kiite hiza ga (furafura/gatagata/zokuzoku) furue, ippo
   mo arukenakatta.

   銃声を聞いてひざが（ふらふら/がたがた/ぞくぞく）震え、一
   歩も歩けなかった。

   At the report of a gun, my knees trembled and I couldn't move even
   one step.

5.38 **wakuwaku わくわく**   "be excited"

Wakuwaku describes a feeling of excitement, joy or expectation.

EXAMPLES:

1. Ashita wa gakkō no ensoku na node kodomo wa **waku-waku** shite imasu.

   明日は学校の遠足なので子供は**わくわく**しています。

   My child is excited about tomorrow's school field trip.

2. Kare kara tegami o uketotta toki, kanojo wa yorokobi de mune ga **wakuwaku** shita.

   彼から手紙を受け取った時、彼女は喜びで胸が**わくわく**した。

   When she received a letter from him, her heart leaped with joy.

5.39 **isoiso いそいそ**   "cheerfully," "joyfully"

Isoiso describes a cheerful manner.

EXAMPLES:

1. Musume wa **isoiso** (to) dēto ni dekaketa.

   娘は**いそいそ**(と)デートに出かけた。

   My daughter went out for a date looking very happy.

2. O-kyaku ga kuru kara, haha wa **isoiso** (to) shokuji no shitaku o shite imasu.

   お客が来るから、母は**いそいそ**(と)食事の支度をしています。

   Guests are coming, so my mother is cheerfully preparing food.

5.40 | **ikiiki いきいき** | "be lively," "be full of life"

Ikiiki describes someone who is full of energy or in high spirits (Examples 1, 2), or something such as a plant that is fresh or full of life (Example 3).

EXAMPLES:

1. Kyanpu kara kaetta kodomo-tachi wa jitsu ni **ikiiki** shite iru.
キャンプから帰った子供達は実に**いきいき**している。
The children who have come back from camp are truly in high spirits.

2. Yamanaka-san wa wakai josei to saikon shite **ikiiki** shite imasu.
山中さんは若い女性と再婚して**いきいき**しています。
Mr. Yamanaka remarried a young woman and has been full of life ever since.

3. Haru ni natte kigi ga **ikiiki** shi hajimeta.
春になって木々が**いきいき**し始めた。
With spring here, the trees have begun to come to life again.

5.41 | **nobinobi のびのび**

"feel relieved," "feel refreshed," "be at ease"

Nobinobi describes the feeling of being relieved, refreshed or at ease.

EXAMPLES:

1. Sūjitsu onsen de sugoshite jitsu ni **nobinobi** shita.
数日温泉で過ごして実に**のびのび**した。

I spent a few days at a hot spring and felt truly refreshed.

2. Tokai o hanarete inaka de **nobinobi** kurashitai.
都会を離れて田舎で**のびのび**暮らしたい。

I want to leave the city and live a carefree life in the country.

5.42 | **dokidoki どきどき**

"thump-thump," "feel nervous," "feel excited"

Dokidoki describes the sound of someone's heart thumping due to anxiety, excitement or intense physical exertion.

EXAMPLES:

1. Shiken no mae ni wa itsumo **dokidoki** shimasu.
試験の前にはいつも**どきどき**します。

I'm always nervous before an exam.

2. Sanchō ni tsuita toki mune ga **dokidoki** shite shibaraku hanasenakatta.
山頂に着いた時胸が**どきどき**してしばらく話せなかった。

When I reached the mountaintop, my heart was pounding so hard that I couldn't speak for a while.

5.43 | harahara はらはら | "feel nervous," "feel uneasy"

Harahara describes the feeling of fear, suspense or excitement that comes with observing a situation of uncertain outcome.

EXAMPLES:

1. Watashi wa **harahara** shinagara musume ga sukēto o suru no o mite ita.

   私は**はらはら**しながら娘がスケートをするのを見ていた。

   I was watching nervously as my daughter skated.

2. Kinō no shiai ni wa saigo made **harahara** saserareta.

   昨日の試合には最後まで**はらはら**させられた。

   Yesterday's game kept me in suspense to the end.

5.44 | bikubiku びくびく | "nervously," "timidly"

Bikubiku describes the feeling of being nervous or ill at ease.

EXAMPLES:

1. Sono otoko wa **bikubiku** shinagara keisatsu ni shuttō shita.

   その男は**びくびく**しながら警察に出頭した。

   He appeared at the police station looking apprehensive.

2. Kono ko wa ōkii inu ga chikazuku to **bikubiku** shimasu.

   この子は大きい犬が近づくと**びくびく**します。

   This child gets nervous when a big dog comes near.

5.45 | **iraira いらいら** | "be irritated," "be impatient"

Iraira describes the feeling of being irritated or impatient.

EXAMPLES:

1. Hikōki no shuppatsu ga okurete **iraira** shita.
   飛行機の出発が遅れて**いらいら**した。
   The departure of the airplane was delayed, and I got irritated.

2. Shachō wa kōshō ga hakadoranai node **iraira** shite iru.
   社長は交渉がはかどらないので**いらいら**している。
   Because the negotiations are not progressing, the company president is losing patience.

5.46 | **muzumuzu むずむず** | "impatiently (eager)"

Muzumuzu describes the feeling of being impatiently eager.

EXAMPLES:

1. Akira wa atarashii kamera de shashin o toritakute **muzumuzu** shite iru.
   明は新しいカメラで写真をとりたくて**むずむず**している。
   Akira is eager to take pictures with his new camera.

2. Masako wa Pari de katta jaketto o tomodachi ni misetakute **muzumuzu** shite iru.
   正子はパリで買ったジャケットを友達に見せたくて**むずむず**している。
   Masako is eager to show her friends the jacket she bought in Paris.

5.47 | mojimoji もじもじ | "hesitantly"

Mojimoji describes the feeling of being hesitant or embarrassed.

EXAMPLES:

1. Kare wa **mojimoji** shite shitsumon ni kotaenakatta.

   彼は**もじもじ**して質問に答えなかった。

   He hesitated to answer the question.

2. Kanojo wa sukina dansei no mae dewa **mojimoji** shite hanashi mo dekinai.

   彼女は好きな男性の前では**もじもじ**して話も出来ない。

   She feels flustered in front of the man she likes and can't even talk to him.

5.48 | magomago まごまご | "be confused"

Magomago describes a state of agitated confusion.

EXAMPLES:

1. Jon wa Nihongo de hanashikakerarete **magomago** shite shimatta.

   ジョンは日本語で話しかけられて**まごまご**してしまった。

   John got totally confused when he was spoken to in Japanese.

2. O-kane o harau toki, saifu ga mitsukaranakute **magomago** shita.

   お金を払うとき、財布が見付からなくて**まごまご**した。

   Just as I was about to pay, I couldn't find my wallet and panicked.

Circle the correct adverb among the choices given in parentheses.

1. Kanjo wa pātī no shōtaijō o moratte (mojimoji/isoiso/muzu-
   muzu) henji o dashita.

   彼女はパーティーの招待状をもらって（もじもじ/いそいそ/む
   ずむず）返事を出した。

   Having received an invitation to the party, she cheerfully sent a reply.

2. Shiken ga owatta node, gakusei wa (wakuwaku/nobinobi/
   isoiso) shite imasu.

   試験が終わったので、学生は（わくわく/のびのび/いそいそ）
   しています。

   With exams finished, the students are feeling relieved.

3. Kachō wa buka no shigoto ga osoi to (iraira/muzumuzu/
   mojimoji) suru.

   課長は部下の仕事が遅いと（いらいら/むずむず/もじもじ）する。

   The section chief gets impatient when his subordinates are slow in
   their work.

4. Watashi wa kodomo ga tsunawatari suru no o (wakuwaku/
   iraira/harahara) shinagara mite ita.

   私は子供が綱渡りするのを（わくわく/いらいら/はらはら）し
   ながら見ていた。

   I was nervously watching a boy tightrope walking.

5. Koko e kuru yō ni itta noni, ano ko wa toguchi de (mojimoji/
   magomago/muzumuzu) shite tatte iru.

ここへ来るように言ったのに、あの子は戸口で（もじもじ/まごまご/むずむず）して立っている。

I told the girl to come here, but she remained standing hesitantly in the doorway.

6. Shinsenna yama no kūki o sutte (wakuwaku/ikiiki/harahara) shita.

新鮮な山の空気を吸って（わくわく/いきいき/はらはら）した。

Breathing the fresh mountain air, I felt alive.

7. Yonaka ni ayashii ashioto o kiita toki, mune ga (bikubiku/dokidoki/isoiso) shita.

夜中に怪しい足音を聞いた時、胸が（びくびく/どきどき/いそいそ）した。

When I heard strange footsteps in the middle of the night, my heart pounded with fear.

8. Zasshi o mite ita Jon wa sensei ni shitsumon sarete (wakuwaku/magomago/harahara) shita.

雑誌を見ていたジョンは先生に質問されて（わくわく/まごまご/はらはら）した。

John, who had been looking at a magazine, was asked a question by the teacher and got confused.

5.49 | **zāzā ざあざあ** | "(rain) in torrents," "(rain) cats and dogs"

Zāzā describes the sound of pouring rain or torrents of water.

EXAMPLES:

1. Yamagoya de yasunde iru toki, ame ga **zāzā** futte kimashita.

   山小屋で休んでいる時、雨が**ざあざあ**降ってきました。

   When we were resting in a mountain hut, the rain came pouring down.

2. Otoko no hito ga mise no mae no tōri ni **zāzā** mizu o nagashite iru.

   男の人が店の前の通りに**ざあざあ**水を流している。

   A man is dumping water on the street in front of the store.

5.50 | **shitoshito しとしと** | "drizzle"

Shitoshito describes a gentle rain.

EXAMPLES:

1. Gozenchū wa ame ga **shitoshito** futte ita ga gogo kara hareta.

   午前中は雨がしとしと降っていたが午後から晴れた。

   It was drizzling in the morning, but it cleared up in the afternoon.

2. **Shitoshito** furu ame no naka o kodomo-tachi ga hashitte iku.

   しとしと降る雨の中を子供達が走って行く。

   The children are running around in the drizzling rain.

5.51 | chirachira ちらちら | "flicker," "flutter," "(fall) lightly"

Chirachira describes the way something flickers or flashes or becomes momentarily visible and then disappears again (Example 1). It also describes the way small, light flakes fall (Examples 2, 3), or the way dim lights appear in clusters far away (Example 4).

EXAMPLES:

1. Tokidoki terebi no gamen ga **chirachira** suru.
   時々テレビの画面が**ちらちら**する。
   Sometimes the TV screen flickers.

2. Asa okiru to, yuki ga **chirachira** futte ita.
   朝起きると、雪が**ちらちら**降っていた。
   When I got up in the morning, it was snowing lightly.

3. Kōen no sakura no hana ga kaze ni **chirachira** chitte iru.
   公園の桜の花が風に**ちらちら**散っている。
   The cherry blossoms in the park are scattering in the wind.

4. Tōku ni machi no hi ga **chirachira** mieru.
   遠くに街の灯が**ちらちら**見える。
   You can see the lights of the city in the distance.

5.52 | kirakira きらきら | "twinkle," "sparkle"

Kirakira describes the way something twinkles or sparkles.

1. Yozora ni hoshi ga **kirakira** kagayaki hajimeta.

   夜空に星が**きらきら**輝き始めた。

   The stars came out twinkling in the evening sky.

2. Mori no naka no mizuumi wa tsuki no hikari de **kirakira** hikatte ita.

   森の中の湖は月の光で**きらきら**光っていた。

   The lake in the woods was sparkling in the moonlight.

3. Kanojo no hitomi wa **kirakira** shite ita.

   彼女の瞳は**きらきら**していた。

   Her eyes sparkled beautifully.

5.53 | pokapoka ぽかぽか | "nice and warm"

Pokapoka describes the state of being comfortably warm.

EXAMPLES:

1. Kono heya wa minamimuki na node asa wa **pokapoka** atatakai desu.

   この部屋は南向きなので朝は**ぽかぽか**暖かいです。

   Because this room faces to the south, it is nice and warm in the morning.

2. Wain o sukoshi nondara karada ga **pokapoka** shite kita.

   ワインを少し飲んだら体が**ぽかぽか**してきた。

   When I had a little wine, my body warmed up.

5.54 | rinrin りんりん | "jingle," "tinkle"

Rinrin describes the jingling of a bell.

EXAMPLES:

1. Tonari no heya de denwa ga **rinrin** natte iru.
   隣の部屋で電話が**りんりん**鳴っている。

   The phone is ringing in the next room.

2. Fūrin ga **rinrin** natte hirune no jama o shita.
   風鈴が**りんりん**鳴って昼寝の邪魔をした。

   The tinkling of a wind chime disturbed my nap.

5.55 | gōgō ごうごう | "with a roar," "with a rumble"

Gōgō describes the roaring of a machine or of flowing water.

EXAMPLES:

1. Ressha ga **gōgō** oto o tatete tōrisugita.
   列車が**ごうごう**音をたてて通り過ぎた。

   A train came roaring past.

2. Ōame de mizu ga mashita kawa wa **gōgō** nagarete iru.
   大雨で水が増した川は**ごうごう**流れている。

   Swollen with heavy rain, the river is roaring by.

5.56 | guruguru ぐるぐる | "around and around"

Guruguru describes the way something turns in circles or revolves around something else.

EXAMPLES:

1. Yūenchi no merī-gō-raundo ga **guruguru** mawatte iru.
   遊園地のメリーゴーラウンドが**ぐるぐる**回っている。
   The merry-go-round in the amusement park is going around and around.

2. Kodomo ga te ni nigitta kazaguruma ga chiisana oto o tatete **guruguru** mawatta.
   子供が手に握った風車が小さな音をたてて**ぐるぐる**回った。
   The pinwheel in the child's hand went around and around making a little sound.

5.57 | guragura ぐらぐら | "shake"

Guragura describes the manner in which something shakes.

EXAMPLES:

1. Jishin de ie ga **guragura** yureta.
   地震で家が**ぐらぐら**ゆれた。
   The house shook as a result of the earthquake.

2. Sono isu wa **guragura** shite iru kara tsukawanai hō ga ii desu yo.
   そのいすは**ぐらぐら**しているから使わないほうがいいですよ。
   That chair is shaky, so it is better not to use it.

5.58 | **korokoro** ころころ | "roll"

Korokoro describes the manner in which a small, round object, such as a ball or a marble, rolls (Example 1). It is also used figuratively of emotion (Example 2).

EXAMPLES:

1. Bōru ga **korokoro** korogatte mizo ni ochita.
   ボールが**ころころ**転がって溝に落ちた。
   The ball rolled and fell into a ditch.

2. Kanojo no kimochi wa itsu demo **korokoro** kawaru.
   彼女の気持ちはいつでも**ころころ**変わる。
   Her feelings keep changing.

PRACTICE 19 (5.49–5.58)

Circle the correct adverb among the choices given in parentheses.

1. Orenji ga tēburu kara ochite yuka no ue o (guragura/korokoro/guruguru) korogatta.
   オレンジがテーブルから落ちて床の上を（ぐらぐら/ころころ/ぐるぐる）転がった。
   An orange fell off the table and rolled on the floor.

2. Hi ga (pokapoka/shitoshito/kankan) teru hi ni wa gaishutsu shitaku arimasen.

日が（ぽかぽか/しとしと/かんかん）照る日には外出したくありません。

I don't want to go out on days when the sun shines hot.

3. Renjitsu ame ga (shitoshito/zāzā/chirachira) futta node, ike no mizu ga ippai ni natta.

連日雨が（しとしと/ざあざあ/ちらちら）降ったので、池の水がいっぱいになった。

Because it rained cats and dogs for days, the pond swelled.

4. Umibe no hoteru de hitobanjū nami no oto ga (guragura/gōgō/rinrin) kikoeta.

海辺のホテルで一晩中波の音が（ぐらぐら/ごうごう/りんりん）聞こえた。

I could hear the roaring sound of waves all night at the seaside hotel.

5. Saikin kon'yaku shita ane no yubi ni daiya no yubiwa ga (chirachira/kirakira/rinrin) kagayaite ita.

最近婚約した姉の指にダイヤの指輪が（ちらちら/きらきら/りんりん）輝いていた。

A diamond ring glittered on the finger of my older sister, who recently became engaged.

6. Tetsudō senro no soba no ie wa densha ga tōru tabi ni (guruguru/gōgō/guragura) shimasu.

鉄道線路のそばの家は電車が通るたびに（ぐるぐる/ごうごう/ぐらぐら）します。

The houses near the railroad tracks shake whenever a train passes.

7. Heya no mado kara (kirakira/chirachira/shitoshito) furu yuki o nagemete iru to, kyū ni kokyō ga natsukashiku natta.

部屋の窓から（きらきら/ちらちら/しとしと）降る雪を眺めていると、急に故郷が懐かしくなった。

I suddenly felt homesick, looking out the window of my room and seeing the snow falling gently.

 6 Adverbs Used with Negatives

The following adverbs are used with negatives such as *nai* or *muri* to express negation or denial.

6.1 | **sukoshi mo 少しも** | "(not) at all," "(not) in the least"

Sukoshi mo in the form *sukoshi mo … nai* expresses total negation.

EXAMPLES:

1. Kono kusuri wa takai bakari de **sukoshi mo** kikime ga nai.

この薬は高いばかりで**少しも**効き目がない。

This medicine is just expensive; it's not effective at all.

2. Kanojo wa konpyūtā no chishiki ga **sukoshi mo** arimasen.

彼女はコンピューターの知識が**少しも**ありません。

She hasn't the slightest knowledge of computers.

6.2 | chittomo ちっとも | "(not) at all," "(not) in the least"

Chittomo in the form *chittomo ... nai* expresses total negation. It is more colloquial than *sukoshi mo*.

EXAMPLES:

1. Konogoro buchō wa **chittomo** gorufu o shinai.
   この頃部長は**ちっとも**ゴルフをしない。
   These days the division chief doesn't play golf at all.

2. Ano eiga wa **chittomo** omoshirokunakatta.
   あの映画は**ちっとも**面白くなかった。
   That movie wasn't interesting at all.

6.3 | sappari さっぱり | "(not) at all," "(not) in the least"

Sappari in the form *sappari ... nai* expresses total negation and indicates an unfavorable situation. It is, like *chittomo*, more colloquial than *sukoshi mo*.

EXAMPLES:

1. Saikin Rinda ni **sappari** awanai.
   最近リンダに**さっぱり**会わない。
   I haven't seen Linda at all lately.

2. Konogoro **sappari** okyaku ga konai.
   このごろ**さっぱり**お客が来ない。
   There are no customers these days.

6.4 | kesshite 決して | "never," "absolutely (not)," "by no means"

Kesshite in the form *kesshite ... nai* expresses total negation. Unlike with *sukoshi mo*, *chittomo* or *sappari*, sentences with *kesshite* may involve the speaker's volition (Example 2).

EXAMPLES:

1. Kono dēta wa **kesshite** machigatte inai to omou.
   このデータは**決して**間違っていないと思う。

   I think that there is no way this data is wrong.

2. Mō **kesshite** koi nado shitakunai.
   もう**決して**恋などしたくない。

   I never want to fall in love again.

6.5 | tōtei とうてい | "(cannot) possibly"

Tōtei in the form *tōtei ... nai* or *tōtei ... muri* expresses the speaker's belief that something is impossible.

EXAMPLES:

1. Kono shigoto wa mikka de wa **tōtei** dekimasen.
   この仕事は三日では**とうてい**出来ません。

   I can't possibly do this work in three days.

2. Kono tenki de wa **tōtei** pikunikku wa muri desu ne.
   この天気では**とうてい**ピクニックは無理ですね。

   In weather like this, we can't possibly have a picnic, can we?

6.6 taishite 大して   "(not) very," "(not) much"

Taishite in the form *taishite ... nai* expressses the speaker's belief that something is not particularly significant or outstanding.

EXAMPLES:

1. Shachō wa **taishite** gorufu ga jōzu ja arimasen.
   社長は**大して**ゴルフが上手じゃありません。
   Our company president is not very good at golf.

2. Taifū no higai wa **taishite** nakatta.
   台風の被害は**大して**なかった。
   There was not much damage from the typhoon.

6.7 metta ni めったに   "rarely," "seldom"

Metta ni in the form *metta ni ... nai* expresses the speaker's belief that someone or something hardly ever does something or that something rarely happens.

EXAMPLES:

1. Noda-san wa **metta ni** sake o nomanai.
   野田さんは**めったに**酒を飲まない。
   Mr. Noda seldom drinks alcohol.

2. Jimu ga kurasu ni okureru koto wa **metta ni** arimasen.
   ジムがクラスに遅れることは**めったに**ありません。
   It rarely happens that Jim is late for class.

6.8 | kanarazu shi mo 必ずしも |

"(not) always," "(not) necessarily"

Kanarazu shi mo in the form *kanarazu shi mo ... nai/ienai/kagiranai* qualifies an assumption by negating it in part.

EXAMPLES:

1. Yasui mono ga **kanarazu shi mo** shitsu ga warui to wa ienai.
   安い物が**必ずしも**質が悪いとは言えない。

   One cannot always say that inexpensive things are inferior in quality.

2. Yoku benkyō suru gakusei ga **kanarazu shi mo** yoi seiseki o ageru to wa kagiranai.
   良く勉強する学生が**必ずしも**良い成績を上げるとは限らない。

   A student who studies hard does not necessarily get good grades.

6.9 | rokuni ろくに | "(not) enough," "(not) properly"

Rokuni in the form *rokuni ... nai* expresses the speaker's belief that someone or something does not or cannot do something sufficiently or properly.

EXAMPLES:

1. Rinda wa **rokuni** hiragana mo yomenai.
   リンダは**ろくに**ひらがなも読めない。

   Linda cannot read even hiragana properly.

2. **Rokuni** junbi mo shinai de shiken o uketa ga kanari yoku dekita.

ろくに準備もしないで試験を受けたがかなり良く出来た。

I took the exam without properly preparing for it, but I did fairly well.

6.10 | **manzara まんざら** | "(not) altogether," "(not) wholly"

Manzara in the form *manzara ... nai* expresses the speaker's belief that someone or something is not totally what he or it would seem to be.

EXAMPLES:

1. Ano otoko wa **manzara** baka de wa nai.

あの男は**まんざら**馬鹿ではない。

That man is not altogether stupid.

2. Kanojo wa **manzara** kare ga kirai ja nai rashii.

彼女は**まんざら**彼が嫌いじゃないらしい。

It seems that she does not dislike him altogether.

6.11 | **masaka まさか** | "Incredible!" "I never thought ..."

Masaka in the form *masaka ... hazu ga nai* (Example 1) expresses the speaker's belief that something will never happen. In the form *masaka ... omowanakatta* (Example 2), it expresses the speaker's disbelief or surprise about something that has already happened.

EXAMPLES:

1. **Masaka** Toda-san ga ima kaisha o yameru hazu ga nai.
   まさか戸田さんが今会社を辞めるはずがない。

   There is no way Miss Toda would quit the company now.

2. **Masaka** Oda-san no ie ga kaji de yakeru to wa omowanakatta.
   まさか小田さんの家が火事で焼けるとは思わなかった。

   I never thought that Mr. Oda's house would be destroyed by fire.

6.12 | imasara 今さら | "now (when it is too late)"

Imasara in the form *imasara … nai* expresses the speaker's belief that it is too late for someone or something to do something or for something to happen.

EXAMPLES:

1. Kanojo to no yakusoku o **imasara** torikesu koto wa dekimasen.
   彼女との約束を今さら取り消すことは出来ません。

   It is too late now to take back the promise you made to her.

2. **Imasara** yatta koto o kōkai shite mo shikata ga nai.
   今さらやったことを後悔しても仕方がない。

   It's no use now to regret what you have done.

Circle the correct adverb among the choices given in parentheses.

1. Chikagoro Midori-san wa watashi-tachi no atsumari ni (kesshite/taishite/sappari) kimasen ne.

近頃みどりさんは私達の集まりに（決して/大して/さっぱり）来ませんね。

These days Midori doesn't show up at all for our gatherings, does she?

2. Ano otoko ga itte iru koto wa (sukoshi mo/manzara/tōtei) uso de wa nai.

あの男が言っていることは（少しも/まんざら/とうてい）うそではない。

What that man is saying is not altogether a lie.

3. Ano ko wa mainichi piano o renshū shite iru noni (metta ni/chittomo/taishite) jōtatsu shinai.

あの子は毎日ピアノを練習しているのに（めったに/ちっとも/大して）上達しない。

Although the girl is practicing piano every day, she doesn't improve much.

4. Watashi wa (kesshite/kanarazu shi mo/imasara) kare no kangaekata ni dōi shinai tsumori desu.

私は（決して/必ずしも/今さら）彼の考え方に同意しないつもりです。

I will never go along with his ideas.

5. (Metta ni/masaka/rokuni) kanojo ga gaikokujin to kekkon suru to wa omowanakatta.

（めったに/まさか/ろくに）彼女が外国人と結婚するとは思わなかった。

I never thought she would marry a foreigner.

6. Isoide mo niji no ressha ni wa (manzara/tōtei/kesshite) maniaimasen yo.

急いでも二時の列車には（まんざら/とうてい/決して）間に合いませんよ。

Even if you hurry, you won't possibly be in time for the two o'clock train.

7. Kenkōna hito ga (sukoshi mo/kanarazu shi mo/metta ni) nagaiki suru to wa kagiranai.

健康な人が（少しも/必ずしも/めったに）長生きするとは限らない。

Healthy people do not necessarily live long.

8. Kare wa hanashikakete mo isogashii to (chitto mo/rokuni/masaka) henji mo shinai.

彼は話しかけても忙しいと（ちっとも/ろくに/まさか）返事もしない。

Even if I talk to him, he does not give a decent answer when he is busy.

9. Ichido chūdan sareta kōshō o (masaka/imasara/tōtei) hajimete mo shikata ga nai.

一度中断された交渉を（まさか/今さら/とうてい）始めても仕方がない。

It's no use now to restart negotiations once they have fallen apart already.

Adverbs with Different Meanings in Positive and Negative Expressions

The following adverbs convey different and sometimes opposite meanings depending on whether they are used in positive or negative expressions.

7.1 | **mada まだ** | "still," "(not) yet"

In a positive expression, *mada* indicates continuation of an action or a state. In a negative expression, it indicates that an action or event has not yet occurred or that a state has not yet been achieved.

EXAMPLES:
1. Kaze wa **mada** fuite imasu.
   風は**まだ** 吹いています。
   The wind is still blowing.

2. Kanojo wa **mada** kuruma o unten shita koto ga nai.
   彼女は**まだ**車を運転したことがない。
   She hasn't driven a car yet.

7.2 | **mō もう** | "already," "(not) anymore"

In a positive expression, *mō* indicates that an action or event has occurred or that a state has been achieved. In a negative expression, it indicates that an action or event has stopped occurring or that someone or something no longer exists in the state he or it has been in.

EXAMPLES:

1. Bangohan wa **mō** owarimashita.
   晩御飯は**もう**終わりました。

   We have already finished dinner.

2. Buraun-san wa **mō** ano ie ni sunde inai sō da.
   ブラウンさんは**もう**あの家に住んでいないそうだ。

   I heard that Mr. Brown no longer lives in that house.

7.3 | **totemo とても** | "very," "(cannot) possibly"

In a positive expression, *totemo* emphasizes degree. In a negative expression, it expresses the speaker's belief that something is difficult or impossible.

EXAMPLES:

1. Kōgi wa nagakute **totemo** taikutsu datta.
   講義は長くて**とても**退屈だった。

   The lecture was long and very boring.

2. Koko kara bijutsukan made **totemo** aruite ikemasen yo.
   ここから美術館まで**とても**歩いて行けませんよ。

   You can't possibly walk to the museum from here, I tell you.

7.4 | **amari あまり** | "very," "much," "(not) very," "(not) much"

In a positive expression, *amari* expresses the speaker's belief that something is excessive. In a negative expression, it indicates that a degree or extent is not as great as it is assumed or expected to be.

EXAMPLES:

1. Kodomotachi ga **amari** sawagu kara shikatta.

   子供たちが**あまり**騒ぐから叱った。

   The children were being so noisy that I scolded them.

2. Ane wa ryōri ga **amari** tokui de wa nai.

   姉は料理が**あまり**得意ではない。

   My older sister is not very good at cooking.

7.5 | **dōmo どうも** | "somehow," "very," "much"

In a positive or negative expression, *dōmo* introduces a guess that is not based on direct evidence, but is nevertheless felt to be true (Example 1). It can also simply emphasize degree (Example 2). In a negative expression, it indicates that something is beyond one's ability or control (Example 3).

EXAMPLES:

1. Neruson-sensei wa **dōmo** kikoku shitai rashii.

   ネルソン先生は**どうも**帰国したいらしい。

   I somehow sense that Professor Nelson wants to return to his country.

2. **Dōmo** arigatō gozaimasu. **Dōmo** mōshiwake gozaimasen.

   どうも有り難うございます。**どうも**申し訳ございません。

   Thank you very much. I am very sorry.

3. Nando yonde mo **dōmo** wakaranai.

   何度読んでも**どうも**分からない。

   No matter how many times I read it, I just don't understand it.

7.6 hotondo ほとんど   "almost," "hardly"

In a positive expression, *hotondo* means "almost." In a negative expression, it means "hardly."

EXAMPLES:

1. Ashita no shukudai wa mō **hotondo** dekimashita.
   明日の宿題はもう**ほとんど**出来ました。
   I have almost finished tomorrow's homework already.

2. Fukutsū de **hotondo** nani mo taberarenakatta.
   腹痛で**ほとんど**何も食べられなかった。
   I could hardly eat anything due to a stomachache.

7.7 nakanaka なかなか

"considerably," "quite," "(not) easily," "(not) readily"

In a positive expression, *nakanaka* indicates that someone or something is admirable, impressive or exceptional. In a negative expression, it indicates that a favorable situation does not come about easily.

EXAMPLES:

1. Abe-san no atarashii ie wa **nakanaka** rippa desu ne.
   阿部さんの新しい家は**なかなか**立派ですね。
   Mr. Abe's new house is quite impressive, isn't it?

2. Kanji wa mainichi renshū shite iru noni, **nakanaka** oboerarenai.
   漢字は毎日練習しているのに、**なかなか**覚えられない。
   Although I practice kanji every day, I can't learn them easily.

7.8 | zenzen 全然 | "totally," "quite," "(not) at all"

In a positive expression, *zenzen* emphasizes degree. In a negative expression, it indicates strong negation. Note that the use of *zenzen* in a positive expression is extremely colloquial.

EXAMPLES:

1. Kono shōsetsu wa **zenzen** omoshiroi kara, yonde mitara.
   この小説は**全然**面白いから、読んで見たら。
   This novel is quite interesting, so why not read it?

2. Sonna koto wa **zenzen** shirimasen.
   そんなことは**全然**知りません。
   I know absolutely nothing about the matter.

7.9 | issai 一切 | "all," "(not) at all"

In a positive expression, *issai* indicates a total number or amount. In a negative expression, it indicates strong denial and is esssentially interchangeable with *zenzen.*

EXAMPLES:

1. Kare wa tōshi ni shippai shite zaisan o **issai** ushinatta.
   彼は投資に失敗して財産を**一切**失った。
   He failed in his investment and lost all his fortune.

2. Kare wa sono jiken ni wa **issai** kankei ga arimasen.
   彼はその事件には**一切**関係がありません。
   He has nothing whatsoever to do with that incident.

271

7.10 | betsu ni 別に |

"separately," "(not) especially," "(not) particularly"

In a positive expression, *betsu ni* indicates that an action occurs separately or independently. In a negative expression, it indicates that someone or something is not exceptional or unusual.

EXAMPLES:

1. Kore wa **betsu ni** tsutsunde kudasai.

   これは**別に**包んでください。

   Please wrap this separately.

2. Ima no tokoro **betsu ni** mondai wa arimasen.

   今のところ**別に**問題はありません。

   There are no problems in particular right now.

PRACTICE 21 (7.1–7.10)

Circle the correct adverb among the choices given in parentheses.

1. Ono-san wa (mō/hotondo/mada) ano furui kuruma o unten shite iru.

   小野さんは（もう/ほとんど/まだ）あの古い車を運転している。

   Mr. Ono is still driving that old car.

2. Watashi wa kare no iken ni (nakanaka/zenzen/totemo) hantai desu.

私は彼の意見に（なかなか/全然/とても）反対です。

I am totally against his opinion.

3. Kono tegami wa kanji ga ōkute (totemo/mada/amari) yomenai.

この手紙は漢字が多くて（とても/まだ/あまり）読めない。

This letter has too many kanji, so I can hardly read it.

4. Kusuri o nonda noni netsu ga (amari/mada/nakanaka) sagarimasen.

薬を飲んだのに熱が（あまり/まだ/なかなか）下がりません。

Although I took some medicine, my fever just won't go down.

5. Yūbe wa ha ga itakute (mō/hotondo/issai) nemurenakatta.

ゆうべは歯が痛くて（もう/ほとんど/一切）眠れなかった。

Last night I hardly slept due to a toothache.

6. Kyō wa (dōmo/amari/hotondo) atsukunakatta node, ichinichijū niwa de hataraita.

今日は（どうも/あまり/ほとんど）暑くなかったので、一日中庭で働いた。

Since today wasn't very hot, I worked in the yard all day.

7. Mori-san wa (mada/dōmo/nakanaka) watashi-tachi to issho ni ikitakunai rashii.

森さんは（まだ/どうも/なかなか）私達と一緒に行きたくないらしい。

I somehow feel that Miss Mori doesn't want to come with us.

8. Kare wa arubaito de kaseida o-kane o (issai/betsu ni/ hotondo) ryokō ni tsukatta.

彼はアルバイトで稼いだお金を（一切/別に/ほとんど）旅行に使った。

He took all the money he had earned working part-time and spent it on his trip.

9. Kachō no uta o hajimete kikimashita ga (mada/issai/naka-naka) jōzu desu ne.

課長の歌を初めて聞きましたが（まだ/一切/なかなか）上手ですね。

I heard the section chief sing for the first time. He is quite good, isn't he?

10. Gogo (mō/betsu ni/hotondo) yōji ga nakereba, kaimono ni demo ikimasen ka.

午後（もう/別に/ほとんど）用事がなければ、買い物にでも行きません か。

If you don't have anything in particular to do this afternoon, would you like to go shopping or something?

8 Interrogative Adverbs and Adverbs Used with Conditionals

8.1 | **dō どう** | "how," "in what way," "how about"

Dō is used to inquire about the state of someone or something (Example 1) or the way in which something is done (Example 2). It is also used to elicit someone's opinion or to offer something to someone (Example 3).

EXAMPLES:

1. Kikai no chōshi wa **dō** desu ka.
   機械の調子は**どう**ですか。

   How is the condition of the machine?

2. Kono kanji wa **dō** yomimasu ka.
   この漢字は**どう**読みますか。

   How do you read this kanji?

3. Wain wa **dō** desu ka.
   ワインは**どう**ですか。

   How about some wine?

8.2 | **ikaga いかが** | "how," "how about"

Ikaga is used in polite speech to inquire about the state of someone or something or to offer something to someone.

EXAMPLES:

1. O-tōsama wa **ikaga** desu ka.
   お父様は**いかが**ですか。

   How is your father?

2. Kēki wa **ikaga** desu ka.
   ケーキは**いかが**ですか。

   How about some cake?

8.3 | dōshite どうして | "why," "how," "in what way"

Dōshite is used to inquire about a reason or cause or the way in which something is done.

EXAMPLES:

1. **Dōshite** kurasu ni okureta no desu ka.
   どうしてクラスに遅れたのですか。
   Why were you late for class?

2. Kore wa **dōshite** taberu no desu ka.
   これはどうして食べるのですか。
   How do you eat this?

8.4 | naze なぜ | "why"

Naze is used to inquire about a reason or cause. It is more formal than *dōshite*.

EXAMPLES:

1. Ogawa-san wa **naze** chūshokukai ni sanka shinai no desu ka.
   小川さんは**なぜ**昼食会に参加しないのですか。
   Why won't Miss Ogawa attend the luncheon?

2. Hayashi-san wa **naze** hayaku kaetta no desu ka.
   林さんは**なぜ**早く帰ったのですか。
   Why did Mr. Hayashi leave early?

8.5 | ittai 一体 | "What on earth!"

Ittai expresses the speaker's disbelief, astonishment or total lack of comprehension.

EXAMPLES:

1. **Ittai** dare ga sonna hidoi koto o shita no desu ka.
   一体だれがそんなひどいことをしたのですか。
   Who on earth did such a terrible thing?

2. **Ittai** sono jiko no genin wa nan desu ka.
   一体その事故の原因は何ですか。
   What on earth was the cause of that accident?

8.6 | moshi もし | "if"

Moshi in the form *moshi ... ba/ tara* indicates a condition or supposition.

EXAMPLES:

1. **Moshi** Kida-san ga tsugō ga warukereba, watashi ga kawari ni shusseki shimasu.
   もし木田さんが都合が悪ければ、私が代わりに出席します。
   If Mr. Kida is not available, I'll attend in his place.

2. **Moshi** ashita ame ga futtara, pikunikku no kawari ni koko de pātī o shimashō.
   もし明日雨が降ったら、ピクニックの代わりにここでパーティーをしましょう。
   If it rains tomorrow, let's have a party here in place of a picnic.

8.7 man'ichi/mangaichi 万一/万が一

"by any chance," "In the event ..."

Man'ichi or *mangaichi* in the form *man'ichi/mangaichi ... tara/te mo* indicates a hypothetical situation that is either highly unlikely or a worst-case scenario.

EXAMPLES:

1. **Man'ichi** gaikoku de byōki ni nattara dō shimasu ka.
   万一外国で病気になったらどうしますか。

   If you were to get sick in a foreign country, what would you do?

2. **Mangaichi** kare ga shusseki dekinaku te mo, kaigi wa okonai-masu.
   万が一彼が出席できなくても、会議は行います。

   Even if he should not be present—which is highly unlikely—the meeting will still take place.

8.8 tatoe たとえ   "even if"

Tatoe in the form *tatoe ... te mo* indicates a supposition.

EXAMPLES:

1. Jimu wa **tatoe** gakkō o yamete mo benkyō o tsuzukeru darō.
   ジムはたとえ学校を辞めても勉強を続けるだろう。

   Even if he quits school, Jim will probably continue his studies.

2. Kare wa **tatoe** yūmei ni natte mo mukashi no tomodachi o wasurenai to omou.

彼は**たとえ**有名になっても昔の友達を忘れないと思う。

I think that even if he becomes famous, he won't forget his old friends.

PRACTICE 22 (8.1–8.8)

Circle the correct adverb among the choices given in parentheses.

1. Kono yasai wa (ikaga/dō/naze) kirimashō ka.
   この野菜は（いかが/どう/なぜ）切りましょうか。
   How shall I cut this vegetable?

2. Samu wa (dō/naze/ikaga) sensei ni shikarareta no kashira.
   サムは（どう/なぜ/いかが）先生に叱られたのかしら。
   I wonder why Sam was scolded by his teacher.

3. Mō goji sugi na noni ano ko wa mada kaeranai. (Naze/man'ichi/ittai) dō shita no deshō.
   もう五時過ぎなのにあの子はまだ帰らない。（なぜ/万一/一体）どうしたのでしょう。
   It's already past five o'clock, but my child hasn't come back yet. What on earth could have happened?

4. (Dōshite/ikaga/naze) kono bin no futa o akeru no desu ka.
   （どうして/いかが/なぜ）このびんのふたを開けるのですか。
   How do you take the lid off this bottle?

5. (Tatoe/moshi/dōshite) kikai ga areba, Hokkaidō no yuki-matsuri o mitai.
   （たとえ/もし/どうして）機会があれば、北海道の雪祭りを見たい。
   If I have the opportunity, I'd like to see the Snow Festival in Hokkaido.

6. (Ittai/dō/man'ichi) jishin ga okotte mo kono chiiki wa hikaku-teki anzen darō.

（一体/どう/万一）地震が起こってもこの地域は比較的安全だろう。

In the event of an earthquake, this area would be relatively safe.

7. (Tatoe/dōshite/ittai) kachō ni tanomarete mo kono shigoto wa shitakunai.

（たとえ/どうして/一体）課長に頼まれてもこの仕事はしたくない。

I wouldn't do this work even if asked to by the section chief.

 # 9 Adverbs Expressing Desire, Conjecture or Resemblance

9.1 | dōzo どうぞ | "please"

Dōzo is used to offer something to someone or to ask someone to do something in a polite way.

EXAMPLES:

1. **Dōzo** o-sukina dake o-tori kudasai.
どうぞお好きなだけお取りください。

   Please take as much as you like.

2. **Dōzo** kochira de shibaraku o-machi kudasai.
どうぞこちらでしばらくお待ちください。

   Please wait here for a while.

9.2 | dōka どうか | "please"

Dōka is used to ask a favor in an emphatic way.

EXAMPLES:

1. **Dōka** dekiru dake hayaku kakutō o o-negai shimasu.
   どうか出来るだけ早く確答をお願いします。

   Please give us a definite answer as soon as possible.

2. **Dōka** shiharai o ato ikkagetsu nobashite kudasai.
   どうか支払いを後一か月延ばしてください。

   Please put off the payment for another month.

9.3 | zehi ぜひ | "by all means," "without fail," "definitely"

Zehi expressses a person's strong desire to do something.

EXAMPLES:

1. Kare wa rainen wa **zehi** Eberesuto ni noboritai to itte iru.
   彼は来年はぜひエベレストに登りたいと言っている。

   He says that he definitely wants to climb Mt. Everest next year.

2. Watashi wa musume no Akiko ni **zehi** barē o narawasetai.
   私は娘の秋子にぜひバレーを習わせたい。

   I really want to have my daughter Akiko learn ballet.

9.4 | tabun 多分 | "probably"

Tabun expresses the speaker's fairly confident conjecture.

EXAMPLES:

1. Kabushiki shijō wa **tabun** nennai ni kaifuku suru darō.
   株式市場は**多分**年内に回復するだろう。
   The stock market will probably revive within the year.

2. Kazuko-san wa sasotte mo **tabun** konai deshō.
   和子さんは誘っても**多分**来ないでしょう。
   Even if we invite her, Kazuko probably won't come.

9.5 | osoraku 恐らく | "probably"

Osoraku expresses the speaker's less-than-confident conjecture.

EXAMPLES:

1. Kimura-san wa **osoraku** raishū wa mada shukkin dekinai deshō.
   木村さんは**恐らく**来週はまだ出勤出来ないでしょう。
   Mr. Kimura probably won't be able to come to work next week.

2. Kono koto wa sensei to sōdan shinakereba, **osoraku** kaiketsu shinai darō.
   このことは先生と相談しなければ、**恐らく**解決しないだろう。
   This matter probably won't be solved unless we consult with our teacher.

9.6 | tashika 確か | "perhaps," "I suppose"

Tashika expresses the speaker's conjecture based on memory.

EXAMPLES:

1. Tanabe-san no kekkonshiki wa **tashika** rokugatsu itsuka datta to omoimasu.

   田辺さんの結婚式は**確か**六月五日だったと思います。

   As I recall, Mr. Tanabe's wedding ceremony was on June 5th.

2. Sono satsujin jiken wa **tashika** yonen mae no koto deshita.

   その殺人事件は**確か**四年前のことでした。

   That murder case was four years ago, if I remember right.

9.7 | dōyara どうやら | "likely"

Dōyara expresses the speaker's conjecture based on what he sees or feels.

EXAMPLES:

1. **Dōyara** ano futari wa mata giron shita rashii.

   どうやらあの二人はまた議論したらしい。

   It seems that those two had an argument again.

2. Kare wa **dōyara** watashi no kotoba o gokai shita rashii.

   彼は**どうやら**私の言葉を誤解したらしい。

   It is likely that he misunderstood my words.

9.8 | **chōdo ちょうど** | "just like," "as if," "just right"

Chōdo in the form *chōdo … no yōna* indicates a close resemblance between two things. In the *chōdo … no yōna* pattern, the form, nature or quality of one thing is being compared to that of another to show that the one is similar to the other in one respect or more.

EXAMPLES:

1. Ano kumo wa **chōdo** tori no yōna katachi o shite iru.
   あの雲は**ちょうど**鳥のような形をしている。
   That cloud is shaped just like a bird.

2. Ani wa **chōdo** nakunatta chichi no yō na kao o shite iru.
   兄は**ちょうど**亡くなった父のような顔をしている。
   My older brother has a face just like our late father.

9.9 | **marude まるで** | "just like," "as if"

Marude in the form *marude … no yōna* indicates a close resemblance between two things. In the *marude … no yōna* pattern, the form, nature or quality of one thing is being compared to that of another to show that the one is similar to the other in all respects, not just in one.

EXAMPLES:

1. Ano shōjo wa **marude** Nihon ningyō no yō ni kawaii.
   あの少女は**まるで**日本人形のようにかわいい。
   That girl is lovely, just like a Japanese doll.

2. Kaigan no keshiki wa utsukushiku **marude** ehagaki no yō da.

海岸の景色は美しく**まるで**絵葉書のようだ。

The coastal landscape is beautiful, just like a postcard.

9.10 | samo さも | "as if"

Samo indicates someone's behaving as if he were someone else or in a way that is out of character.

EXAMPLES:

1. Kare wa isogashikunai noni **samo** isogashi sō ni shite iru.

彼は忙しくないのに**さも**忙しそうにしている。

He behaves as if he were busy even though he is not.

2. Hayashi-san wa shokuba de wa **samo** kanemochi no yō ni furumatte iru.

林さんは職場では**さも**金持ちのようにふるまっている。

In her workplace, Miss Hayashi is behaving as if she were rich.

9.11 | atakamo あたかも | "as if"

Atakamo indicates someone's behaving as if he were someone else or in a way that is out of character. It is more formal than *samo*.

EXAMPLES:

1. Buchō ga rusu no aida, Sagawa-san wa **atakamo** buchō no yō ni furumatta.

部長が留守の間、佐川さんは**あたかも**部長のようにふるまった。

Mr. Sagawa behaved as if he were the division chief while the real division chief was away.

2. **Kanojo wa sono sakka to ichido atta dake na noni, atakamo shin'yū no yō ni itte iru.**

彼女はその作家と一度会っただけなのに、**あたかも**親友のように言っている。

Although she has only met the writer once, she speaks as if they were close friends.

PRACTICE 23 (9.1–9.11)

Circle the correct adverb among the choices given in parentheses.

1. **Jikan ga dekitara (dōzo/tabun/zehi) kaigai ryokō ga shitai.**

時間ができたら（どうぞ/多分/ぜひ）海外旅行がしたい。

If I could make some time, I sure would like to travel abroad.

2. **Ame wa (tabun/dōyara/tashika) yami sō desu.**

雨は（多分/どうやら/確か）止みそうです。

The rain is likely to stop.

3. **Ano kumo wa (samo/chōdo/osoraku) tori no yō ni miemasu ne.**

あの雲は（さも/ちょうど/恐らく）鳥のように見えますね。

That cloud looks just like a bird, doesn't it?

4. Honda-san wa (dōyara/tabun/tashika) nisannen mae ni
intai shita hazu desu.

本田さんは（どうやら/多分/確か）二三年前に引退したはずで
す。

I am quite sure that Mr. Honda retired a few years ago.

5. (Dōka/atakamo/zehi) kono michi ni kuruma o tomenai yō ni
o-negai shimasu.

（どうか/あたかも/ぜひ）この道に車を止めないようにお願い
します。

Please don't park your car on this street.

6. Kore kara kono kōjō no seisan wa (tashika/osoraku/dōyara)
genshō suru darō.

これからこの工場の生産は（確か/恐らく/どうやら）減少する
だろう。

The production at this plant will probably decrease from now on.

7. Kanojo wa yakusoku o yabutte mo (tashika/tabun/samo)
wasurete shimatta yō ni furumau.

彼女は約束を破っても（確か/多分/さも）忘れてしまったよう
にふるまう。

Even if she breaks her promise, she'll behave as if she had forgotten
all about it.

8. Nimotsu o hakobu noni (zehi/tabun/chōdo) motto ōkii
torakku ga iru deshō.

荷物を運ぶのに（ぜひ/多分/ちょうど）もっと大きいトラック
が要るでしょう。

We'll probably need a bigger truck to transport the goods.

9. Kare wa shashin wa ama na noni (chōdo/atakamo/osoraku) puro no yō ni hanashite iru.

彼は写真はアマなのに（ちょうど/あたかも/恐らく）プロのように話している。

Although he is an amateur photographer, he talks as if he were a pro.

A P P E N D I X E S

ADJECTIVES

ANSWERS TO PRACTICES (PART I, CONJUGATION)

Practice 1

A.

1. atsukunai 暑くない 2. mushiatsukunai 蒸し暑くない 3. atatakakunai 暖かくない
4. suzushikunai 涼しくない

B.

1. nagakatta 長かった, nagakunakatta 長くなかった 2. mijikakatta 短かった, mijika-
kunakatta 短くなかった 3. ōkatta 多かった, ōkunakatta 多くなかった 4. suku-
nakatta 少なかった, sukunakunakatta 少なくなかった

C.

1. hayakute 早くて 2. hayakute 速くて 3. osokute 遅くて 4. takakute 高くて 5. yasu-
kute 安くて 6. hikukute 低くて

D.

1. yoku よく 2. waruku 悪く 3. isogashiku 忙しく 4. yakamashiku やかましく

E.

1. muzukashikereba 難しければ, muzukashikattara 難しかったら 2. yasashikereba
易しければ, yasashikattara 易しかったら 3. omoshirokereba 面白ければ, omoshirokatta 面白かったら 4. tsumaranakereba つまらなければ, tsumaranakattara つま
らなかったら

F.

1. atarashikattari 新しかったり 2. furukattari 古かったり 3. omokattari 重かったり
4. karukattari 軽かったり

G.

1. tōsa 遠さ 2. chikasa 近さ 3. wakasa 若さ 4. tanoshisa 楽しさ

Practice 2

A.

1. kantan de (wa) nai 簡単で(は)ない 2. fukuzatsu de (wa) nai 複雑で(は)ない

B.

1. jōzu datta 上手だった, jōzu de (wa) nakatta 上手で(は)なかった 2. heta datta 下手
だった, heta de (wa) nakatta 下手で(は)なかった 3. benri datta 便利だった, benri

de (wa) nakatta 便利で(は)なかった 4. fuben datta 不便だった, fuben de (wa) nakatta 不便で(は)なかった

C.

1. anzen de 安全で 2. kiken de 危険で 3. hitsuyō de 必要で

D.

1. hima ni ひまに 2. taihen ni 大変に 3. mendō ni 面倒に

E.

1. suki nara(ba) 好きなら(ば), sukidattara 好きだったら 2. kirai nara (ba) 嫌いなら(ば), kiraidattara 嫌いだったら 3. jūdai nara (ba) 重大なら(ば), jūdaidattara 重大だったら

F.

1. shiawase dattari 幸せだったり 2. fukō dattari 不幸だったり 3. kenkō dattari 健康だったり

G.

1. rippasa 立派さ 2. seikakusa 正確さ

Practice 3

A.

1. kaitai 買いたい 2. uritai 売りたい 3. mitai 見たい

B.

1. yametakunai 辞めたくない 2. okuritakunai 送りたくない 3. arukitakunai 歩きたくない

C.

1. naraitakatta 習いたかった, naraitakunakatta 習いたくなかった 2. benkyō shitakatta 勉強したかった, benkyō shitakunakatta 勉強したくなかった

D.

1. kakitakute 書きたくて 2. yomitakute 読みたくて

E.

1. tabetakereba 食べたければ, tabetakattara 食べたかったら 2. nomitakereba 飲みたければ, nomitakattara 飲みたかったら 3. kitakereba 来たければ, kitakattara 来たかったら

F.

1. asobitasa 遊びたさ 2. aitasa 会いたさ

Practice 4

A.

1. oishi sō da おいしそうだ 2. mazu sō da まずそうだ 3. daiji sō da 大事そうだ

B.

1. ama sō de (wa) nai 甘そうで(は)ない 2. kara sō de (wa) nai 辛そうで(は)ない 3. kiken sō de (wa) nai 危険そうで(は)ない

C.

1. tsuyo sō datta 強そうだった, tsuyo sō de (wa) nakatta 強そうで(は)なかった

2. benri sō datta 便利そうだった, benri sō de (wa) nakatta 便利そうで(は)なかった
3. hitsuyō sō datta 必要そうだった, hitsuyō sō de (wa) nakatta 必要そうで(は)なかった

D.
1. yawaraka sō de 柔かそうで 2. mezurashi sō de 珍しそうで 3. kōka sō de 高価そうで

E.
1. kanashi sō ni 悲しそうに 2. omoshiro sō ni 面白そうに 3. meiwaku sō ni 迷惑そうに

F.
1. yowa sō nara 弱そうなら, yowa sō dattara 弱そうだったら 2. hiro sō nara 広そうなら, hiro sō dattara 広そうだったら 3. fukuzatsu sō nara 複雑そうなら, fukuzatsu sō dattara 複雑そうだったら

ANSWERS TO PRACTICES (PART II, USAGE OF ADJECTIVES)

Practice 1

A.
1. Kōen no ike wa fukakunai. 公園の池は深くない。
2. Kono kaban wa benri de wa arimasen. このかばんは便利ではありません。
3. Watashi-tachi no kyōshitsu wa akarukunai desu/akaruku arimasen.
   私達の教室は明るくないです/明るくありません。
4. Kono heya wa tenjō ga takakunai. この部屋は天井が高くない。

B.
1. Ano resutoran wa yūmei datta. あのレストランは有名だった。
2. Kare no heya wa semakatta desu. 彼の部屋は狭かったです。
3. Depāto no ten'in wa shinsetsu deshita. デパートの店員は親切でした。
4. Jimu wa tenisu ga heta datta. ジムはテニスが下手だった。

C.
1. Watashi no kaisha wa eki kara tōkunakatta.
   私の会社は駅から遠くなかった。
2. Kinō no shiken wa muzukashikunakatta desu/muzukashiku arimasen deshita.
   昨日の試験は難しくなかったです/難しくありませんでした。
3. Sono machi no chikatetsu wa kirei de wa nakatta.
   その町の地下鉄はきれいではなかった。
4. Buraun-san wa sashimi ga kirai de wa/ja arimasen deshita.
   ブラウンさんはさしみが嫌いでは/じゃありませんでした。

D.
1. yasashikat 易しかっ 2. ondan 温暖 3. tashika 確か 4. oishiku おいしく 5. yasu-kunakat 安くなかっ 6. hitsuyō dat 必要だっ 7. kanashikat 悲しかっ

Practice 2

1. kantan 簡単   2. subarashikatta すばらしかった   3. shinsen 新鮮   4. tōku 遠く
5. shizuka 静か, fuben 不便   6. yūmei da 有名だ, oishiku おいしく   7. kirei da きれいだ, jōbu 丈夫

Practice 3

1. kiraina 嫌いな   2. kireina きれいな, yoku よく   3. fukai 深い, kiken 危険   4. nigai 苦い, oishiku おいしく   5. isogashikatta 忙しかった, hima ひま   6. genkaku da 厳格だ, shinsetsuna 親切な   7. kashikoi かしこい, sunao de wa/janai 素直では/じゃない   8. omokunakatta 重くなかった, tashika 確か

Practice 4

1. tsumetakatta 冷たかった, takakat 高かっ   2. jōzu dat 上手だっ, kirai 嫌い
3. kashikokat かしこかっ, shōjiki dat 正直だっ   4. suzushii 涼しい, atatakai 暖かい, kaiteki 快適   5. kantan dat 簡単だっ, yokunakat よくなかっ

Practice 5

1. semai 狭い   2. utsukushii 美しい   3. aokatta 青かった   4. hikui to 低いと
5. fukuzatsu da kara 複雑だから   6. shōjikina node 正直なので   7. nagai tori 長い鳥
8. himana toki ひまな時   9. jōzuna Amerikajin 上手なアメリカ人

Practice 6

1. kibishii kamoshirenai 厳しいかもしれない   2. atataka sō da 暖かそうだ   3. mendō datta rashii 面倒だったらしい   4. yosa sō da よさそうだ, takai ni chigainai 高いにちがいない   5. fuka sō 深そう, tsumetai kamoshirenai 冷たいかもしれない   6. damena yō da 駄目なようだ   7. kanashi sō 悲しそう, warukatta ni chigainai 悪かったにちがいない

Practice 7

1. ō sugiru 多すぎる, tekitō de/ja nai kamoshire 適当では/じゃないかもしれ   2. asasugiru 浅すぎる, oyoginikui 泳ぎにくい   3. mochiyasui 持ちやすい, benri 便利   4. fuka sō 深そう, wakasugiru 若すぎる   5. hitsuyō 必要, takasugiru 高すぎる   6. sawagashikat さわがしかっ, kikinikukat 聞きにくかっ   7. hoshii 欲しい, hoshigat 欲しがっ   8. ikitai 行きたい, ikitaku 行きたく   9. karasugiru 辛すぎる, tabetagara 食べたがら

Practice 8

1. chiisaku 小さく, furukat 古かっ   2. shizuka 静か, kaiteki 快適   3. shinsetsu de wa/ja 親切では/じゃ, fuyukai 不愉快   4. abunaku 危なく   5. kiken 危険, takute たくて   6. nagaku 長く, mijikaku 短く   7. binbō de 貧乏で, yūfuku de 裕福で   8. takaku 高く, mushiatsukute 蒸し暑くて   9. ganjō 頑丈, anzen de 安全で

Practice 9

1. mijikaku 短く   2. genki ni 元気に   3. osoku 遅く   4. sugoku すごく, benri ni 便利に

5. ō kiku 大きく   6. isogashikat 忙しかっ, hima ni ひまに   7. hidoku ひどく, sabishiku さびしく   8. atsu 厚, usuku 薄く

Practice 10
1. chikakere 近けれ   2. tsumetakat 冷たかっ   3. hitsuyō 必要, takaku 高く   4. kirai dat 嫌いだっ   5. fukuzatsu 複雑, fukuzatsuna 複雑な   6. ganjō 頑丈, ganjōna 頑丈な, anzen 安全   7. wakakereba 若ければ, daitan ni 大胆に   8. yūfuku nara/yūfuku de areba 裕福なら/裕福であれば, zeitaku ni ぜいたくに

Practice 11
1. omoshirokat 面白かっ, omoshirokunakat 面白くなかっ   2. isogashikat 忙しかっ, hima dat ひまだっ   3. sunao dat 素直だっ, sunao de nakat 素直でなかっ   4. suki dat 好きだっ, kirai dat 嫌いだっ   5. amakat 甘かっ, karakat 辛かっ, oishiku おいしく
6. kaiteki dat 快適だっ, kaiteki de nakat 快適でなかっ

Practice 12
1. omosa 重さ   2. hirosa 広さ   3. jūdaisa 重大さ   4. amami 甘み   5. itami 痛み
6. seiketsusa 清潔さ   7. wakasa 若さ, tsuyomi 強み

Practice 13
A.
1. Mori-san no okosan wa kawaikute irasshaimasu.
   森さんのお子さんはかわいくていらっしゃいます。
2. Ano kata wa borantia no o-shigoto ni nesshin de irasshaimasu.
   あの方はボランティアのお仕事に熱心でいらっしゃいます。
3. Shachō wa sanji made o-isogashikute irasshaimasu.
   社長は三時までお忙しくていらっしゃいます。
4. Sumisu-san wa Nihon ryōri ga o-suki de irasshaimasu.
   スミスさんは日本料理がお好きでいらっしゃいます。
5. Ogawa-sensei wa gakusei katsudō ni kyōryokuteki de irasshaimasu.
   小川先生は学生活動に協力的でいらっしゃいます。

B.
1. Rainen wa Itaria e ikitō gozaimasu.
   来年はイタリアへ行きとうございます。
2. Chichi no byōki wa karū gozaimashita.
   父の病気は軽うございました。
3. Kono hen de jūgatsu ni yuki ga furu no wa mezurashū gozaimasu.
   この辺で十月に雪が降るのは珍しゅうございます。
4. Tetsuzuki wa omotta yori mendō de gozaimashita.
   手続きは思ったより面倒でございました。
5. Ano resutoran wa takō gozaimasu ne.
   あのレストランは高うございますね。

SENTENCE PATTERNS

1. Noun Modifiers
1.1   Adj + N, 35
1.2   Adj + no の "one", 36
1.3   motto もっと + Adj "-er," "more", 37
1.4   ichiban 一番 + Adj "-est," "most", 37

2. Adjectival Predicates
2.1   N wa/ga は/が + Adj aff "NOUN is ADJECTIVE", 39
2.2   N wa/ga は/が + Adj neg "NOUN is not ADJECTIVE", 40
2.3   N1 wa は N2 ga が + Adj "As for NOUN 1, NOUN 2 is ADJECTIVE", 41

3. Expressions Following Adjectival Predicates
3.1   Adj pred + darō だろう "probably", 45
3.2   Adj pred + ka か "…?", 46
3.3   Adj pred + ne ね "… isn't it/he?" "… is it/he?", 47
3.4   Adj pred + yo よ "I tell you", 48
3.5   Adj pred + ga が "but", 48
3.6   Adj pred + keredomo けれども "although", 49
3.7   Adj pred + dake da だけだ "only," "just," "that's all", 51
3.8   Adj pred + hazu da はずだ "I expect that ～", 52
3.9   Adj pred + koto ga aru ことがある "There are/were times when ～", 53
3.10 Adj pred + no/koto の/こと "that ～", 54
3.11 Adj pred + kashira/kana かしら/かな "I wonder", 55
3.12 Adj pred + sō da そうだ "I heard that ～", 56
3.13 Adj pred + shi し "and what's more," "so," "moreover", 59
3.14 Adj pred + ka dō ka かどうか "whether or not", 59
3.15 Adj pred + noni のに "although", 60
3.16 Adj pred + toki 時 "when", 63
3.17 Adj pred + uchi ni うちに "while", 64
3.18 Adj pred + to と "if", 65
3.19 Adj pred + kara から "because," "so", 66
3.20 Adj pred + node ので "because," "so", 67
3.21 Adj pred + dake de naku だけでなく "not only ～, but also ～", 68
3.22 Adj pred + N to make a relative clause, 69

4. Auxiliary Adjectives
4.1   Adj pred + kamoshirenai かもしれない "might", 71
4.2   Adj pred + ni chigainai にちがいない "must be," "no doubt", 72
4.3   Adj pred + rashii らしい "seem," "look like", 73

BASIC JAPANESE ADJECTIVES

1. I-Adjectives

abunai, 危ない dangerous

akai, 赤い red

akarui, 明るい bright

amai, 甘い sweet

aoi, 青い blue

arai, 荒い rude

arai, 粗い coarse

arigatai, ありがたい thankful

asai, 浅い shallow

atarashii, 新しい new, fresh

atatakai, 暖かい warm (weather)

atatakai, 温かい warm (water)

atsui, 暑い hot (weather)

atsui, 熱い hot (coffee)

atsui, 厚い thick (board)

awatadashii, あわただしい hurried

bakarashii, ばからしい foolish, silly

chiisai, 小さい small

chikai, 近い near

darashinai, だらしない untidy

darui, だるい languid

egatai, 得難い hard to obtain

erai, 偉い great

fukai, 深い deep

furui, 古い old

fusawashii, ふさわしい suitable

futoi, 太い thick (thread)

gikochinai, ぎこちない awkward

hageshii, 激しい violent

hakanai, はかない ephemeral

haradatashii, 腹立たしい provoking

hayai, 早い early

hayai, 速い speedy

hazukashii, 恥ずかしい bashful, shameful

hidoi, ひどい terrible

hikui, 低い low

hiroi, 広い large, spacious

hisashii, 久しい long-continued

hitoshii, 等しい equal

hokorashii, 誇らしい proud

hoshii, 欲しい want

hosoi, 細い thin, narrow

ichijirushii, 著しい remarkable

ii, いい good

ikagawashii, いかがわしい doubtful

isagiyoi, 潔い upright, brave

isamashii, 勇ましい brave

isogashii, 忙しい busy

itai, 痛い painful

jirettai, じれったい irritating

josainai, 如才ない shrewd, tactful

kanashii, 悲しい sad

karai, 辛い salty, hot

karui, 軽い light

kashikoi, かしこい wise, bright, intelligent

kawaii, かわいい cute, lovely

katai, かたい tough, hard
kayowai, か弱い delicate, feeble
kayui, かゆい itchy
kedakai, 気高い noble
kemui, けむい smoky
kemutai, けむたい smoky
kewashii, 険しい steep
kibishii, 厳しい strict
kiiroi, 黄色い yellow
kimuzukashii, 気難しい fastidious
kitanai, きたない dirty
kitsui, きつい tight, strict
kiyoi, 清い clean, pure
kiyowai, 気弱い fainthearted
kizuyoi, 気強い stouthearted
kōbashii, 香ばしい fragrant
kodakai, 小高い slightlyelevated
kōgōshii, 神々しい divine
koi, 濃い dark, thick
kokorobosoi, 心細い lonely, uneasy
kokoroyasui, 心安い intimate, friendly
kokoroyoi, 快い pleasant
komakai, 細かい small, detailed
konomashii, 好ましい desirable
kowai, こわい fearful
kurai, 暗い dark
kuroi, 黒い black
kurushii, 苦しい painful
kusai, くさい stinking
kuwashii, 詳しい detailed
kuyashii, くやしい regrettable

maatarashii, 真新しい brand-new
mabushii, まぶしい dazzling
machidōshii, 待ち遠しい long in waiting
magirawashii, まぎらわしい confusing
marui, 丸い round
mazui, まずい unsavory
mazushii, 貧しい poor
meatarashii, 目新しい novel
memagurushii, 目まぐるしい dizzy
memeshii, 女々しい unmanly

mezamashii, 目覚しい remarkable
mezurashii, 珍しい rare
mijikai, 短い short
minikui, みにくい ugly
misuborashii, みすぼらしい shabby
mittomonai, みっともない ugly
mizumizushii, みずみずしい fresh
mizuppoi, 水っぽい watery
monomonoshii, 物々しい showy
mugoi, むごい cruel
munashii, むなしい empty
mushiatsui, 蒸し暑い humid
muzukashii, 難しい difficult

nadakai, 名高い famous
nagai, 長い long
namagusai, 生臭い fishy
nasakebukai, 情け深い benevolent
natsukashii, なつかしい dear, longed for
nayamashii, 悩ましい distressful
nebarizuyoi, 粘り強い tenacious
negurushii, 寝苦しい wakeful
nemui, 眠い sleepy
nemutai, 眠たい sleepy
netamashii, ねたましい jealous
nezuyoi, 根強い deep-rooted
niawashii, 似合わしい suitable
nibui, 鈍い dull
nigai, 苦い bitter
niganigashii, 苦々しい disgusting
nikui, 憎い hateful
nikurashii, 憎らしい hateful
noroi, のろい slow
nozomashii, 望ましい desirable
nurui, ぬるい lukewarm

ōi, 多い many, much
oishii, おいしい delicious, good, tasty
okashii, おかしい funny
ōkii, 大きい big
omoi, 重い heavy, serious
omoshiroi, 面白い interesting

omotai, 重たい heavy
osoi, 遅い late, slow
osoroshii, 恐ろしい fearful
otokorashii, 男らしい manly
otonashii, おとなしい gentle, obedient

rikutsuppoi, 理屈っぽい argumentative
ririshii, りりしい gallant

sabishii, さびしい lonely
samui, 寒い cold
sawagashii, 騒がしい noisy
semai, 狭い narrow, small
shibui, 渋い astringent
shibutoi, しぶとい stubborn
shimeppoi, 湿っぽい damp
shiroi, 白い white
shitashii, 親しい intimate
sosokkashii, そそっかしい careless
sōzōshii, 騒々しい noisy
subarashii, 素晴らしい splendid
sugasugashii, すがすがしい refreshing
sugoi, すごい terrific
sukunai, 少ない few, little
suppai, 酸っぱい sour
surudoi, 鋭い sharp
susamajii, すさまじい dreadful
suzushii, 涼しい cool

tadashii, 正しい correct
tadotadoshii, たどたどしい faltering
takai, 高い high, expensive
takumashii, たくましい robust
tanomoshii, 頼もしい reliable, promising
tanoshii, 楽しい enjoyable
tegowai, 手ごわい formidable
toboshii, 乏しい scarce
togetogeshii, とげとげしい sharp, harsh
tōi, 遠い far
tōtoi, 尊い noble, valuable
tsumaranai, つまらない boring

tsumashii, つましい frugal
tsumetai, 冷たい cold
tsurenai, つれない heartless
tsutanai, つたない unskillful
tsutsumashii, つつましい modest
tsuyoi, 強い strong

umai, うまい delicious, skillful
urayamashii, うらやましい enviable
ureshii, 嬉しい glad, happy
urusai, うるさい annoying, troublesome
uruwashii, 麗しい beautiful
usugurai, 薄暗い dusky
usui, 薄い thin, light
utagawashii, 疑わしい doubtful
utsukushii, 美しい beautiful

wabishii, わびしい miserable, lonely
wakai, 若い young
wakawakashii, 若々しい youthful
warugashikoi, 悪がしこい cunning
warui, 悪い bad

yakamashii, 喧しい noisy
yasashii, 易しい easy
yasashii, 優しい gentle
yasui, 安い inexpensive
yasuppoi, 安っぽい cheap
yawarakai, 柔かい soft
yayakoshii, ややこしい complicated
yoi, よい good
yōjinbukai, 用心深い careful, prudent
yorokobashii, 喜ばしい happy
yosoyososhii, よそよそしい aloof
yowai, 弱い weak
yowayowashii, 弱々しい weak-looking, fragile
yurui, 緩い loose

zurui, ずるい cunning
zūzūshii, ずうずうしい impudent

2. *Na*-Adjectives

aimaina, あいまいな ambiguous
akirakana, 明らかな apparent
angaina, 案外な unexpected
anshinna, 安心な relieved
anzenna, 安全な safe
asahakana, 浅はかな shallow-minded
atatakana, 暖かな warm
awarena, あわれな pitiful, miserable
azayakana, 鮮やかな bright

bakana, ばかな foolish
bakudaina, 莫大な enormous
benrina, 便利な convenient
bimina, 美味な delicious
binbōna, 貧乏な poor
binkanna, 敏感な sensitive
binsokuna, 敏速な quick
bitekina, 美的な aesthetic
buenryona, 無遠慮な unreserved
bujina, 無事な safe
bukimina, 無気味な uncanny
bukiyōna, 無器用な unskillful
bukkirabōna, ぶっきらぼうな abrupt
bunkatekina, 文化的な cultural
byōdōna, 平等な equal
byōtekina, 病的な morbid

chachina, ちゃちな cheap
chamena, 茶目な mischievous
chāminguna, チャーミングな charming
chiisana, 小さな small
chinpuna, 陳腐な trite
chitekina, 知的な intellectual
chōhōna, 重宝な valuable
chūjitsuna, 忠実な faithful
chūshōtekina, 抽象的な abstract

daihyōtekina, 代表的な representative
daijina, 大事な important
dainamikkuna, ダイナミックな dynamic
daitanna, 大胆な bold

damena, 駄目な useless
danpentekina, 断片的な fragmentary
danseitekina, 男性的な manly
dasantekina, 打算的な calculative
datōna, 妥当な appropriate
dentōtekina, 伝統的な traditional
derikētona, デリケートな delicate
dokutokuna, 独特な peculiar
doramachikkuna ドラマチックな dramatic
dōtokutekina, 道徳的な moral

eikyūtekina, 永久的な permanent
eirina, 鋭利な sharp
ekizocikkuna, エキゾチックな exotic
enerugisshuna, エネルギッシュな energetic
enmanna, 円満な harmonious
eregantona, エレガントな elegant
erochikkuna, エロチックな erotic

fuanna, 不安な uneasy
fuanteina, 不安定な unstable
fubenna, 不便な inconvenient
fudōtokuna, 不道徳な immoral
fugōrina, 不合理な unreasonable
fuhōna, 不法な illegal
fujitsuna, 不実な unfaithful
fujūbunna, 不十分な insufficient
fujunna, 不順な unseasonable
fujunna, 不純な impure
fukakaina, 不可解な incomprehensible
fukanōna, 不可能な impossible
fukanzenna, 不完全な imperfect
fuketsuna, 不潔な dirty
fukisokuna, 不規則な irregular
fukitsuna, 不吉な ominous
fukōheina, 不公平な unfair
fukōna, 不幸な unhappy
fukuzatsuna, 複雑な complicated
furesshuna, フレッシュな fresh
fuseikakuna, 不正確な inaccurate
fushiawasena, 不幸せな unhappy
fushigina, 不思議な mysterious

fushinsetsuna, 不親切な unkind
fushizenna, 不自然な unnatural
futsugōna, 不都合な inconvenient
fuunna, 不運な unfortunate
fuyukaina, 不愉快な unpleasant

ganjōna, 頑丈な strong, durable
gankona, 頑固な stubborn
gehinna, 下品な vulgar
gekitekina, 劇的な dramatic
genjitsutekina, 現実的な realistic
genkakuna, 厳格な strict
genkina, 元気な healthy
genshitekina, 原始的な primitive
genshukuna, 厳粛な solemn
gōjōna, 強情な stubborn
gōkana, 豪華な gorgeous
gōmanna, ごう慢な arrogant
gōritekina, 合理的な rational
guretsuna, 愚劣な foolish
gurōbaruna, グローバルな global
gurotesukuna, グロテスクな grotesque
gutaitekina, 具体的な concrete
gūzenna, 偶然な accidental

hadena, 派手な showy
hakujōna, 薄情な coldhearted
hankana, 繁華な bustling
hansamuna, ハンサムな handsome
heibonna, 平凡な commonplace
heiseina, 平静な calm
hetana, 下手な unskillful
hibonna, 非凡な uncommon
hidōna, 非道な inhuman
hikantekina, 悲観的な pessimistic
hikutsuna, 卑屈な mean
hikyōna, 卑怯な cowardly
himana, ひまな free (not busy)
hitsuyōna, 必要な necessary
hōfuna, 豊富な abundant
hōkentekina, 封建的な feudal
hoshutekina, 保守的な conservative

hōtekina, 法的な legal

ichijitekina, 一時的な temporary
idaina, 偉大な great
igaina, 意外な unexpected
ijiwaruna, 意地悪な ill-natured
ijōna, 異常な abnormal
ikanna, 遺憾な regrettable
ikina, 粋な chic
inkenna, 陰険な cunning
inkina, 陰気な gloomy
iroirona, 色々な various
itazurana, いたずらな mischievous
iyana, 嫌な distasteful

jakenna, 邪険な cruel
jidōtekina, 自動的な automatic
jimutekina, 事務的な businesslike
jindōtekina, 人道的な humane
jinkōtekina, 人工的な artificial
jisshitsutekina, 実質的な substantial
jiyūna, 自由な free
jōbuna, 丈夫な healthy, durable
jōhinna, 上品な refined
joseitekina, 女性的な feminine
jōzuna, 上手な skillful
jūbunna, 十分な sufficient
jūdaina, 重大な important
jūjunna, 従順な obedient
junjōna, 純情な purehearted
jūyōna, 重要な important

kaihōtekina, 開放的な openhearted
kaikatsuna, 快活な cheerful
kaitekina, 快適な comfortable
kakkitekina, 画期的な epoch-making
kandaina, 寛大な generous
kanjōtekina, 感情的な emotional
kanshōtekina, 感傷的な sentimental
kantanna, 簡単な simple
kanzenna, 完全な perfect
kappatsuna, 活発な lively

kattena, 勝手な selfish
kawaisōna, かわいそうな pitiful
keisotsuna, 軽率な hasty
keizaitekina, 経済的な economical
kekkōna, 結構な good
kenkōna, 健康な healthy
kenmeina, 賢明な wise
kibatsuna, 奇抜な original
kikenna, 危険な dangerous
kinbenna, 勤勉な industrious, diligent
kindaitekina, 近代的な modern
kiraina, 嫌いな distasteful
kirakuna, 気楽な carefree
kireina, きれいな pretty, clean
kisokutekina, 規則的な regular
kiyōna, 器用な skillful
kōdaina, 広大な vast
kōfukuna, 幸福な happy
kofūna, 古風な old-fashioned
kōkana, 高価な expensive
kōkina, 高貴な noble
kokusaitekina, 国際的な international
kōkyūna, 高級な high-class
konnanna, 困難な difficult
kōshōna, 高尚な refined
kōunna, 幸運な fortunate
kyodaina, 巨大な huge
kyōikutekina, 教育的な educational
kyōryokuna, 強力な powerful
kyōryokutekina, 協力的な cooperative

majimena, まじめな serious
makkana, 真っ赤な deep red
makkurana, 真っ暗な pitch-dark
makkurona, 真っ黒な deep black
manzokuna, 満足な satisfactory
marena, まれな rare
massaona, 真っ青な deep blue/green
masshirona, 真っ白な pure white
massuguna, 真っ直ぐな straight
meihakuna, 明白な clear
meiwakuna, 迷惑な troublesome, annoy-
　　ing

mendōna, 面倒な troublesome
minshutekina, 民主的な democratic
miryokutekina, 魅力的な charming
modanna, モダンな modern
mōretsuna, 猛烈な terrible
mottomona, もっともな reasonable
muchina, 無知な ignorant
mudana, 無駄な wasteful
muekina, 無益な useless
mugaina, 無害な harmless
muimina, 無意味な meaningless
mujakina, 無邪気な innocent
munōna, 無能な incompetent
murina, 無理な unreasonable
musekininna, 無責任な irresponsible

nadarakana, なだらかな gently sloping
nagoyakana, 和やかな peaceful
naībuna, ナイーブな naïve
namerakana, 滑らかな smooth
nesshinna, 熱心な enthusiastic
nigatena, 苦手な unskillful
nigiyakana, にぎやかな bustling
nodokana, のどかな peaceful
nōritsutekina, 能率的な efficient
nyūnenna, 入念な careful

ōgesana, 大げさな exaggerated
ōheina, 横柄な arrogant
ondanna, 温暖な mild
onshirazuna, 恩知らずな ungrateful
onwana, 温和な gentle
orijinaruna, オリジナルな original
ōtomachikkuna, オートマチックな auto-
　　matic

popyurāna, ポピュラーな popular
puraibētona, プライベートな private

rakkantekina, 楽観的な optimistic
rakuna, 楽な comfortable
ranbōna, 乱暴な violent
reiseina, 冷静な cool

rekishitekina, 歴史的な historical
rikōna, 利口な bright, intelligent
rikotekina, 利己的な selfish
rippana, 立派な fine
riseitekina, 理性的な rational
risōtekina, 理想的な ideal
romanchikkuna, ロマンチックな romantic
ronritekina, 論理的な logical
rōrenna, 老練な veteran
ryōshintekina, 良心的な conscientious

saiwaina, 幸いな fortunate
samazamana, 様々な various
sawayakana, さわやかな refreshing
seidaina, 盛大な grand
seijitsuna, 誠実な faithful
seijōna, 正常な normal
seiketsuna, 清潔な clean, pure
seikakuna, 正確な accurate
seikōna, 精巧な exquisite
seishintekina, 精神的な spiritual
seitōna, 正当な just
sekaitekina, 世界的な worldwide
sekkyokutekina, 積極的な positive
senchimentaruna センチメンタルな sentimental
senjōtekina, 扇情的な sensational
shakōtekina, 社交的な sociable
shiawasena, 幸せな happy
shinchōna, 慎重な prudent
shinkenna, 真剣な serious
shinmitsuna, 親密な intimate
shinpaina, 心配な uneasy
shinpina, 神秘な mysterious
shinpotekina, 進歩的な progressive
shinpuruna, シンプルな simple
shinseina, 神聖な divine
shinsenna, 新鮮な fresh
shinsetsuna, 親切な kind
shitekina, 私的な private
shizenna, 自然な natural
shizukana, 静かな quiet, calm

shōjikina, 正直な honest
shōkyokutekina, 消極的な negative
shōsaina, 詳細な detailed
shukantekina, 主観的な subjective
sōgonna, 荘厳な grand
sōjukuna, 早熟な precocious
somatsuna, 粗末な humble
sotchokuna, 率直な frank
sukina, 好きな favorite
sunaona, 素直な obedient
sutekina, 素敵な splendid

tabōna, 多忙な busy
taidana, 怠惰な lazy
taihenna, 大変な difficult
taikutsuna, 退屈な boring
tairana, 平らな even
taisetsuna, 大切な important
tanchōna, 単調な monotonous
tanjunna, 単純な simple
tankina, 短気な short-tempered
tasaina, 多才な versatile
tashikana, 確かな accurate
teikyūna, 低級な low-class
teineina, ていねいな polite
tekisetsuna, 適切な appropriate
tekitōna, 適当な appropriate
tokubetsuna, 特別な special
tokuina, 得意な skillful
tōmeina, 透明な transparent
tsūkaina, 痛快な thrilling
tsūzokuna, 通俗な popular

ubuna, うぶな naïve

wagamamana, 我がままな selfish
waridakana, 割高な comparatively high-priced
wariyasuna, 割安な comparatively low-priced
wazukana, 僅かな little, few

yabanna, 野蛮な barbarous
yahina, 野卑な vulgar
yasurakana, 安らかな peaceful
yawarakana, 柔らかな soft
yōchina, 幼稚な infantile
yōina, 容易な easy
yūbōna, 有望な promising
yūdokuna, 有毒な poisonous
yūekina, 有益な useful
yūfukuna, 裕福な rich
yūgaina, 有害な harmful
yūgana, 優雅な elegant
yukaina, 愉快な delightful
yūkanna, 勇敢な brave
yūkōna, 有効な effective
yūkōtekina, 友好的な friendly

yūmeina, 有名な famous
yunīkuna, ユニークな unique
yūnōna, 有能な competent
yūrina, 有利な profitable
yūryokuna, 有力な powerful
yūshūna, 優秀な superior
yutakana, 豊かな abundant
yūutsuna, ゆううつな melancholic

zankokuna, 残酷な cruel
zannenna, 残念な regrettable
zeitakuna, ぜいたくな luxurious
zenryōna, 善良な good
zokuakuna, 俗悪な vulgar
zuborana, ずぼらな negligent
zuiina, 随意な optional

ENGLISH-JAPANESE ADJECTIVE LIST

abnormal, ijōna 異常な
abrupt, bukkirabōna ぶっきらぼうな
abstract, chūshōtekina 抽象的な
abundant, yutakana 豊かな, hōfuna 豊富な
accidental, gūzenna 偶然な
accurate, tashikana 確かな, seikakuna 正確な
aesthetic, bitekina 美的な
aloof, yosoyososhii よそよそしい
ambiguous, aimaina あいまいな
annoying, urusai うるさい
apparent, akirakana 明らかな
appropriate, tekitōna 適当な, tekisetsuna 適切な, datōna 妥当な
argumentative, rikutsuppoi 理屈っぽい
arrogant, gōmanna ごう慢な, ōheina 横柄な
artificial, jinkōtekina 人工的な
astringent, shibui 渋い

automatic, jidōtekina 自動的な, ōtomachikkuna オートマチックな
awkward, gikochinai ぎこちない

bad, warui 悪い
barbarous, yabanna 野蛮な
bashful, hazukashii 恥ずかしい
beautiful, utsukushii 美しい, uruwashii 麗しい
benevolent, nasakebukai 情け深い
big, ōkii 大きい
bitter, nigai 苦い
black, kuroi 黒い
blue, aoi 青い
bold, daitanna 大胆な
boring, tsumaranai つまらない, taikutsuna 退屈な
brand-new, maatarashii 真新しい
brave, isamashii 勇ましい, yūkanna 勇敢な, isagiyoi 潔い

bright, akarui 明るい, azayakana 鮮やかな, kashikoi かしこい, rikōna 利口な

businesslike, jimutekina 事務的な

bustling, nigiyakana にぎやかな, hankana 繁華な

busy, isogashii 忙しい, tabōna 多忙な

calculative, dasantekina 打算的な

calm, shizukana 静かな, heiseina 平静な

carefree, kirakuna 気楽な

careful, yōjinbukai 用心深い, nyūnenna 入念な

careless, sosokkashii そそっかしい

charming, miryokutekina 魅力的な, chāminguna チャーミングな

cheap, yasuppoi 安っぽい, chachina ちゃちな

cheerful, kaikatsuna 快活な

chic, ikina 粋な

clean, kireina きれいな, seiketsuna 清潔な, kiyoi 清い

clear, meihakuna 明白な

coarse, arai 粗い

cold, samui 寒い, tsumetai 冷たい

coldhearted, hakujōna 薄情な

comfortable, rakuna 楽な, kaitekina 快適な

commonplace, heibonna 平凡な

comparatively high-priced, waridakana 割高な

comparatively low-priced, wariyasuna 割安な

competent, yūnōna 有能な

complicated, yayakoshii ややこしい, fukuzatsuna 複雑な

concrete, gutaitekina 具体的な

confusing, magirawashii まぎらわしい

conscientious, ryōshintekina 良心的な

conservative, hoshutekina 保守的な

convenient, benrina 便利な

cool, suzushii 涼しい, reiseina 冷静な

cooperative, kyōryokutekina 協力的な

correct, tadashii 正しい

cowardly, hikyōna 卑怯な

cruel, mugoi むごい, zankokuna 残酷な, jakenna 邪険な

cultural, bunkatekina 文化的な

cunning, zurui ずるい, warugashikoi 悪がしこい, inkenna 陰険な

cute, kawaii かわいい

damp, shimeppoi 湿っぽい

dangerous, abunai 危ない, kikenna 危険な

dark, kurai 暗い, koi 濃い

dazzling, mabushii まぶしい

dear, natsukashii 懐かしい

deep, fukai 深い

deep black, makkurona 真っ黒な

deep blue/green, massaona 真っ青な

deep red, makkana 真っ赤な

deep-rooted, nezuyoi 根強い

delicate, kayowai か弱い, derikētona デリケートな

delicious, oishii おいしい, umai うまい, bimina 美味な

delightful, yukaina 愉快な

democratic, minshutekina 民主的な

desirable, konomashii 好ましい, nozomashii 望ましい

detailed, komakai 細かい, kuwashii 詳しい, shōsaina 詳細な

difficult, muzukashii 難しい, konnanna 困難な, taihenna 大変な

diligent, kinbenna 勤勉な

dirty, kitanai 汚い, fuketsuna 不潔な

disgusting, niganigashii 苦々しい

distasteful, iyana 嫌な, kiraina 嫌いな

distressful, nayamashii 悩ましい

divine, kōgōshii 神々しい, shinseina 神聖な

dizzy, memagurushii 目まぐるしい

doubtful, utagawashii 疑わしい, ikaga-
　washii いかがわしい
dramatic, gekitekina 劇的な, dorama-
　chikkuna ドラマチックな
dreadful, susamajii すさまじい
dull, nibui 鈍い
durable, jōbuna 丈夫な, ganjōna 頑丈な
dusky, usugurai 薄暗い
dynamic, dainamikkuna ダイナミックな

early, hayai 早い
easy, yasashii 易しい, yōina 容易な
economical, keizaitekina 経済的な
educational, kyōikutekina 教育的な
effective, yūkōna 有効な
efficient, nōritsutekina 能率的な
elegant, yūgana 優雅な, fūryūna 風流な,
　eregantona エレガントな
emotional, kanjōtekina 感情的な
empty, munashii むなしい
energetic, enerugisshuna エネルギッシュな
enjoyable, tanoshii 楽しい
enormous, bakudaina 莫大な
enthusiastic, nesshinna 熱心な
enviable, urayamashii うらやましい
ephemeral, hakanai はかない
epoch-making, kakkitekina 画期的な
equal, hitoshii 等しい, byōdōna 平等な
erotic, erochikkuna エロチックな
even, tairana 平らな
exaggerated, ōgesana 大げさな
exotic, ekizochikkuna エキゾチックな
exquisite, seikōna 精巧な

fainthearted, kiyowai 気弱い
faithful, chūjitsuna 忠実な, seijitsuna 誠
　実な
faltering, tadotadoshii たどたどしい
famous, yūmeina 有名な, nadakai 名高い
far, tōi 遠い
fastidious, kimuzukashii 気難しい

favorite, sukina 好きな
fearful, kowai こわい, osoroshii 恐ろしい
feeble, kayowai か弱い
feminine, joseitekina 女性的な
feudal, hōkentekina 封建的な
few, sukunai 少ない, wazukana わずかな
fine, rippana 立派な
fishy, namagusai 生臭い
foolish, bakarashii ばからしい, bakana
　ばかな
formidable, tegowai 手ごわい
fortunate, saiwaina 幸いな, kōunna 幸運
　な
fragile, yowayowashii 弱々しい
fragmentary, danpentekina 断片的な
fragrant, kōbashii 香ばしい
frank, sotchokuna 率直な
free (not busy), himana ひまな, jiyūna
　自由な
fresh, atarashii 新しい, shinsenna 新鮮な,
　mizumizushii みずみずしい, furesshu-
　na フレッシュな
friendly, kokoroyasui 心安い, yūkōtekina
　友好的な
frugal, tsumashii つましい
funny, okashii おかしい

gallant, ririshii りりしい
generous, kandaina 寛大な
gentle, otonashii おとなしい, yasashii 優
　しい, onwana 温和な
gently sloping, nadarakana なだらかな
glad, ureshii 嬉しい
global, gurōbaruna グローバルな
gloomy, inkina 陰気な
good, ii いい, yoi よい, kekkōna 結構な,
　zenryōna 善良な
gorgeous, gōkana 豪華な
grand, seidaina 盛大な, sōgonna 荘厳な
great, erai 偉い, idaina 偉大な
grotesque, gurotesukuna グロテスクな

handsome, hansamuna ハンサムな

happy, ureshii 嬉しい, yorokobashii 喜ばしい, shiawasena 幸せな, kōfukuna 幸福な

hard, katai かたい

hard to obtain, egatai 得難い

harmless, mugaina 無害な

harmonious, enmanna 円満な

harsh, togetogeshii とげとげしい

hasty, keisotsuna 軽率な

hateful, nikui 憎い, nikurashii 憎らしい

healthy, genkina 元気な, jōbuna 丈夫な, kenkōna 健康な

heartless, tsurenai つれない

heavy, omoi 重い, omotai 重たい

high, takai 高い

high-class, kōkyūna 高級な

hot, atsui 暑い, atsui 熱い, karai 辛い

huge, kyodaina 巨大な

humane, jindōtekina 人道的な

humble, somatsuna 粗末な

humid, mushiatsui 蒸し暑い

hurried, awatadashii あわただしい

ideal, risōtekina 理想的な

ignorant, muchina 無知な

illegal, fuhōna 不法な

ill-natured, ijiwaruna 意地悪な

immoral, fudōtokuna 不道徳な

imperfect, fukanzenna 不完全な

important, daijina 大事な, taisetsuna 大切な, jūdaina 重大な, jūyōna 重要な

impossible, fukanōna 不可能な

impudent, zūzūshii ずうずうしい

impure, fujunna 不純な

inaccurate, fuseikakuna 不正確な

incompetent, munōna 無能な

incomprehensible, fukakaina 不可解な

inconvenient, fubenna 不便な, futsugō-na 不都合な

industrious, kinbenna 勤勉な

inexpensive, yasui 安い

infantile, yōchina 幼稚な

inhuman, hidōna 非道な

innocent, mujakina 無邪気な

insufficient, fujūbunna 不十分な

intellectual, chitekina 知的な

intelligent, kashikoi かしこい, rikōna 利口な

interesting, omoshiroi 面白い

international, kokusaitekina 国際的な

intimate, kokoroyasui 心安い, shitashii 親しい, shinmitsuna 親密な

irregular, fukisokuna 不規則な

irresponsible, musekininna 無責任な

irritating, jirettai じれったい

itchy, kayui かゆい

jealous, netamashii ねたましい

just, seitōna 正当な

kind, shinsetsuna 親切な

languid, darui だるい

large, hiroi 広い

late, osoi 遅い

lazy, taidana 怠惰な

legal, hōtekina 法的な

light, karui 軽い, usui 薄い

little, sukunai 少ない, wazukana わずかな

lively, kappatsuna 活発な

logical, ronritekina 論理的な

lonely, sabishii さびしい, wabishii わびしい, kokorobosoi 心細い

long, nagai 長い

long-continued, hisashii 久しい

long in waiting, machidōshii 待ち遠しい

longed for, natsukashii 懐かしい

loose, yurui 緩い

lovely, kawaii かわいい

low, hikui 低い

low-class, teikyūna 低級な

lukewarm, nurui ぬるい

luxurious, zeitakuna ぜいたくな

manly, otokorashii 男らしい, danseiteki-na 男性的な

many, ōi 多い

mean, hikutsuna 卑屈な

meaningless, muimina 無意味な

melancholic, yūutsuna ゆううつな

mild, ondanna 温暖な

mischievous, itazurana いたずらな, cha-mena 茶目な

miserable, awarena あわれな, wabishii わびしい

modern, kindaitekina 近代的な, mo-danna モダンな

modest, tsutsumashii つつましい

monotonous, tanchōna 単調な

moral, dōtokutekina 道徳的な

morbid, byōtekina 病的な

much, ōi 多い

mysterious, fushigina 不思議な, shin-pitekina 神秘的な

naïve, ubuna うぶな, naïbuna ナイーブな

narrow, hosoi 細い, semai 狭い

natural, shizenna 自然な

near, chikai 近い

necessary, hitsuyōna 必要な

negative, shōkyokutekina 消極的な

negligent, zuborana ずぼらな

new, atarashii 新しい

noble, kedakai 気高い, tōtoi 尊い, kōki-na 高貴な

noisy, yakamashii やかましい, sawaga-shii 騒がしい, sōzōshii 騒々しい

normal, seijōna 正常な

novel, meatarashii 目新しい

obedient, otonashii おとなしい, sunao-na 素直な, jūjunna 従順な

old, furui 古い

old-fashioned, kofūna 古風な

ominous, fukitsuna 不吉な

openhearted, kaihōtekina 開放的な

optimistic, rakkantekina 楽観的な

optional, zuiina 随意な

original, kibatsuna 奇抜な, orijinaruna オリジナルな

painful, itai 痛い, kurushii 苦しい

peaceful, nagoyakana 和やかな, nodoka-na のどかな, yasurakana 安らかな

peculiar, dokutokuna 独特な

perfect, kanzenna 完全な

permanent, eikyūtekina 永久的な

pessimistic, hikantekina 悲観的な

pitch-dark, makkurana 真っ暗な

pitiful, kawaisōna かわいそうな, awarena あわれな

pleasant, kokoroyoi 快い

poisonous, yūdokuna 有毒な

polite, teineina ていねいな

poor, mazushii 貧しい, binbōna 貧乏な

popular, tsūzokuna 通俗な, popyurāna ポピュラーな

positive, sekkyokutekina 積極的な

powerful, kyōryokuna 強力な

precocious, sōjukuna 早熟な

pretty, kireina きれいな

primitive, genshitekina 原始的な

private, shitekina 私的な, puraibētona プライベートな

progressive, shinpotekina 進歩的な

promising, tanomoshii 頼もしい, yūbō-na 有望な

proud, hokorashii 誇らしい

provoking, haradatashii 腹立たしい

prudent, yōjinbukai 用心深い, shinchō-na 慎重な

pure, kiyoi 清い, seiketsuna 清潔な

purehearted, junjōna 純情な

pure white, masshirona 真っ白な

quick, hayai 速い, binsokuna 敏速な

quiet, shizukana 静かな

rare, mezurashii 珍しい, marena まれな

rational, riseitekina 理性的な, gōritekina 合理的な

realistic, genjitsutekina 現実的な

reasonable, mottomona もっともな

red, akai 赤い

refined, jōhinna 上品な, kōshōna 高尚な

refreshing, sawayakana さわやかな, suga-sugashii すがすがしい

regrettable, kuyashii くやしい, zannenna 残念な, ikanna 遺憾な

regular, kisokutekina 規則的な

reliable, tanomoshii 頼もしい

relieved, anshinna 安心な

remarkable, ichijirushii 著しい, mezama-shii 目覚ましい

representative, daihyōtekina 代表的な

robust, takumashii たくましい

romantic, romanchikkuna ロマンチックな

round, marui 丸い

rich, yūfukuna 裕福な

rude, arai 荒い

sad, kanashii 悲しい

safe, anzenna 安全な, bujina 無事な

salty, karai 辛い

satisfactory, manzokuna 満足な

scarce, toboshii 乏しい

selfish, kattena 勝手な, wagamamana 我がままな, rikotekina 利己的な

sensational, senjōtekina 扇情的な

sensitive, binkanna 敏感な

sentimental, kanshōtekina 感傷的な, sen-chimentaruna センチメンタルな

serious, majimena まじめな, shinkenna 真剣な, omoi 重い

shabby, misuborashii みすぼらしい

shallow, asai 浅い

shallow-minded, asahakana 浅はかな

shameful, hazukashii 恥ずかしい

sharp, surudoi 鋭い, eirina 鋭利な, toge-togeshii とげとげしい

short, mijikai 短い

short-tempered, tankina 短気な

showy, hadena 派手な, monomonoshii 物々しい

shrewd, josainai 如才ない

silly, bakarashii ばからしい

simple, kantanna 簡単な, tanjunna 単純な, shinpuruna シンプルな

skillful, jōzuna 上手な, umai うまい, ki-yōna 器用な, tokuina 得意な

sleepy, nemui 眠い, nemutai 眠たい

slightly elevated, kodakai 小高い

slow, osoi 遅い, noroi のろい

small, chiisai 小さい, chiisana 小さな, komakai 細かい, semai 狭い

smoky, kemui けむい, kemutai けむたい

smooth, namerakana 滑らかな

sociable, shakōtekina 社交的な

soft, yawarakai 柔かい, yawarakana 柔らかな

solemn, genshukuna 厳粛な

sour, suppai 酸っぱい

spacious, hiroi 広い

special, tokubetsuna 特別な

spiritual, seishintekina 精神的な

splendid, subarashii 素晴らしい, suteki-na 素敵な

steep, kewashii 険しい

stinking, kusai 臭い

stouthearted, kizuyoi 気強い

straight, massuguna 真っ直ぐな

strict, kibishii 厳しい, genkakuna 厳格な

strong, tsuyoi 強い, ganjōna 頑丈な

stubborn, shibutoi しぶとい, gankona 頑固な, gōjōna 強情な

subjective, shukantekina 主観的な

substantial, jisshitsutekina 実質的な

sufficient, jūbunna 十分な

suitable, fusawashii ふさわしい, niawashii 似合わしい

superior, yūshūna 優秀な

sweet, amai 甘い

tactful, josainai 如才ない

tasty, oishii おいしい

temporary, ichijitekina 一時的な

tenacious, nebarizuyoi 粘り強い

terrible, hidoi ひどい

terrific, sugoi すごい, mōretsuna 猛烈な

thankful, arigatai ありがたい

thick, atsui 厚い, futoi 太い, koi 濃い

thin, hosoi 細い, usui 薄い

thrilling, tsūkaina 痛快な

tough, katai かたい

traditional, dentōtekina 伝統的な

transparent, tōmeina 透明な

trite, chinpuna 陳腐な

troublesome, urusai うるさい, mendōna 面倒な, meiwakuna 迷惑な

ugly, minikui みにくい, mittomonai みっともない

uncanny, bukimina 無気味な

uncommon, hibonna 非凡な

uneasy, fuanna 不安な, shinpaina 心配な, kokorobosoi 心細い

unexpected, igaina 意外な, angaina 案外な

unfair, fukōheina 不公平な

unfaithful, fujitsuna 不実な

unfortunate, fuunna 不運な

ungrateful, onshirazuna 恩知らずな

unhappy, fukōna 不幸な, fushiawasena 不幸せな

unique, unīkuna ユニークな

unkind, fushinsetsuna 不親切な

unmanly, memeshii 女々しい

unnatural, fushizenna 不自然な

unpleasant, fuyukaina 不愉快な

unreasonable, murina 無理な, fugōrina 不合理な

unreserved, buenryona 無遠慮な

unsavory, mazui まずい

unseasonable, fujunna 不順な

unskillful, hetana 下手な, nigatena 苦手な, bukiyōna 無器用な, tsutanai つたない

untidy, darashinai だらしない

upright, isagiyoi 潔い

useful, yūekina 有益な

useless, muekina 無益な

valuable, tōtoi 尊い, chōhōna 重宝な

various, iroirona 色々な, samazamana 様々な

vast, kōdaina 広大な

versatile, tasaina 多才な

veteran, rōrenna 老練な

violent, hageshii 激しい, ranbōna 乱暴な

vulgar, gehinna 下品な, zokuakuna 俗悪な, yahina 野卑な

wakeful, negurushii 寝苦しい

want, hoshii 欲しい

warm, atatakai 暖かい, atatakai 温かい, atatakana 暖かな

wasteful, mudana 無駄な

watery, mizuppoi 水っぽい

weak, yowai 弱い

white, shiroi 白い

wise, kashikoi かしこい, kenmeina 賢明な

worldwide, sekaitekina 世界的な

yellow, kiiroi 黄色い

young, wakai 若い

youthful, wakawakashii 若々しい

ADVERBS

ANSWERS TO PRACTICES

Practice 1
1. tokidoki 時々 2. tsune ni 常に 3. shikiri ni しきりに 4. shibashiba しばしば
5. tama ni たまに 6. taezu 絶えず

Practice 2
1. sono uchi そのうち 2. shūshi 終始 3. sugu ni すぐに 4. zutto ずっと 5. shibaraku しばらく 6. tadachi ni ただちに 7. mamonaku 間もなく 8. tachimachi たちまち 9. sassoku 早速

Practice 3
1. hajimete 初めて 2. tatta ima たった今 3. mata また 4. mazu 先ず 5. kanete かねて 6. sudeni すでに

Practice 4
1. saki ni 先に 2. gūzen 偶然 3. tōtō とうとう 4. ittan いったん 5. arakajime あらかじめ 6. yōyaku ようやく 7. ichiō 一応 8. tsui ni ついに

Practice 5
1. subete すべて 2. takusan たくさん 3. minna みんな 4. jūbun 十分 5. mitchiri みっちり 6. sukunakarazu 少なからず 7. hotondo ほとんど

Practice 6
1. wazuka わずか 2. tatta たった 3. tada ただ 4. chotto ちょっと 5. sukunakutomo 少なくとも 6. tsui つい 7. tan ni 単に

Practice 7
1. hobo ほぼ 2. zatto ざっと 3. taitei たいてい 4. daitai 大体 5. ōyoso おおよそ

Practice 8
1. kiwamete 極めて 2. sōtō 相当 3. daibu 大分 4. ōini 大いに 5. taihen 大変 6. jitsu ni 実に 7. nakanaka なかなか

Practice 9

1. motto もっと　2. zutto ずっと　3. toku ni 特に　4. sara ni 更に　5. mottomo 最も
6. masumasu ますます　7. ichiban 一番

Practice 10

1. hakkiri はっきり　2. sassato さっさと　3. narubeku なるべく　4. yukkuri ゆっくり
5. tsuide ni ついでに　6. tonikaku とにかく　7. sotto そっと　8. wazawaza わざわざ
9. sekkaku せっかく　10. kossori こっそり

Practice 11

1. gakkari がっかり　2. sappari さっぱり　3. shonbori しょんぼり　4. hotto ほっと
5. mutto むっと　6. hatto はっと

Practice 12

1. chōdo ちょうど　2. dandan だんだん　3. kitchiri きっちり　4. pittari ぴったり
5. chakuchaku to 着々と　6. hissori ひっそり　7. zokuzoku 続々

Practice 13

1. kitto きっと　2. yahari やはり　3. mochiron もちろん　4. aikawarazu 相変わらず
5. kekkyoku 結局　6. saiwai 幸い　7. tatoeba 例えば　8. kaette かえって

Practice 14

1. punpun ぷんぷん　2. kankan ni かんかんに　3. kusukusu くすくす　4. nikoniko
にこにこ　5. wāwā わあわあ　6. niyaniya にやにや　7. gamigami がみがみ

Practice 15

1. gabugabu がぶがぶ　2. pekopeko ぺこぺこ　3. perapera ぺらぺら　4. pechakucha
ぺちゃくちゃ　5. morimori もりもり　6. berabera べらべら　7. poripori ぽりぽり

Practice 16

1. zorozoro ぞろぞろ　2. urouro うろうろ　3. burabura ぶらぶら　4. utouto うとうと
5. yoroyoro よろよろ　6. gūgū ぐうぐう

Practice 17

1. zukizuki ずきずき　2. zokuzoku ぞくぞく　3. pinpin ぴんぴん　4. gangan がんがん
5. fūfū ふうふう　6. gatagata がたがた

Practice 18

1. isoiso いそいそ　2. nobinobi のびのび　3. iraira いらいら　4. harahara はらはら
5. mojimoji もじもじ　6. ikiiki いきいき　7. dokidoki どきどき　8. magomago まご
まご

Practice 19

1. korokoro ころころ   2. kankan かんかん   3. zāzā ざあざあ   4. gōgō ごうごう
5. kirakira きらきら   6. guragura ぐらぐら   7. chirachira ちらちら

Practice 20

1. sappari さっぱり   2. manzara まんざら   3. taishite 大して   4. kesshite 決して
5. masaka まさか   6. tōtei とうてい   7. kanarazu shi mo 必ずしも   8. rokuni ろくに
9. imasara 今さら

Practice 21

1. mada まだ   2. zenzen 全然   3. totemo とても   4. nakanaka なかなか   5. hotondo
ほとんど   6. amari あまり   7. dōmo どうも   8. issai 一切   9. nakanaka なかなか
10. betsu ni 別に

Practice 22

1. dō どう   2. naze なぜ   3. ittai 一体   4. dōshite どうして   5. moshi もし   6. man'ichi
万一   7. tatoe たとえ

Practice 23

1. zehi ぜひ   2. dōyara どうやら   3. chōdo ちょうど   4. tashika 確か   5. dōka どうか
6. osoraku 恐らく   7. samo さも   8. tabun 多分   9. atakamo あたかも

LIST OF ADVERBS

1. Adverbs Expressing Time

2. Adverbs Expressing Quantity

3. Adverbs Expressing Degree

4. Adverbs Expressing Circumstance

5. Onomatopoeic Words

COMMON JAPANESE ADVERBS

NOTE: Sometimes Japanese adverbs translate into verbs in English.

aikawarazu, 相変わらず as usual, as always

ainiku, あいにく unfortunately

amari, あまり very, much, (not) very, (not) much

arakajime, あらかじめ beforehand, in advance

atakamo, あたかも as if

ato de, 後で later, afterward

berabera, べらべら (talk) on and on, blab

betsu ni, 別に separately, (not) especially, (not) particularly

bikubiku, びくびく nervously, timidly

bonyari, ぼんやり vacantly, absentmindedly

burabura, ぶらぶら leisurely, idly

chakuchaku, 着々 steadily, step by step

chibichibi, ちびちび (sip) little by little, in sips

chirachira, ちらちら flicker, flutter, (fall) lightly

chittomo, ちっとも (not) at all, (not) in the least

chōdo, ちょうど exactly, just like, as if, just right

chotto, ちょっと a little, a bit

daibu, 大分 fairly, quite

daitai, 大体 almost, roughly

dandan, だんだん gradually, slowly

dō, どう how, in what way, how about

dōka, どうか please

dokidoki, どきどき thump-thump, feel nervous, feel excited

dōmo, どうも very, much, somehow

dōshite, どうして why, how, in what way

dōyara, どうやら likely

dōzo, どうぞ please

fūfū, ふうふう puffing and panting, gasping for breath

furafura, ふらふら feel dizzy, be unsteady

gabugabu, がぶがぶ quaff, (drink) thirstily

gakkari, がっかり be disappointed, be discouraged

gamigami, がみがみ (snap at someone) angrily

gangan, がんがん have a splitting headache, hear a ringing in one's ears

gatagata, がたがた rattle, tremble

gatsugatsu, がつがつ hungrily, gluttonously, (eat) like a pig

geragera, げらげら (laugh) loudly

gōgō, ごうごう with a roar, with a rumble

gūgū, ぐうぐう z-z-z, (sleep) soundly, snore

guragura, ぐらぐら shake

guruguru, ぐるぐる around and around

gūzen, 偶然 unexpectedly, by chance

hajimete, 初めて for the first time

hakihaki, はきはき clearly, unambiguously

hakkiri, はっきり clearly, unambiguously

harahara, はらはら feel nervous, feel uneasy

hatto, はっと be startled, be taken aback

hisohiso, ひそひそ in whispers

hissori, ひっそり quietly, still

hobo, ほぼ almost, nearly

hotondo, ほとんど almost, nearly, hardly

hotto, ほっと be relieved

ichiban, 一番 most

ichiō, 一応 once, briefly, for the time being

ikaga, いかが how, how about

ikiiki, いきいき be lively, be full of life

imasara, 今さら now (when it is too late)

ippai, いっぱい full

iraira, いらいら be irritated, be impatient

isoiso, いそいそ cheerfully, joyfully

issai, 一切 all, (not) at all

issō, いっそう more, all the more

itsumo, いつも always, habitually

ittai, 一体 What on earth!

ittan, いったん once, temporarily

izure, いずれ soon, one of these days

jitsu ni, 実に truly, indeed

jojo ni, じょじょに gradually, slowly

jūbun (ni), 十分（に）enough, fully

kaette, かえって on the contrary

kanarazu, 必ず surely, certainly, without fail

kanarazu shi mo, 必ずしも (not) always, (not) necessarily

kanari, かなり fairly, considerably

kanete, かねて before, beforehand, for some time

kankan, かんかん (fume) with anger, (shine) hot

kekkyoku, 結局 after all, finally, in the end

kesshite, 決して never, absolutely (not)

kichinto, きちんと regularly, neatly

kippari, きっぱり flatly, once and for all

kirakira, きらきら twinkle, sparkle

kirikiri, きりきり have a sharp pain

kitchiri, きっちり exactly, perfectly

kitto, きっと surely, certainly, without fail

kiwamete, 極めて very, extremely

korokoro, ころころ roll

kossori, こっそり quietly, stealthily, secretly

kusukusu, くすくす giggle, chuckle

mada, まだ still, (not) yet

maemotte, 前もって beforehand, in advance

magomago, まごまご be confused

mamonaku, 間もなく soon, shortly, before long

man'ichi/mangaichi, 万一/万が一 by any chance, In the event …

manzara, まんざら (not) altogether, (not) wholly

marude, まるで just like, as if

masaka, まさか Incredible!, I never thought …

masumasu, ますます more and more, increasingly

mata, また again, once more

mazu, 先ず first

metta ni, めったに rarely, seldom

minna/mina, みんな/みな all, entirely

mitchiri, みっちり thoroughly

mō, もう already, (not) anymore

mochiron, もちろん of course, no doubt

mojimoji, もじもじ hesitantly

morimori, もりもり (eat) like a horse, have a hearty appetite

moshi, もし if

mō sugu, もうすぐ soon, before long

motto, もっと more

mottomo, 最も most

mutto, むっと get angry, be offended

muzumuzu, むずむず impatiently (eager)

nakanaka, なかなか quite, fairly, considerably, (not) easily, (not) readily

narubeku, なるべく as … as possible, if possible

naze, なぜ why

nikoniko, にこにこ with a smile, happily

niyaniya, にやにや with a grin, with a smirk

nobinobi, のびのび feel relieved, feel refreshed, be at ease

nochihodo, 後ほど later, afterward

ōini, 大いに very much, greatly, largely

osoraku, 恐らく probably

oyoso/ōyoso, およそ/おおよそ about, roughly

pechakucha, ぺちゃくちゃ (talk) noisily, chatter

pekopeko, ぺこぺこ on an empty stomach, with one's head bowed

perapera, ぺらぺら fluently, rapidly

pinpin, ぴんぴん be lively, be full of life

pittari, ぴったり exactly, perfectly

pokapoka, ぽかぽか nice and warm

poripori, ぽりぽり munch

poroporo, ぽろぽろ (shed tears) in large drops

punpun, ぷんぷん in anger, in a huff

rinrin, りんりん jingle, tinkle

rokuni, ろくに (not) enough, (not) properly

saiwai, 幸い fortunately

sakihodo, 先ほど a (little) while ago

saki ni, 先に before, ahead of, first

sakki, さっき a (little) while ago

samo, さも as if

sappari, さっぱり (not) at all, (not) in the least, feel refreshed, feel relieved

sara ni, 更に even more, further

sassato, さっさと quickly, hurriedly

sassoku, 早速 immediately

seizei, せいぜい at most

sekkaku, せっかく with effort, kindly, especially

sesseto, せっせと diligently, laboriously

shibaraku, しばらく for a while, for a long time

shikiri ni, しきりに constantly, strongly, eagerly

shikkari, しっかり steadily, firmly

shikushiku, しくしく sob, weep

shitoshito, しとしと drizzle

shonbori, しょんぼり dejectedly

shūshi, 終始 from beginning to end, throughout

sono uchi (ni), そのうち（に）soon, one of these days, before long

sōtō, 相当 fairly, considerably

sotto, そっと quietly, softly

subete, すべて all

sudeni, すでに already

sugu (ni), すぐ（に）right away

sukkiri, すっきり feel fine, feel refreshed

sukoshi, 少し a little, a bit

sukoshi mo, 少しも (not) at all, (not) in the least

sukunakarazu, 少なからず not a few, not a little

sukunakutomo, 少なくとも at least

suyasuya, すやすや (sleep) calmly, (sleep) peacefully

tabitabi, 度々 often, frequently

tabun, 多分 probably

tada, ただ only, merely

tadachi ni, ただちに immediately, at once

taezu, 絶えず constantly, incessantly, consistently

taihen, 大変 very, extremely

taishite, 大して (not) very, (not) much

taitei, たいてい usually, mostly

takusan, たくさん many, much, enough

tama ni, たまに occasionally, once in a great while

tan ni, 単に only, merely

tappuri, たっぷり full

tashika, 確か perhaps, I suppose

tatoe, たとえ even if

tatoeba, 例えば for instance

tatta, たった only

tatta ima, たった今 just now, a moment ago

tobotobo, とぼとぼ trudge

tokidoki, 時々 sometimes, once in a while

toku ni, 特に specially, especially

tonikaku, とにかく at any rate, anyway

tōtei, とうてい (cannot) possibly

totemo, とても very, terribly, (cannot) possibly

tōtō, とうとう at last, finally, after all, in the end

tsugitsugi, 次々 one after another, in succession

tsui, つい just, only

tsuide ni, ついでに while (I am/you are at it), at the same time

tsui ni, ついに at last, finally, after all

tsumari, つまり in brief, in other words, that is to say

tsune ni, 常に always, habitually

urouro, うろうろ wander about, hang about

utouto, うとうと drowse, doze

uttori, うっとり absorbedly, in a trance

wakuwaku, わくわく be excited

wāwā, わあわあ (weep) loudly, wail, cheer

wazawaza, わざわざ expressly, specially

wazuka, わずか a little, only

yagate, やがて soon, before long, at (long) last, in the end

yahari/yappari, やはり/やっぱり as expected, after all

yaku, 約 about, approximately

yatto, やっと at last, finally, barely

yoroyoro, よろよろ stagger

yukkuri, ゆっくり slowly, leisurely

yuttari, ゆったり be spacious, be loose

zatto, ざっと about, roughly

zāzā, ざあざあ (rain) in torrents, (rain) cats and dogs

zehi, ぜひ by all means, without fail, definitely

zenzen, 全然 totally, quite, (not) at all

zokuzoku, 続々 one after another, in succession

zokuzoku, ぞくぞく feel excited, shiver

zorozoro, ぞろぞろ in succession, in streams

zuibun, ずいぶん very, awfully

zukizuki, ずきずき sting, throb

zutto, ずっと throughout, all the time, all the way, by far, far more

ENGLISH-JAPANESE ADVERB LIST

NOTE: Not all the adverbs presented in this book are listed below.

a bit, chotto ちょっと, sukoshi 少し

about, oyoso/ōyoso およそ/おおよそ, yaku 約, zatto ざっと

a little, chotto ちょっと, sukoshi 少し, wazuka わずか

a (little) while ago, sakki さっき, sakihodo 先ほど

a moment ago, tatta ima たった今

absentmindedly, bonyari ぼんやり

absolutely not, kesshite ~ nai 決して~ない

absorbedly, uttori うっとり

after all, tōtō とうとう, tsui ni ついに, yahari/yappari やはり/やっぱり, kekkyoku 結局

afterward, ato de 後で, nochihodo 後ほど

again, mata また

ahead of, saki ni 先に

all, minna/mina みんな/みな, subete すべて, issai 一切

all the more, issō いっそう

all the time, zutto ずっと

all the way, zutto ずっと

almost, hotondo ほとんど, hobo ほぼ, daitai 大体

already, mō もう, sude ni すでに

always, itsumo いつも, tsune ni 常に

angrily, gamigami がみがみ

anyway, tonikaku とにかく

approximately, yaku 約

around and around, guruguru ぐるぐる

as always, aikawarazu 相変わらず

as ... as possible, narubeku なるべく

as expected, yahari/yappari やはり/やっぱり

as if, chōdo ちょうど, marude まるで, atakamo あたかも, samo さも

as usual, aikawarazu 相変わらず

at any rate, tonikaku とにかく

at last, tōtō とうとう, tsui ni ついに, yagate やがて, yatto やっと

at least, sukunakutomo 少なくとも

at most, seizei せいぜい

at once, tadachi ni ただちに

at the same time, tsuide ni ついでに

awfully, zuibun ずいぶん

barely, yatto やっと

before, saki ni 先に, kanete かねて

beforehand, maemotte 前もって, arakajime あらかじめ, kanete かねて

before long, izure いずれ, mamonaku 間もなく, mō sugu もうすぐ, sono uchi (ni) そのうち(に), yagate やがて

briefly, ichiō 一応

by all means, zehi ぜひ

by any chance, man'ichi/mangaichi 万一/万が一

by chance, gūzen 偶然

by far, zutto ずっと

cannot possibly, tōtei ～ nai/muri とうて い～ない/無理, totemo ～ nai/muri とても～ない/無理

certainly, kitto きっと, kanarazu 必ず

cheerfully, isoiso いそいそ

clearly, hakihaki はきはき, hakkiri はっきり

considerably, kanari かなり, nakanaka なかなか, sōtō 相当

consistently, taezu 絶えず

constantly, taezu 絶えず, shikiri ni しきりに

dejectedly, shonbori しょんぼり

diligently, sesseto せっせと

(drink) thirstily, gabugabu がぶがぶ

eagerly, shikiri ni しきりに

(eat) like a horse, morimori もりもり

(eat) like a pig, gatsugatsu がつがつ

enough, jūbun (ni) 十分 (に), takusan たくさん

entirely, minna/mina みんな/みな

especially, toku ni 特に, sekkaku せっかく

even if, tatoe たとえ

even more, sara ni 更に

exactly, chōdo ちょうど, kitchiri きっちり, pittari ぴったり

expressly, wazawaza わざわざ

extremely, taihen 大変, kiwamete 極めて

fairly, daibu 大分, kanari かなり, nakanaka なかなか, sōtō 相当

(fall) lightly, chirachira furu ちらちら

far more, zutto ずっと

finally, tōtō とうとう, tsui ni ついに, yatto やっと, kekkyoku 結局

firmly, shikkari しっかり

first, mazu 先ず, saki ni 先に

flatly, kippari きっぱり

fluently, perapera ぺらぺら

for a long time, shibaraku しばらく

for a while, shibaraku しばらく

for instance, tatoeba 例えば

for some time, kanete かねて

for the first time, hajimete 初めて

for the time being, ichiō 一応

fortunately, saiwai 幸い

frequently, tabitabi 度々

from beginning to end, shūshi 終始

full, ippai いっぱい, tappuri たっぷり

full of life, ikiiki いきいき, pinpin ぴんぴん

fully, jūbun (ni) 十分 (に)

(fume) with anger, kankan かんかん

further, sara ni 更に

gasping for breath, fūfū ふうふう

gluttonously, gatsugatsu がつがつ

gradually, dandan だんだん, jojo ni じょじょに

greatly, ōini 大いに

habitually, itsumo いつも, tsune ni 常に

happily, nikoniko にこにこ

hardly, hotondo ～ nai ほとんど～ない

hesitantly, mojimoji もじもじ

how, dō どう, dōshite どうして, ikaga いかが

how about, dō どう, ikaga いかが

hungrily, gatsugatsu がつがつ

hurriedly, sassato さっさと

idly, burabura ぶらぶら

if, moshi もし

if possible, narubeku なるべく

immediately, sassoku 早速, tadachi ni ただちに

impatiently (eager), muzumuzu むずむず

in advance, maemotte 前もって, arakajime あらかじめ

in a huff, punpun ぷんぷん

in anger, punpun ぷんぷん

in a trance, uttori うっとり

in brief, tsumari つまり
incessantly, taezu 絶えず
increasingly, masumasu ますます
Incredible!/I never thought …, masaka まさか
indeed, jitsu ni 実に
in other words, tsumari つまり
in sips, chibichibi ちびちび
in streams, zorozoro ぞろぞろ
in succession, tsugitsugi 次々, zokuzoku 続々, zorozoro ぞろぞろ
in the end, yagate やがて, kekkyoku 結局, tōtō とうとう
In the event …, man'ichi/mangaichi 万一/万が一
in what way, dō どう, dōshite どうして
in whispers, hisohiso ひそひそ

just, tsui つい, chōdo ちょうど
just like, chōdo ちょうど, marude まるで
just now, tatta ima たった今

kindly, sekkaku せっかく

laboriously, sesseto せっせと
largely, ōini 大いに
later, ato de 後で, nochihodo 後ほど
(laugh) loudly, geragera げらげら
leisurely, burabura ぶらぶら, yukkuri ゆっくり
likely, dōyara どうやら
lively, ikiiki いきいき, pinpin ぴんぴん

many, takusan たくさん
merely, tada ただ, tan ni 単に
more, motto もっと, issō いっそう
more and more, masumasu ますます
most, ichiban 一番, mottomo 最も
mostly, taitei たいてい
much, takusan たくさん, dōmo どうも

nearly, hobo ほぼ, hotondo ほとんど

neatly, kichinto きちんと
nervously, bikubiku びくびく
never, kesshite ～ nai 決して～ない
no doubt, mochiron もちろん
not a few, sukunakarazu 少なからず
not a little, sukunakarazu 少なからず
not altogether, manzara ～ nai まんざら ～ない
not always, kanarazu shi mo ～ nai 必ずしも～ない
not anymore, mō ～ nai もう ～ ない
not at all, chittomo ～ nai ちっとも ～ ない, sappari ～ nai さっぱり ～ ない, issai ～ nai 一切 ～ ない, zenzen ～ nai 全然 ～ ない
not easily, nakanaka ～ nai なかなか ～ ない
not enough, rokuni ～ nai ろくに ～ ない
not especially, betsu ni ～ nai 別に～ない
not in the least, chittomo ～ nai ちっとも ～ ない, sappari ～ nai さっぱり ～ ない
not much, amari ～ nai あまり ～ ない, taishite ～ nai 大して ～ ない
not necessarily, kanarazu shi mo ～ nai 必ずしも～ない
not particularly, betsu ni ～ nai 別に～ない
not properly, rokuni ～ nai ろくに ～ ない
not readily, nakanaka ～ nai なかなか ～ ない
not very, amari ～ nai あまり ～ ない, taishite ～ nai 大して ～ ない
not wholly, manzara ～ nai まんざら～ない
not yet, mada ～ nai まだ～ない
now (when it is too late), imasara 今さら

occasionally, tama ni たまに
of course, mochiron もちろん
often, tabitabi 度々

on an empty stomach, pekopeko ぺこぺこ

on the contrary, kaette かえって

once, ichiō 一応, ittan いったん

once and for all, kippari きっぱり

once in a great while, tama ni たまに

once in a while, tokidoki 時々

once more, mata また

one after another, tsugitsugi 次々, zoku-zoku 続々

one of these days, izure いずれ, sono uchi (ni) そのうち(に)

only, tada ただ, tan ni 単に, tatta たった, tsui つい, wazuka わずか

perfectly, kitchiri きっちり, pittari ぴったり

perhaps, tashika 確か

please, dōzo どうぞ, dōka どうか

probably, osoraku 恐らく, tabun 多分

puffing and panting, fūfū ふうふう

quickly, sassato さっさと

quietly, hissori ひっそり, kossori こっそり, sotto そっと

quite, nakanaka なかなか, daibu 大分, zenzen 全然

(rain) in torrents, zāzā ざあざあ

rapidly, perapera ぺらぺら

rarely, metta ni 〜 nai めったに〜ない

regularly, kichinto きちんと

right away, sugu (ni) すぐ(に)

roughly, oyoso/ōyoso およそ/おおよそ, zatto ざっと, daitai 大体

secretly, kossori こっそり

seldom, metta ni 〜 nai めったに〜ない

separately, betsu ni 別に

(shed tears) in large drops, poroporo ぽろぽろ

(shine) hot, kankan かんかん

shortly, mamonaku 間もなく

(sip) little by little, chibichibi ちびちび

(sleep) calmly/peacefully, suyasuya すやすや

(sleep) soundly, gūgū ぐうぐう

slowly, yukkuri ゆっくり, dandan だんだん, jojo ni じょじょに

(snap at someone) angrily, gamigami がみがみ

sob, shikushiku しくしく

somehow, dōmo どうも

sometimes, tokidoki 時々

soon, yagate やがて, izure いずれ, ma-monaku 間もなく, mō sugu もうすぐ, sono uchi (ni) そのうち(に)

specially, toku ni 特に, wazawaza わざわざ

steadily, shikkari しっかり, chakuchaku 着々

stealthily, kossori こっそり

step by step, chakuchaku 着々

still, mada まだ

strongly, shikiri ni しきりに

surely, kitto きっと, kanarazu 必ず

(talk) on and on, berabera べらべら

(talk) noisily, pechakucha ぺちゃくちゃ

temporarily, ittan いったん

terribly, totemo とても

that is to say, tsumari つまり

thoroughly, mitchiri みっちり

throughout, zutto ずっと, shūshi 終始

thump-thump, dokidoki どきどき

timidly, bikubiku びくびく

totally, zenzen 全然

truly, jitsu ni 実に

twinkle, kirakira きらきら

unambiguously, hakihaki はきはき

unexpectedly, gūzen 偶然

unfortunately, ainiku あいにく

usually, taitei たいてい

vacantly, bonyari ぼんやり

very, taihen 大変, totemo とても, zuibun ずいぶん, kiwamete 極めて, dōmo どうも

very much, ōini 大いに

(weep) loudly, wāwā わあわあ

What on earth!, ittai 一体

while (I am/you are at it), tsuide ni ついでに

why, dōshite どうして, naze なぜ

with a grin/smirk, niyaniya にやにや

with a roar/rumble, gōgō ごうごう

with a smile, nikoniko にこにこ

with effort, sekkaku せっかく

with one's head bowed, pekopeko ぺこぺこ

without fail, kitto きっと, kanarazu 必ず, zehi ぜひ

z-z-z, gūgū ぐうぐう

KODANSHA USA DICTIONARIES

Easy-to-use Dictionaries Designed for Learners of Japanese

THE KODANSHA KANJI LEARNER'S COURSE
A Step-by-Step Guide to Mastering 2300 Characters
A complete, logical system for acquiring all the kanji characters needed for genuine literacy
- Includes all 2,136 official jōyō kanji plus 164 most useful non-jōyō characters
- Summarizes kanji meanings in concise, easy-to-memorize keywords
- Mnemonic annotations for each kanji help in remembering its meaning(s)
- Cross-references, character meanings, readings, and sample vocabulary drawn from The Kodansha Kanji Learner's Dictionary

Paperback, 720 pages, ISBN: 978-1-56836-526-8

KODANSHA'S FURIGANA JAPANESE DICTIONARY
JAPANESE-ENGLISH / ENGLISH-JAPANESE
Both of Kodansha's popular furigana dictionaries in one portable, affordable volume. A truly comprehensive and practical dictionary for English-speaking learners, and an invaluable guide to using the Japanese language.
- 30,000-word basic vocabulary
- Hundreds of special words, names, and phrases
- Clear explanations of semantic and usage differences
- Special information on grammar and usage

Hardcover, 1318 pages, ISBN 978-1-56836-457-5

KODANSHA'S FURIGANA JAPANESE-ENGLISH DICTIONARY
The essential dictionary for all students of Japanese.
- Furigana readings added to all kanji
- 16,000-word basic vocabulary

Paperback, 592 pages, ISBN 978-1-56836-422-3

KODANSHA'S FURIGANA ENGLISH-JAPANESE DICTIONARY
The companion to the essential dictionary for all students of Japanese.
- Furigana readings added to all kanji
- 14,000-word basic vocabulary

Paperback, 728 pages, ISBN 978-1-56836-506-0

A DICTIONARY OF BASIC JAPANESE SENTENCE PATTERNS
Author of the best-selling *All About Particles* explains fifty of the most common, basic patterns and their variations along with numerous contextual examples. Both a reference and a textbook for students at all levels.
- Formulas delineating basic pattern structure
- Commentary on individual usages

Paperback, 320 pages, ISBN 978-1-56836-510-7

KODANSHA USA DICTIONARIES

Easy-to-use Dictionaries Designed for Learners of Japanese

THE KODANSHA KANJI LEARNER'S DICTIONARY
Revised and Expanded
A revised and expanded edition of the best-selling Japanese-English character dictionary
- 3,002 character entries – 772 more than in the previous edition
- Includes all the current jōyō and jinmei kanji
- 5 lookup methods, including the revolutionary SKIP method; 3 indexes
- Displays readings of kanji in kana instead of romanized Japanese

Paper, 1,248 pages (2 color), ISBN: 978-1-56836-407-0

THE KODANSHA KANJI DICTIONARY
The most sophisticated kanji dictionary ever developed
- Includes all the current jōyō and jinmei kanji
- 5,458 character entries – all the kanji that advanced learners are likely to encounter
- 6 lookup methods, including the SKIP method; 3 indexes; 13 appendixes
- Features core meanings or concise keywords that convey the dominant sense of each character

Hardcover, 2,112 pages (53 in 2 color), ISBN: 978-1-56836-408-7

THE KODANSHA KANJI USAGE GUIDE
An A to Z of Kun Homophones
The first Japanese-English reference work devoted exclusively to kun homophones
- Presents detailed usage articles that show the differences and similarities for 675 homophone groups, or 1590 kanji headings
- Entries are numbered sequentially and arranged in Japanese *a-i-u-e-o* order
- Includes thousands of illustrative examples of kanji in context

Paperback, 352 pages, ISBN 978-1-56836-559-6

KODANSHA'S ESSENTIAL KANJI DICTIONARY
A functional character dictionary that is both compact and comprehensive.
- Complete guide to the 1,945 essential jōyō kanji
- 20,000 common compounds
- Three indices for finding kanji

Paperback, 928 pages, ISBN 978-1-56836-397-4

A DICTIONARY OF JAPANESE PARTICLES
Treats over 100 particles in alphabetical order, providing sample sentences for each meaning.
- Meets students' needs from beginning to advanced levels
- Treats principal particle meanings as well as variants

Paperback, 368 pages, ISBN 978-1-56836-542-8

JAPANESE LANGUAGE GUIDES

Easy-to-use Guides to Essential Language Skills

LL ABOUT PARTICLES   *Naoko Chino*

he most common and less common particles brought together and broken down into some 200
ages, with abundant sample sentences.

aperback, 160 pages, ISBN 978-1-56836-419-3

OW TO TELL THE DIFFERENCE BETWEEN JAPANESE PARTICLES
omparisons and Exercises   *Naoko Chino*

y grouping particles that are similar in function, this book helps students pin down differences in
sage that would ordinarily take years to master. Definitions, sample sentences, usage notes, and
uizzes enable students to move to a higher level of comprehension.

aperback, 200 pages, ISBN 978-1-56836-479-7

IAKING SENSE OF JAPANESE: What the Textbooks Don't Tell You   *Jay Rubin*

3rief, wittily written essays that gamely attempt to explain some of the more frustrating hurdles
of Japanese].... They can be read and enjoyed by students at any level."   —*Asahi Evening News*

aperback, 144 pages, ISBN 978-1-56836-492-6

APANESE SENTENCE PATTERNS FOR EFFECTIVE COMMUNICATION
Self-Study Course and Reference   *Taeko Kamiya*

resents 142 essential sentence patterns for daily conversation—all the ones an intermediate student
10uld know, and all the ones a beginner should study to become minimally proficient in speaking.
ll in a handy, step-by-step format with pattern practice every few pages.

aperback, 368 pages, ISBN 978-1-56836-420-9

HE HANDBOOK OF JAPANESE VERBS   *Taeko Kamiya*

n indispensable reference and guide to Japanese verbs, aimed at beginning and intermediate
rudents. Precisely the book that verb-challenged students have been looking for.
Verbs are grouped, conjugated, and combined with auxiliaries
Different forms are used in sentences
Each form is followed by reinforcing examples and exercises

aperback, 256 pages, ISBN 978-1-56836-484-1

HE HANDBOOK OF JAPANESE ADJECTIVES AND ADVERBS   *Taeko Kamiya*

he ultimate reference manual for those seeking a deeper understanding of Japanese adjectives and
dverbs and how they are used in sentences. Ideal, too, for those simply wishing to expand their
ocabulary or speak livelier Japanese.

aperback, 336 pages, ISBN 978-1-56836-416-2

JAPANESE LANGUAGE GUIDES

Easy-to-use Guides to Essential Language Skills

13 SECRETS FOR SPEAKING FLUENT JAPANESE   *Giles Murray*

The most fun, rewarding, and universal techniques of successful learners of Japanese that anyone can put immediately to use. A unique and exciting alternative, full of lively commentaries, comical illustrations, and brain-teasing puzzles.

Paperback, 184 pages, ISBN 978-1-56836-426-1

BREAKING INTO JAPANESE LITERATURE: Seven Modern Classics in Parallel Text
Giles Murray

Read classics of modern Japanese fiction in the original with the aid of a built-in, customized dictionary, free MP3 sound files of professional Japanese narrators reading the stories, and literal English translations. Features Ryunosuke Akutagawa's "Rashomon" and other stories.

Paperback, 240 pages, ISBN 978-1-56836-415-5

EXPLORING JAPANESE LITERATURE: Read Mishima, Tanizaki and Kawabata in the Original
Giles Murray

Provides all the backup you need to enjoy three works of modern Japanese fiction in the original language: Yukio Mishima's "Patriotism," Jun'ichiro Tanizaki's "The Secret," and Yasunari Kawabata's "Snow Country Miniature."

Paperback, 352 pages, ISBN 978-1-56836-541-1

READ REAL JAPANESE FICTION: Short Stories by Contemporary Writers
Edited by Michael Emmerich

Short stories by cutting-edge writers, from Otsuichi to Tawada Yoko. Set in vertical text with translations, notes, and an audio CD containing narrations of the works.

Paperback, 256 pages, ISBN 978-1-56836-529-9

READ REAL JAPANESE ESSAYS: Contemporary Writings by Popular Authors
Edited by Janet Ashby

Essays by Japan's leading writers. Set in vertical text with translations, notes, and an audio CD containing narrations of the works.

Paperback, 240 pages, ISBN 978-1-56836-414-8

BASIC CONNECTIONS: Making Your Japanese Flow   *Kakuko Shoji*

Explains how words and phrases dovetail, how clauses pair up with other clauses, how sentences come together to create harmonious paragraphs. The goal is to enable the student to speak both coherently and smoothly.

Paperback, 160 pages, ISBN 978-1-56836-421-6

JAPANESE CORE WORDS AND PHRASES: Things You Can't Find in a Dictionary
Kakuko Shoji

Some Japanese words and phrases, even though they lie at the core of the language, forever elude the student's grasp. This book brings these recalcitrants to bay.

Paperback, 144 pages, ISBN 978-1-56836-488-9

JAPANESE SPIRITUALITY

BUSHIDO The Soul of Japan *Inazo Nitobe*

Written specifically for a Western audience in 1900 by Japan's under-secretary general to the League of Nations, *Bushido* explains concepts such as honor and loyalty within traditional Japanese ethics. The book is a classic, and as such throws a great deal of light on Japanese thinking and behavior, both past and present.

Hardcover, 160 pages, ISBN 978-1-56836-440-7

MUSASHI An Epic Novel of the Samurai Era *Eiji Yoshikawa*

This classic work tells of the legendary samurai who was the greatest swordsman of all time. "... a stirring saga... one that will prove popular not only for readers interested in Japan but also for those who simply want a rousing read." —*The Washington Post*

Hardcover, 978 pages, ISBN 978-1-56836-427-8

SEPPUKU A History of Samurai Suicide *Andrew Rankin*

A collection of thrilling samurai tales tracing the history of seppuku from ancient times to the twentieth century.

Hardcover, 256 pages, ISBN 978-4-7700-3142-6

EAT SLEEP SIT My Year at Japan's Most Rigorous Zen Temple *Kaoru Nonomura*

The true story of one ordinary man's search for meaning to life at Japan's strictest Zen Temple.

Paperback, 328 pages, ISBN 978-1-56836-565-7

THE ESSENCE OF SHINTO Japan's Spiritual Heart *Motohisa Yamakage*

The author explains the core values of Shinto, as well as exploring the very profound aspects of the original Shinto of ancient times. He also carefully analyzes the relationships of the spirit and soul, which will provide readers with informed and invaluable insight into how spirituality affects our daily existence.

Hardcover, 232 pages, ISBN 978-1-56836-437-7

THE TWENTY GUIDING PRINCIPLES OF KARATE
The Spiritual Legacy of the Master *Gichin Funakoshi*

Gichin Funakoshi, "the father of karate," penned his now legendary twenty principles more than 60 years ago. While the principles have circulated for years, a translation of the accompanying commentary has never found its way into publication—until now.

Hardcover, 128 pages, ISBN 978-1-56836-496-4

MIND OVER MUSCLE Writings from the Founder of Judo *Jigoro Kano*

In 1882 Jigoro Kano founded Kodokan Judo in Tokyo. This book is a collection of the essential teachings by the founder, selected and compiled from his wealth of writings and lectures spanning a period of fifty-one years. Throughout his life, Kano repeatedly emphasized grasping the correct meaning of judo and putting it into practice.

Hardcover, 160 pages, ISBN 978-1-56836-497-1